# HANGING CAPTAIN GORDON

# HANGING CAPTAIN GORDON

## THE LIFE AND TRIAL OF AN AMERICAN SLAVE TRADER

# RON SOODALTER

ATRIA BOOKS

NEW YORK    LONDON    TORONTO    SYDNEY

**ATRIA** BOOKS
1230 Avenue of the Americas
New York, NY 10020

Library of Congress Cataloging-in-Publication Data
Soodalter, Ron.
   Hanging Captain Gordon : the life and trial of an American slave trader / Ron Soodalter.
   1st Atria Books hardcover ed.
      p.   cm.
   Includes bibliographical references and index.
   1. Gordon, Nathaniel, 1826–1862—Trials, litigation, etc.   2. Slave traders—Legal status,
laws, etc.—United States—History—19th century.   3. Trials—New York (State)—New York.
4. Slave trade—United States—History—19th century.   5. Slave traders—United States—
Biography.   I. Title.

KF223.G67 S67   2006
149—dc22         2005055897

ISBN-13: 978-0-7432-6727-4
ISBN-10:    0-7432-6727-3

First Atria Books hardcover edition February 2006

10  9  8  7  6  5  4  3  2  1

**ATRIA** BOOKS is a trademark of Simon & Schuster, Inc.

Manufactured in the United States of America

For information about special discounts for bulk purchases,
please contact Simon & Schuster Special Sales at
1-800-456-6798 or business@simonandschuster.com.

*For Jane*

# CONTENTS

# PREFACE

As an undergraduate majoring in American History in the mid-1960s, I was allowed to take a graduate course entitled "Lincoln Day by Day." One week, we were researching the pressures placed on Lincoln when he was president, and on the outline was a simple two-word reference: "Gordon Case." I attempted to research the story, but found that practically nothing had been written about it at the time; consequently, I spent countless hours in front of microfilm readers, deciphering the newspapers and journals of the period, until I had put together a reliable chronology of the events relating to Captain Nathaniel Gordon and his unique fate. I was captured by the drama of the story: a young Yankee sea captain with a beautiful wife and son, caught in the machinery of a government determined to hang him as a slaver. Intending eventually to write the Gordon story, I copied every relevant frame of microfilm that Boston University's Mugar Memorial Library offered. Unfortunately, by the time I retrieved my scrolls (and they had indeed scrolled with the passage of time), the copies had faded to white; my source material had literally disappeared. Discouraged, I shelved the project.

It is only with the perspective of age and experience that I can look back and understand that this was a blessing. As a callow, White, middle-class New England youth of 19, I had nothing to bring to the story. I was more concerned with what I considered the tragedy of Nathaniel Gordon himself than with the far greater tragedy that allowed men like Gordon to prosper for decades on the countless bodies of captured Africans, even while the laws of the land prescribed death for their crime. With the passage of time, it became clear to me that Gordon's story is a very small part of the story of the American slave trade of the nineteenth century and of our government's stunning and continuous failure to stop it.

I never dreamed that Gordon would haunt me for almost 40 years. During that time, various articles were written for history journals; college papers were presented on the subject; and books on Lincoln, the Civil War, and the slave trade devoted anywhere from a sentence to a page or two to Captain Gordon. These studies and references ranged from the scholarly to the juvenile and reflected varying degrees of historical accuracy. During those four decades, I pursued graduate degrees in education and American folk culture; taught history for a time; worked as a museum curator; and collected the traditional ballads of the United States, Scotland, and Ireland. When I finally sat down to write the Gordon story, it was with the accumulated information—and perspective—gleaned and gathered through these pursuits. I'd like to think there are touches of all of them in this book.

Which leads me to the ballad that follows. From the seventeenth through the nineteenth century, it was common for ballads—"broadsides," as they were called—to appear around the executions of condemned pirates. Hawkers would sell them for a penny at the gallows. Probably the most famous of these is "Captain Kidd." To my knowledge, there was no such broadside written for Captain Gordon, so I took it upon myself to create one—a "come-all-ye"—in the traditional mode.

## Captain Gordon, or, the Slaver's Doom

Come all ye sons of freedom, and list while I relate
The tale of Captain Gordon and his untimely fate.
He sailed the Middle Passage, his fortune for to try,
But now he stands condemned by law, in grief and shame to die.

'Twas in the year of '60, lads, the wars had not begun,
We shipped aboard the *Erie*, of full 500 ton.
We sailed forth from Havana's port, where soft the breezes blow,
Tho' where away, no man on board save Gordon then did know.

Now, some of us did grow alarmed as eastward we did sail,
To find our course a strange one, boys, so Gordon we did hail,
And put it to him straightaway, and whither are we bound?
Alas, no answer did he give, but drove our queries down.

Within the week, he called us forth, and summoned us around.
Says he, "My lads, your fortune's made, we're on the slaving ground.
A dollar to each man of you, no captain would do more,
For every child of Africa you land on Cuba's shore."

Now some of us were willing, boys, and some of us were not,
For tho' the wages grand appeared, it seemed a dismal plot
To steal them from their native homes, consigning them to hell,
And sell them into slavery, in mis'ry for to dwell.

The choice was not our own to make, for Gordon made it plain
That whosoever should refuse on shore he would remain—
No loved ones or relations, 5,000 miles from home,
With nothing but the Afric wastes for us poor lads to roam.

Another week we sailed the seas, until we sighted land,
And mixed were our emotions, lads, as on the deck we stand.
For tho' each sailor loves the sight and smell of island glade,
We all did know, but little spoke, the horrors of our trade.

We reached the Congo River, and up her we did go,
To take on board a load of slaves, 900 head or so.

One hundred fifty barrelsful of whiskey in the hold
All for to trade for niggers, boys, to traffic in black gold.


And when Sharks Point it came in view, we then did throw our hook,
And what we saw upon the bank did try our hearts to look.
But wretched as them blacks appeared, 'twas nothing to the sight
Of packing them close under decks, all on that hellish night.


And some did weep, while others prayed and clutched their heathen charms.
Full half of them were children, lads, some babes in mother's arms.
And dazed were they to find themselves consigned to such a state,
But little knew the bondage vile that was to be their fate.


Now Gordon waited on the deck, and by the rail did stand,
His eyes as hard as granite stone, a knife all in his hand.
And as those wretched souls did board, bound down in agony,
He cut the rags from off their backs, and cast them in the sea.


Next day we sailed upon the tide, the breezes fairly blew.
We bade farewell to Afric shores, the River Congo, too.
But ere we sailed scarce 50 miles, a ship we did espy;
A naval vessel hove in view, and from her we did fly.


The *Erie* bore to north'ard, and swiftly we did run,
When a round of shot did cross our bows from out their forward gun.
She ran us down and hove us to, no answer could we make,
And soon did board the *Erie,* lads, possession for to take.


And Gordon was arrested, his mates detained as well,
The niggers all brought up on deck, from out that burning hell.
For fifteen days, we sailed them north, bound for Monrovia's shore,
And there released from slavery, to wear the chains no more.


And on that trip, full 37 of the buggers died.
We stripped the chains from off their limbs, and dropped them overside.
Their blood is all on Gordon's hands, the blame is his alone,
For so it goes whene'er the seeds of slavery are sown.

'Twas back to New York City Captain Gordon he was borne,
And in the Tombs remanded, boys, in infamy and scorn.
The jury found him guilty, and the judge he did decree
That by the rope he'd perish for the crime of piracy.

He leaves a pious mother, whom grief has bended low.
His wife she sits and weeps, my lads, his son does mourn also.
But pity more those tragic souls who walk the world no more,
Whose lives were traded off for gold, upon the Afric shore.

So now my song has ended, boys, I guess I'll sing no more.
I'll sail creation's oceans wide, just as I did before,
I'll climb the rigging as I'm bid, and scorn to lag below,
And swear by all that's holy, I'll no more a-slaving go.

# HANGING CAPTAIN GORDON

# INTRODUCTION

# ONE FOOT IN THE WATER

Six hundred niggers I bought dirt-cheap
   Where the Senegal River is flowing;
Their flesh is firm, and their sinews tough
   As the finest iron going.

I got them by barter, and gave in exchange
   Glass beads, steel goods, and some brandy;
I shall make at least eight hundred per cent,
   With but half of them living and handy.
                    —Christian Johann Heinrich Heine,
                    "The Slave Ship"[1]

On a frosty day in late February 1862, at a little past noon, 400 people stood solemnly in the walled-in stone courtyard of the Tombs, New York City's prison. Eighty were marines, dressed in Union blue and standing rigidly at attention with loaded rifles and fixed bayonets. The rest of the crowd consisted of reporters, politicians, and observers who had procured invitations to an unusual execution. The condemned, flanked by government officials, was a small, dark-haired man in a black frock coat. His arms were pinioned, a black hood covered his face, and a noose encircled his neck. The other end of the rope connected to the crossbeam of a gallows. He had been convicted of "piratically confining and detaining negroes with intent of making them slaves." His name was Nathaniel Gordon, and he was about to become the only man in the history of the United States to be hanged for the crime of slave trading.

Gordon's unique fate has been called a "fluke," resulting from "the chance conjunction of all the forces necessary to hang a pirate."[2] The law under which he was condemned had been passed 42 years earlier, yet previously neither captain nor sailor was ever given more than a dismissal, a perfunctory slap on the wrist, or, at worst, a fine and a brief jail sentence. It was rare that they were arrested in the first place. Considering the thousands of slaving voyages—and the millions of Africans taken—during that period, this record is nothing short of remarkable. When Gordon sailed for the Congo River in the early summer of 1860, he had absolutely no reason to anticipate a hanging in his future.

Nathaniel Gordon's story is inextricably linked with that of the entire history of the slave trade in America. It begins in 1619, when a "dutche man of warre" sold "twenty negars" to the settlers of Jamestown, Virginia, and slavery and the slave trade became an integral part of America's history.[3] Many of the Founding Fathers were slaveholders, and some signers of the Declaration of Independence, such as Philip Livingston of New York, made vast fortunes in the slave trade. This country was born with a devotion to the pursuit of profit, and rarely has there been an enterprise as lucrative as the slave trade. No amount of lip service paid by Washington or Jefferson regarding the offensiveness of the "peculiar institution" could mask the fact that half the country relied upon slave labor for its existence, and entrepreneurs and seamen from the other half provided it. If the South called for slaves, it was largely the New York and New England captains and their ships and crews that delivered them.

Some of our most enduring national figures dealt in the importation and sale of Africans. John Paul Jones, often called the "Father of the American Navy," began his career on a slave ship.[4] Two of America's most enduring folk heroes were active slavers. In our national lore, famed duelist and Texas patriot James Bowie died a hero's death at the Alamo, while Louisiana buccaneer Jean Lafitte fought beside Andrew Jackson to protect New Orleans from the British. Yet, working together, Bowie and Lafitte purchased slaves at one dollar per pound, and introduced them into the new western frontier at a tremendous profit.[5] The United States drew its first national breath as a slave-owning republic, and maintained that status well into the Civil War. Until the election of Abraham Lincoln, the government itself was decidedly proslavery. Ultimately, however, the government—more than willing to accept and often encourage slavery as an inextricable fiber of American life—came to see the trafficking in slaves as a repulsive practice and a blight on the image of the new nation.

The Founding Fathers "had to go through moral, linguistic, and political contortions to explain why their 'land of the free' was only for white people."[6] A masterwork of convoluted logic allowed Americans to morally distinguish between slavery and the slave trade. They found high-minded justification for what was clearly an economic issue. In order for proslavery forces—which included various presidents and large sections of Congress, as well as slave-owning Southerners and business-minded Northerners—to justify the institution of slavery while at the same time condemning the barbaric methods that actually provided the slaves, a distinction had to be made, defensible only if one did not look too closely. Trading in slaves is an act of violent, criminal abduction, ran the argument, and as such should be punishable by law—whereas slavery itself merely represents the preservation of a traditional, beneficent, and time-proven social order. Proponents suggested that slavery was not only good for the owners, but for the Blacks as well. Clergymen gave sermons claiming that bringing the benighted heathen to our shores gave him the opportunity to embrace Christianity. John Brown, a Rhode Island congressman, merchant, and slave trader, stood up in Congress and claimed that slavery "much bettered their condition."[7] After all, just witness how they propagated and thrived!

Near the end of the eighteenth century, the Congress of the recently independent United States passed the first in a series of laws designed to limit and eventually abolish the slave trade. It was called "an act to prohibit the carrying on of the slave trade from the United States to any foreign place or country," and it was voted into law only five years after Washington's inauguration. The 1794 act also specified that no ship's officer or owner, whether an American citizen or a foreigner, could legally "build, fit, equip, load, or otherwise prepare" a vessel within our borders for slave trading.[8]

This action was the first taken by any nation against the slave trade, and the prescribed penalty for conviction was $2,000 and forfeiture of the vessel. Six years later, Congress declared it illegal for Americans to carry slaves from one foreign port to another. There was a brief flurry of concern among the slavers, followed by a significant increase in the slave trade once they realized that nothing had really changed. Typical of the Northeastern states, tiny Rhode Island alone sent out more than

200 slaving expeditions between 1794 and 1804.[9] It was, in fact, this highly lucrative traffic that "enabled Newport to grow into a jewel of affluence."[10]

Although Congress had passed significant legislation, it had failed to provide for adequate enforcement. Legal trickery, creative judicial interpretation, bribery, intimidation, and a general unwillingness to put teeth into the laws resulted in acts that, while impressive on the books, reflected a shameful lack of determination and conviction on the part of the federal government. Sadly, this deficiency would continue unabated until the Civil War put an end to the Atlantic slave trade.

Meanwhile, several developments led to a brief demand for the importation of more slaves into the country. The western frontier was rapidly opening up to settlement, and the Louisiana Purchase added vast territory to the Union, much of which would come under the plow. Additionally, the invention of the cotton gin increased crop production, calling for a larger workforce. South Carolina spearheaded the movement for the increase in slave traffic. In the years 1804–1807, Charleston became the leading port of entry, welcoming at least 200 ships carrying more than 40,000 slaves.[11]

A landmark act was introduced in 1807, outlawing slave traffic between Africa and the United States. As Thomas Jefferson (himself a slaveholder) eloquently put it, it was now possible to "withdraw the citizens of the United States from all further participation in those violations of human rights which have so long continued on the unoffending inhabitants of Africa." With Jefferson's strong support, the 1807 act was passed. It would not take effect, however, for another ten months, thereby giving ships already at sea the opportunity to complete their business before coming under the law. Predictably, this precipitated another burst of activity from South Carolina, with both British and American slave ships delivering their cargoes to Charleston Harbor. South Carolina didn't restrict its activity to the importation of slaves; the number of Africa-bound ships cleared from Charleston rose from nine in 1804 to forty-three in 1807.[12]

The most surprising aspect of the 1807 act is not that it passed, but that it did so almost unanimously. The vote was 113 to 5; three negative votes came from the South, and of these only one was from South Carolina.[13] Given the number of Southerners, as well as proslavery Northerners, in Congress, how can we account for the anomaly?

Humanitarianism had little, if anything, to do with it. Many Southerners feared that any major increase in the Black population might upset the racial balance, and they were afraid of a large-scale slave revolt. They were well aware of what had occurred less than 16 years earlier in Haiti; the slaves there, drawing inspiration from the French Revolution, took over the country. Slave revolts in the American South, such as the 1739 Stono Rebellion near Charleston, had been few, small, local, and easily put down. This, however, did little to assuage the South's concern. The slaveholding South had determined not only that there were enough slaves, but also that the slaves were a self-perpetuating population. As early as 1760, Andrew Burnaby wrote, "The number of Negroes in the southern colonies is upon the whole nearly equal, if not superior, to that of the white men; and they propagate and increase even faster." [14]

In this, America was unique. Just as Africa's climate often proved unhealthy to Whites—journalists of the period referred to it as the "White man's grave"—Brazil and the Caribbean isles spelled death to the African. Historians differ as to the reasons for this. Some point to the many tropical diseases to which the slaves were susceptible, while others stress the relentlessly harsh working conditions imposed by the cultivation of sugar. From the days of the earliest slaving voyages in the mid-1600s until the prohibition of slavery in Jamaica in 1834, slavers introduced an estimated 750,000 slaves onto the island; by 1834, that population had been reduced to 311,000

Although it is impossible to pinpoint with total accuracy the number of Africans brought in chains to America during the country's first 200 years, it is estimated at between 600,000 and 650,000. From this initial importation figure the slave population in the United States, through "natural population growth," had swelled to 1.1 million by 1810. American-born slaves outnumbered imported Africans long before the Revolution. By 1860, the population had more than tripled, to 4 million. Allowing for the relatively small number of slaves imported in the 50 years before the Civil War, this represents an amazing demographic. [15]

The 1807 law promised stiff penalties for those caught importing slaves into the United States. It was a promise rarely kept. The government had no more effectively enforced this act than it had the two that preceded it. Incredibly, 13 years after this act passed, President Monroe's treasury secretary, William H. Crawford, reported to Congress, "It appears, from an examination of the records of this office, that no particular instructions have ever been given, by the Secretary of the Treasury, under the original or supplementary acts prohibiting the introduction of slaves into the United States." Despite the overwhelming support in passing the law, no structure existed to enforce it.[16]

Ironically, slave importation into the United States did decline, but it was due more to a dwindling market than fear of fine, forfeiture, or imprisonment. Over the next 58 years, there would be only sporadic bursts of importation activity, with a real resurgence of the trade in the 1840s and 1850s. But if the American market reflected a downturn, Brazil and Cuba were clamoring for slave labor to work their coffee and sugar crops. Although a slave would bring less on the blocks of Havana or Rio de Janeiro than in Charleston or New Orleans, the market was wide open, and American slavers pursued it avidly. Estimates show that between 1810 and 1850, when roughly 50,000 Africans were being smuggled into the United States, about 2 million were sold into Cuba and Brazil. Americans played a significant role in this traffic.[17]

President Madison, understandably discouraged at the lack of punitive response to the three acts, stated in his 1810 message to Congress

> It appears that American citizens are instrumental in carrying on a traffic in enslaved Africans, equally in violation of the laws of humanity, and in defiance of those of their own country. The same just and benevolent motives which produced the interdiction in force against this criminal conduct, will doubtless be felt by Congress, in devising further means of suppressing the evil.[18]

Eight years later Congress passed yet another act, this time actually *lowering* the penalties for outfitting a slaver or enslaving Africans. The government hoped to make it easier for the courts to more aggressively convict and punish captured offenders. Significantly, however, it prohibited fitting out slave ships in foreign ports. Now, if a ship left the United States with the *intention* of making a slave run, it was in direct violation of the law.

Finally, in 1820, Congress raised the stakes by passing a law that made slave trading a capital offense. It declared, in no uncertain terms, that any U.S. citizen on the crew of a foreign slave ship, or anyone serving on a U.S. ship that seized a "Negro or mulatto . . . shall be adjudged a pirate; and . . . shall suffer death."[19]

When the House Committee on the Slave Trade introduced the bill, committee chairman Henry Mercer wrote,

> [We] cannot perceive wherein the offense of kidnapping an . . . inhabitant of a foreign country; of chaining him down for a series of days, weeks, and months, amidst the dying and the dead, to the pestilential hold of a slave ship; of consigning him, if he chance to live out the voyage, to perpetual slavery, in a remote and unknown land, differs in malignity from piracy, or why a milder punishment should follow the one, than the other crime.[20]

Although the law applied only to American citizens and to foreigners serving on American slavers, it went further than any antislavery law the world had yet seen. It was also the government's final legislative move against the slave trade. One figurative toe at a time, Congress now had an entire foot in the water. The other foot, representing actual enforcement of the five acts, would remain on dry land until the abolition of slavery.

Ironically, an opportunity for strict enforcement of the slave trade laws was available to the United States almost from the beginning, but it meant collaborating with the British. An event occurred in 1807 that would have a stunning impact on the world's shipping, and, more specifically, on the international slave trade. England, the world's largest slaving nation, outlawed its own slave trade. Actual abolition of slavery by Britain would have to wait until 1833, but for now, no slave ships would leave British ports. But the law did not stop there; with a mandate from Parliament, the British navy assumed the role of policeman of the seas. Britain's motives were not especially altruistic. Its policy makers were considered to be "among the world's most brazen hypocrites, attempting to turn purity into profit by using humanitarianism as a cloak for selfish motives."[21] In reality, the British were trying to protect the commerce of their colonies by denying slave labor to their competitors, chiefly Spain, France, Portugal, Brazil, and the United States. By boarding foreign ships and capturing slaves bound for America, Brazil, and the Caribbean, they would not only be depriving their rivals of a much-needed labor force but they also could then add these "rescued" slaves to the half million Blacks already at work in the cane fields, mills, and boiling houses of the British Caribbean. Although a small number of rescued slaves were taken to Sierra Leone, a Crown-operated colony devoted to the repatriation of liberated Africans, thousands more would find themselves toiling in misery on the Cuban cane or Brazilian coffee plantations of British colonials.[22]

Britain demanded the right of search and seizure of all ships, on all international waters. Spain, Portugal, and Brazil eventually complied; France and the United States refused. The United States looked askance at any attempt by Britain to board and search American vessels at sea. One of America's major issues for seeking independence had been the impressment of her seamen into the British navy. In fact, Britain was still actively involved in taking Americans off U.S. merchant and naval ships, and "pressing" them into service. The same year Britain declared the abolition of her slave trade, her warship HMS *Leopard* attacked the American naval frigate *Chesapeake* off the coast of Virginia, killing or wounding 21 men and removing several of her American crew by force. This incident, and the outcry it caused, fueled President Madison's rallying cry "Free Trade and Sailors' Rights" and helped propel the United States into the War of 1812.[23]

As time passed, America's attitude should have mellowed sufficiently for her to accept Britain's help in her antislavery efforts, but this didn't happen. Even John Quincy Adams, whose intense opposition to the slave trade was later demonstrated during the *Amistad* trials, balked at the notion of maritime interference from Britain. When asked by the British foreign minister if he could envision anything more horrendous than the slave trade, Adams replied, "Yes. Admitting the right of search by foreign officers of our vessels upon the seas in time of peace; for that would be making slaves of ourselves."[24] America bristled at interference with her ships, from the inception of Britain's antislave trade policy until Abraham Lincoln's administration—a refusal fueled by equal parts bitter experience, inflated patriotism, and economic self-interest.

The United States irreparably weakened its already feeble antislaving activities in two ways by refusing to work with Britain. First, America denied herself the assistance of Britain's large, aggressive, and amazingly successful navy, whose record of seizures in the first half of the nineteenth century was stunning compared to our own. Regardless of motive, Britain sent its ships after slavers with an almost biblical zeal, seizing more than 500 vessels and 38,000 captive Africans from 1842 to 1850 alone; while the United States, according to the 1850 annual report of Secretary of the Navy William A. Graham, captured 7 ships in the same period.[25]

Second, the United States' consistently anti-British policies required that the few American naval vessels capable of hunting slavers would now be used to protect American shipping from foreign interference. The pursuit and capture of slave ships would take a distant backseat. For decades, slavers enjoyed a virtual holiday from interference, with only rare exceptions.[26]

Had the United States cooperated with Britain at any point, the slave trade would certainly have ended earlier. As it was, the trade flourished throughout the first half of the nineteenth century, as Yankee captains continued to fit out their ships in Providence; New York City; Portland, Maine; Havana; Rio; or any of a dozen other sympathetic ports, and sail to the west coast of Africa for slaves. The Brazilian and Cuban markets were strong, the risks low, and the potential for profits enormous.

Meanwhile, the record of convictions in the courts was as poor as that of seizures at sea. In New York City, where most of the Northern prosecutions took place, only one-sixth of those indicted were convicted. The rest were either acquitted, forfeited bail, escaped from custody, or were released because of hung juries or the court's unwillingness to prosecute. From 1837 to 1861 (when Captain Gordon alone made at least four slaving voyages), around 125 accused slave traders—officers and crewmen—were prosecuted in New York City; only 20 were given prison sentences, averaging two years apiece. Of these men, 10 received presidential pardons, and 3 more—indicted for capital crimes under the piracy act of 1820—were allowed to plead to lesser charges. One was briefly convicted of piracy, but the conviction was overturned on a technicality. Clearly, no one in power *wanted* to hang a man for trafficking in slaves.[27]

The record of the Southern courts was even worse. While the slave trade surged in the 1840s and 1850s, after 1846 not a single person was convicted in a Southern federal court on charges relating to slaving.[28] In 1858, the brig *Putnam,* sailing under the false name *Echo,* was seized off Cuba with 318 sick and suffering Africans chained belowdeck. Her owner/captain and 16 crew members were taken to Charleston, that bastion of proslaving sentiment. Indicted under the 1820 act by a reluctant jury, all 16 crewmen were acquitted despite a mountain of incriminating evidence. The owner/captain was freed when a federal judge instructed the jury to release him on a minor technicality.[29]

From the passage of the first antislaving law, the legal system displayed an almost complete lack of effectiveness. Customs officials and law enforcement officers were bribed outright, and judges frequently took advantage of legal loopholes and subjective interpretations to make a mockery of the slave-trade laws. But by 1860—the year in which Gordon sailed from Havana—a perceptive observer might have sensed a coming change. The new order of things, wrapped in a national war, would be stunning, and bring with it the full weight of social reform. An example would be required to show that the old ways were indeed gone. Nathaniel Gordon was caught up in this most vital turning point in American history, and by standing in exactly the wrong place at the wrong time, he would provide that example: with his death.

Many forces and players came together in the Gordon drama. On the one side, there were those who worked relentlessly to bring Gordon to the gallows: the young and aggressive prosecutor, who made Gordon his personal demon; the U.S. marshal who did everything within his power to ensure Gordon's death; the federal judge who, in *U.S. v. Gordon,* would be presiding over his first slave-trade case; the increasing number of abolitionists, for whom nothing was as important as the extinction of slavery and those who made it possible; and ultimately, President Abraham Lincoln, known for his compassionate nature, beleaguered by pressures from all directions, but always mindful of the larger issues. In the Gordon case, they all saw an opportunity to deal a potentially fatal blow to the slave trade.

On the other side stood those who wanted Gordon spared: the corrupt officials, who, for a bribe, would facilitate a slaver's escape from prison; the lax U.S. attorney, unwilling to send a man to the gallows for trafficking in humans; the old-guard justices, who would bend the law to the breaking point to spare a slave trader; Gordon's devoted young wife and child, torn from a comfortable life and thrown into a nightmare; the moderates, who saw only foolishness in punishing the supplier while allowing the institution of slavery to continue; the successful and respected New York law firm whose specialty was defending accused slavers.

And the drama itself would unfold in New York City—that elegant, sordid, violent bastion of the slave trade.

• • •

The three-year period between Gordon's execution and the actual demise of the African slave trade, as practiced by American slavers, in
1865, saw enough slavers arrested for piracy to assume a similar fate
awaited them. This was not to be. Some were clearly as guilty as Gordon, and yet they were allowed to escape the rope, just as so many had
before. For a brief moment, a portal opened, and only one man fell
through.

# CHAPTER I

# LUCKY NAT

Early in 1860, a young sea captain from Portland, Maine, sailed south to Havana, Cuba, leaving behind a two-year-old son and a pretty young wife. The fourth in as many generations to bear the name, Nathaniel Gordon was a short—five-foot-five—and muscular man with a ruddy complexion, a dark beard, and small piercing eyes. Gordon was not a handsome man; a reporter once described him as "repulsive" in appearance.[1] His demeanor reflected a quiet intensity and a confidence found in one used to giving orders. He was a slave trader—a "blackbirder" in the slang of the time—and upon arriving in Cuba, he would take command of a full-rigged ship and provision her for a voyage to the Congo River, on the west coast of Africa. It would be his fourth slaving expedition.

Nathaniel Gordon's early life is sketchy, where information exists at all. Large numbers of personal records were destroyed in major fires in Portland in 1866 and 1908. Gordon was born on February 6, 1826, almost certainly in Portland.[2] (His attorney would later claim that he was born in British waters, under the British flag, on one of his father's voyages, and was consequently not an American citizen.) Gordon's father was a merchant captain, and his mother would sometimes accompany her husband on board ship. In addition to Nathaniel, she would bear two girls: Dorcas Ellen was four years older than her brother; Mary, named for her mother, was almost exactly eight years younger.[3] The Gordons were an old New England family; Nathaniel's earliest American ancestor arrived at Plymouth nine generations earlier, in 1621, aboard the *Fortune*.

On February 22, 1862, the day after Gordon's death, the *New York Times* published an extensive article about his life. In all likelihood, it represents an amalgam of recollections by the clergymen, doctors, and jailers who knew him briefly, and were retelling Gordon's own accounts of his life. And the writer, presenting the second- or thirdhand story, added the expected Victorian embellishments, to provide both a history and a morality lesson.

> Thirty-five years ago, in the City of Portland, a well-to-do couple were gladdened by the birth of a son. [In fact, Gordon had died just fifteen days past his thirty-sixth birthday.] The boy, who was delicately made, grew rapidly, and in his earliest years, developed unusual vigor of mind, which gave promise of a useful and honorable manhood. At the age of fifteen he manifested suddenly a desire to go to sea. His parents, who had fondly watched his rapid progress at school, demurred, but the boy, already the ruler of the domestic circle, was determined, and to sea he went. His father, Capt. Gordon, had been a seafaring man for years, and soon recovered from the disappointment which, to the mother, has been a source of life-long grief, and which was the means by which the son NATHANIEL GORDON attained [his] disgraceful end.

The writer describes an admirable young Gordon who avidly pursues a sailor's life, and whose skill, loyalty, and abstinence from "vicious habits" win him friends and impress his employers. When, at 20, he is offered a captaincy, he continues to work with zeal, and impresses the citizens of Portland with his "ability, energy, and good reputation." His enthusiasm takes a dark turn, however, as he is consumed with a craving for riches, according to the *Times* account.

Gordon has property worth thousands of dollars, the article continues, and is part owner of a "fine ship" by the time he is 25, but he sells everything, resigns his command, and travels to California in search of greater riches. The writer has Gordon falling in with "certain moneyed parties" on the return trip, who lure the young captain into the slave trade, tempting him with "enormous profits, little risk of detection and certain immunity from punishment."

Gordon ultimately commands at least four slaving voyages, according to the *Times,* two of which made him and his employers an "immense amount" of money. The article describes the young slaver's thrilling life at sea. "Very many hair-breadth escapes, such as daring sailors delight in, were his fortune." Often pursued by both American and British cruisers, Gordon always managed to escape. His life was an exciting one, and he claimed he had found no greater pleasure than when eluding the slave-catchers. "The same adventurous spirit, the same careful study, the same business tact and attentive industry which aided his upward career while engaged in lawful pursuits, marked his disgraceful career, and he was known amongst his fellow traders as 'Lucky Nat.' "[4]

The *Times* account reads like a story from Dickens, seasoned with a healthy dash of Robert Louis Stevenson: a good boy gone bad for the sake of gold. Actually, it might be said that, far from disappointing his father, Nathaniel Gordon was taking over the family business. When Gordon was 12 years old, his father was arrested for attempting to smuggle a slave into the country. The July 7, 1838, issue of the New York newspaper *The Colored American* printed an article entitled "Bringing Slaves into the United States," in which it reported that the senior Gordon was charged with importing a single slave from Point Petre, Guadeloupe, on his brig *Dunlap*. He was "held to bail in $5000," and if convicted, he could have faced the gallows.[5] There is no record of how the case was resolved, but it is safe to say that Captain Gordon never suffered the full weight of the law.[6] Ironically, it was this same circuit court—Southern District of New York—that would see Gordon's son Nathaniel on trial for his own life 23 years later.

There was little in the culture or society of Portland to discourage the Gordons—or any other seamen—from pursuing careers as slavers. New England's sea captains had sailed to Africa for generations in search of native cargoes. And of all the Northern states, Maine was known as the "least likely to burn with the fires of abolition." By virtue of its geography, as well as a minuscule African American population, it was literally the farthest removed from the heat of the slavery issue. In 1840, when Gordon was 14 years of age, Portland counted only 402 African Americans, out of 15,218 residents; by 1860, the year of his final voyage, the number of residents had grown to 26,342, while the African American population had dropped to 318.[7] There was a small but fiercely dedicated core of men, though, who kept the antislavery issue "before an unappreciative public" from the early 1830s until the Civil War.[8] Their impact was minimal, however. Throughout the state, the speeches of such abolitionist luminaries as William Lloyd Garrison, Austin Willey, and Reverend David Thurston were disrupted by mobs throwing eggs and wielding hoses, with the featured speaker exiting ignominiously through the rear door.[9]

Maine's abolitionists were largely involved in fruitless debates with those who favored colonization of the Blacks. As the antislavers saw it, America's responsibility lay with freeing Blacks, not merely removing them from its shores. In the end, their efforts in Maine failed utterly.[10]

The churches of Portland, and of Maine in general, would not begin to adopt an antislavery stance until around 1856. The state's most famous clergyman was the Reverend John W. Chickering, whose High Street Congregational Church numbered the Gordons among its flock. (Young Nathaniel attended Sunday school there.) Of all the churches and denominations in Maine, the Congregationalists were the richest and the most politically conservative, but Reverend Chickering, on a trip to England in 1846, "had passed himself off . . . as a committed anti-slavery man." Whether this was the truth or merely an attempt to impress his hosts, he came under a storm of criticism—which sank to the level of personal vilification—from Maine's die-hard abolitionists. To their way of thinking, Chickering talked a good show abroad, but did nothing for the cause at home, other than speak out against slavery "in the abstract. . . . And who was not against slavery in the abstract?"[11]

Growing up in the city where generations of Gordons had achieved commercial success and social status, and where racial consciousness was practically nonexistent, Nathaniel developed into an enterprising young man. Only two years after he earned his captain's papers, he was involved in a telling incident off the coast of Brazil. The first half of the nineteenth century saw Cuba and Brazil alternating positions as most favored site for outfitting ships and selling slaves. In the late 1840s, the port of choice was Rio de Janeiro, and would remain so until Brazil virtually closed its ports to the slave trade. In June 1848, the 1,000-ton, iron-hulled U.S. Navy steamer *Allegheny* was assigned to the coast of Brazil to patrol for slavers. Gorham Parks, United States consul to Brazil, sent orders to its commander, Lieutenant William W. Hunter, alerting him to the presence of the *Juliet,* captained by Nathaniel Gordon. The street talk in Rio had the *Juliet* carrying shackles, leaving no doubt as to the ship's purpose. According to local gossip, the ship's cook would be willing to show the officers where the chains were hidden. Because the cook supposedly feared reprisals from local slavers, Hunter would have to wait until after the *Juliet* left port before boarding her.

The *Juliet* set sail on June 10; Hunter overtook her five miles out to sea. He sent a contingent aboard her, and ordered a search that lasted nearly 12 hours. But the cook reversed himself, decrying all knowledge of hidden slave chains, and nothing incriminating was found. There were goods and objects that could be used to trade for and sustain slaves on a sea voyage, but these might just as easily serve as legitimate trade goods.

Since there was nothing on board the *Juliet* to provide Lieutenant Hunter with proof that she was bound on a slaving expedition, he had no choice but to let her go, and to assume that the talk in Rio had been unfounded. Later, however, word circulated that the *Juliet* had in fact sailed to Africa, taken on a cargo of slaves, and returned to Brazil. There was never any proof, but this was probably Gordon's first slaving voyage.[12]

Gordon again drew official attention to himself in 1851. As the *Times* article stated, he had indeed gone to California in search of riches. But although the strikes of three years earlier were still luring men by the thousands, he would seek his fortune far from the gold fields. In San Francisco, Gordon met a man named Levi H. Fenner. According to the Fenner family history, Levi Fenner was an ambitious young fellow. Sensing the opportunity for profit in California, he had left his home in Pennsylvania early in 1851 and traveled to New York. There, Fenner and some companions went partners on a brig, the *Camargo,* in which they made the dangerous trip around Cape Horn to San Francisco, where Fenner started a business, possibly a tannery, and prospered. In less than a year, he bought his partners' shares in the *Camargo,* becoming her sole owner. Fenner loaded the brig with a cargo of hides to be taken to New York City for sale. He hired twenty-five-year-old Nathaniel Gordon as captain.

Once at sea, Gordon won over the crew, probably with the promise of gold; he ordered the hides thrown over the side, commandeered the *Camargo,* and sailed to Rio de Janeiro, where he outfitted the ship for a slaving voyage to Africa.[13]

The voyage of the *Camargo* has the distinction of being the last slaving expedition to land Africans on the coast of Brazil.[14] But it was not an overwhelming success. Gordon had sailed from Rio under the watchful and suspicious eye of then U.S. consul Edward Kent. Taking a circuitous route in order to avoid naval patrol vessels, the *Camargo* landed briefly at the Cape of Good Hope, then sailed to the distant *east* coast of Africa. Here, Gordon boarded about 500 Africans, filled his water casks, and made the return voyage to Brazil. Despite Gordon's precautions, however, he was pursued by a British man-of-war as he approached the Brazilian coast, so he quickly landed his cargo and burned the ship. The Africans were soon seized, and some of the crewmen arrested and charged with slave trading. Through interviews with some of the captured sailors, Consul Kent learned that Gordon had "escaped in woman's clothes, hastily put on in the cabin, his small frame rendering the disguise comparatively easy of accomplishment."[15] "It is now reported," Kent wrote, "that Captain Gordon has gone to the United States, but this fact is uncertain."[16]

Even if Gordon had successfully delivered his cargo, he still might have chosen to burn his ship, to avoid prosecution. The 452-ton bark *Sultana* was torched by her owners in 1860, after she had successfully delivered between 850 and 1,300 Africans to the coast of Cuba. The crew, claiming to be castaways, traveled to Key West in a fishing boat, and no trace was ever found of the *Sultana*. Her captain, Francis Bowen, was a known slaver, and rumors of her voyage ran from New York to New Orleans. But the courts could not prosecute on the strength of rumors. The *Sultana,* despite her fiery end, was a successful slaver.[17]

The brig *Sophia* made a successful run from Africa to Brazil in 1841, with a load of 500 captives. Once safely docked, she was burned to the water line, "being a telltale liability worth only a small fraction of [her] recent cargo."[18] Twenty years later, the brig *Nancy,* alternating between legal and slaving voyages, delivered a shipload of 690 Africans to Cuba, and was then set aflame by her captain.[19]

Although the destruction of a fully functional vessel worth upward of $14,000 seems an unnecessary waste, it was a practical decision. If the trip was successful, the profit from the sale of the slaves far exceeded the worth of the ship. Should the voyage prove a disaster, however, the destruction of the ship was often an unfortunate necessity: it was the most expedient way to remove incriminating evidence and eliminate the cost of refitting.

There is no information on Gordon's life between the voyages of the *Juliet* and the *Camargo*. In fact, we know very little about his third trip, beyond what we are told by U.S. Marshal Robert Murray, the man responsible for Gordon during his trials and imprisonment in 1851. Shortly after returning home from the *Camargo* debacle, Gordon made a slaving voyage to Cuba in the bark *Ottawa* after taking on a cargo of Africans. But once again, the vast profits that he had sought eluded him. According to Murray's account, Gordon reached Cuba with only 25 percent of his cargo still alive. Gordon claimed that the others had been poisoned on the Congo River by a rival of the trader from whom he had bought the slaves. Gordon burned this vessel as well, after landing what remained of his "merchandise.'[20]

The loss of so many lives on a single trip is truly horrific, but the captains and crews of the slave ships were steeled to it. As far back as 1706, Sir Dalby Thomas, commander of the Royal Africa Company of England, wrote an instructive to potential slavers: "Your captains and mates . . . must neither have dainty fingers or dainty noses, few men are fit for these voyages but them that are bred up to it. It's a filthy voyage as well as a laborious [one]."[21] In the 160 years that followed, this would not change.

Attrition was the inevitable result of any slaving voyage. There would always be deaths; it was just a question of numbers. The deaths were frequent enough, however, that the crewmen of slavers often told of the schools of sharks that followed their ships all the way from Africa to their final destination. Much has been written about the horrors of the infamous Middle Passage—the voyage from Africa to America, Brazil, or the islands of the Caribbean—so called because it represented the second leg of a three-part trip by the slaver: from home in the United States or Europe to Africa for the cargo of slaves; then from Africa to the place of sale; and, finally, home again. The Middle Passage took anywhere from several weeks to three months. Debilitated, often already ill and half-starved from the trek from the African interior to the coast and the waiting slave ship, the Africans

> are packed below in as dense a mass as it is possible for human beings to be crowded; the space allotted them being . . . about four feet high between decks, there, of course, can be but little ventilation given. These unfortunate beings are obliged to attend to the calls of nature in this place—tubs being provided for the purpose—and here they pass their days, their nights, amidst the most horribly offensive odors of which the mind can conceive, and this under the scorching heat of the tropical sun, without room enough for sleep; with scarcely space to die in; with daily

allowance of food and water barely sufficient to keep them alive. The passage varies from forty to sixty days, and when it has much exceeded the shorter time disease has appeared in its most appalling forms, the provisions and water are nearly exhausted, and their sufferings are terrible.[22]

All ships at sea had their own cacophony of sounds: the wind in the sheets and sails, the groan and crack of wood driven by water and weather, the commands of the officers shouting to be heard above it all, and the responding cries of the crew. Aboard a slaver, the perpetual groans and pleadings of hundreds of desperate, often dying humans were added as well. In 1854, the slaver Captain Theodore Canot, a contemporary of Gordon, recorded his memoirs of a lifetime of trafficking in humans. He tells of the ship *Volador,* which lost 136 of its 747 captives:

> The degree of mortality was not unusual; neither was the overcrowding. The slaves were laid on their sides, spoon-fashion, the bent knees of one fitting into the hamstrings of his neighbour. On some vessels, they could not even lie down; they spent the voyage sitting in each other's laps.[23] The stench was terrific. A British officer testified that one could smell a slaver "five miles down wind."[24]

The death rate among the captives varied, depending on the length of the voyage, the severity of conditions on board, and the callousness of captain and crew. It averaged 17.5 percent among captured American slavers for the period 1844–1864; out of every 1,000 Africans shipped as slaves, approximately 175 perished.[25] Captives died of disease, thirst, starvation, suffocation, exhaustion, suicide, and sometimes simply despair. If a captive attempted suicide and failed, he or she would be mutilated, tortured, or executed to provide an example for the others. Should slaves revolt against the horrific conditions, they would be summarily hanged, shot, or drowned. Between the high rate of mortality aboard ship and that of the slave in his first year ashore—the period of adjustment to a slave's existence that the owners euphemistically called "seasoning"—nearly one in every three people taken from Africa in bondage would die during the process of enslavement.[26]

In 1847, the brig *Senator* boarded 900 slaves. The first night, 74 died of suffocation. Before the three weeks' voyage was done, more than 200 additional captives had perished of thirst. The *Senator* eventually delivered only 600 of her slaves to Brazil. Through neglect and cruelty, one-third had died.[27]

Commanded by Captain Luke Collingwood, the British ship *Zong* picked up 400 African slaves and set sail for Jamaica on September 6, 1781. Within two and a half months, he had lost 60 captives; several more were ill, and he was running short of water. If the slaves were to die on their own, the ship's owners would take the loss. However, if they were thrown over the side while living, it could be claimed that they were washed overboard. This would be attributed to "perils of the sea," and the insurance company would have to pay. Consequently, the captain selected 54 sick slaves and cast them overboard, living and bound. Two days later, he followed with another 42. That same day, it rained, providing the ship with enough water for 11 days. Nonetheless, Collingwood threw 26 more into the sea, bound at the wrists. As he was about to prepare another 10 for a like fate, they elected to take their own lives and jumped overboard. The underwriters of the voyage, suspicious, refused to honor the insurance policy. The ship owners sued them, and the British courts obliged them to pay the premium.[28]

Stories abound of slaver captains who chose to jettison their cargo rather than face fine, imprisonment, or forfeiture of their vessels. One such slaver, an Englishman named Homans, had already completed 10 successful voyages, delivering around 5,000 Africans to the shores of Brazil and Cuba. On the return of his eleventh voyage, he found his brig, the *Brillante,* surrounded by four cruisers. He immediately had his cargo of 600 manacled captives herded to the rail and bound to the anchor chain. When the cruisers' boats lowered and made for the *Brillante,* Homans had the anchor thrown over the side; it plummeted to the ocean floor, carrying every man, woman, and child with it. When the warships' crews boarded the *Brillante,* they found clear evidence that several hundred human beings had occupied the hold only moments before, but they could do nothing. They were forced to release the brig, as Homans "jeered in their faces and defied them as they stood on his deck."[29]

What would allow for such a callous disregard for life? Greed. In fact, a successful slaving voyage was profitable beyond all reason. It has been estimated that during the mid-1800s, when Nathaniel Gordon was pursuing his career, a slave purchased in Africa for approximately $40 worth of trade goods would bring a price ranging from $400 to $1,200. Therefore, the selling price of a cargo of, say, 800 slaves ranged between $320,000 and $960,000. Even after factoring in the cost of outfitting the ship, paying—and paying off—all the people involved in the voyage, and the inevitable loss of "inventory," a successful slaving expedition realized a profit many times in excess of the initial investment. Consider that $100 in the 1850s would be worth around $4,000 today, and the allure of such a venture becomes apparent. Given such returns, a single successful trip could more than compensate for three or four previous failures, and make the fortunes of investors and captain.[30]

Again, nothing is known of Gordon's seafaring activities during the four years after he burned the *Ottawa*. However, the Gordon family Bible records that on March 28, 1855, Nathaniel Gordon embarked upon an adventure of another sort. In Cape Elizabeth, within sight of his native Portland, he married Elizabeth Annie Kenney, by all reports a slight and remarkably pretty young woman. Gordon was twenty-nine years old; Elizabeth was fifteen or sixteen. Just over two years later, on April 28, she would bear him a son; in keeping with family tradition, they named him Nathaniel.[31]

Judging by Gordon's final letters, and Elizabeth's devotion to him during his long period of incarceration, the marriage was a successful one, characterized by mutual love and devotion. Given the failure of his two previous trips, it is unlikely that Gordon could afford to lounge on shore for the four years between voyages. The Gordons' lifestyle was far from lavish; Nathaniel, Elizabeth, and their young son lived in his mother's modest row house, along with an aunt. There were probably opportunities for an experienced captain to command vessels shipping out of Portland, and it's likely that Gordon accepted various commissions during this time. At worst, he could have earned money by signing on as a mate or able-bodied seaman. Then, in 1860, came the opportunity to command another slave ship, and Gordon sailed for Havana to take command of the *Erie*.

The reporter for the *New York Times,* in his highly embroidered article of February 22, 1862, told of Gordon's goal:

Had he reached the port of destination with the usual proportion of living Negroes, an immense fortune would have been made, and in that event, as he declared, he would have returned to the United States rich and contented, with the prospect of a happy shore-life before him. But it was ordained otherwise.[32]

# CHAPTER II

## SLAVERS AND THE LAW

Havana was the capital of Spain's richest and most important colony, and her stone-and-stucco architecture reflected her status. Overwhelmingly Catholic, the city boasted many large and beautiful churches, some going back hundreds of years. One visitor at the time commented that his two strongest impressions of Havana were the constant ringing of the church bells and the taste of guava. Lining Havana's more affluent streets were the mansions of the Spanish aristocrats and the planters and merchants who made their fortunes in sugar. The houses were as finely built and elaborate as any found in Europe, with elegant wrought-iron window bars, gateways, and balconies, from which hung baskets of tropical flowers. The buildings reflected various styles; some featured elaborate stone scrollwork, while others bore the more austere Greek columns made popular in the early 1800s. Large windows and bright colors were the fashion in 1860, and walls throughout the city were painted shades of blue, yellow, pink, and green. In keeping with the custom of the tropics, most of the better structures opened onto courtyards shaded by palms and redolent with the scent of flowers. Havana's middle class, attempting to emulate the styles of the rich, built their houses as smaller, more modest versions of their social betters. Brightly colored awnings were hung between houses on many of the streets to create shade, and vendors offered cool drinks and a wide variety of fruits to passersby.

The city's government buildings embodied the centuries-old but fast-fading majesty of Spain; built of large blocks, they were imposing, no-nonsense structures, constructed for the maintenance of the empire. Two stone *castillos*—El Morro and La Punta—stood on either side of Havana Bay, their cannons guarding the harbor. A huge chain connected them: when the city was threatened, the chain would be raised, effectively closing off the harbor to sea traffic.

Havana was a city of contrasts. The smells of the city were those of flowers and garbage; of spice and mildew; of coffee, tobacco, and perfume. One Cuban author, recalling Havana after a rain, described the "smell of woman, of gravesoil and bedclothes, of kissing and foliage." And while many of the citizens lived in luxury—or at least relative comfort—others lived in utter squalor, in makeshift shacks clustered in muddy alleys that reeked of filth and fostered disease. Malaria and yellow fever epidemics were common.[1]

The city was a bastion of a caste system, determined mainly by race. In order of social prominence, there were the Whites; free persons of color (*"gentes de color"*), including Blacks and mulattos; Chinese brought over as "indentured servants"—slaves, really—after 1847; and, at the bottom rung, the slaves of African descent. Although Spain had officially outlawed the slave trade decades earlier, it was unofficially encouraged as the most efficient means of processing the island's sugar, molasses, and rum.[2] There had been a brief decline in the trade in the 1840s, when the demand had shifted to Brazil, but Cuba experienced a major resurgence in the 1850s, culminating in 1859, when an all-time high of 25,000 Africans were sold to the island's sugar plantations.[3] When Gordon arrived in Havana, Cuba's 2,000 mills were providing one-third of the world's sugar and the slave trade was flourishing as never before.[4] The city, in addition to providing a welcome market for slaves, was also the safest port in which to outfit a slaver. With Spain looking the other way, Cuba's customs officials were lax and corrupt. The captain general of Cuba claimed that the law against slave trading applied only to Spanish ships; consequently, American ships were free to outfit in the harbor with impunity.[5]

Nathaniel Gordon had been hired to sail to Havana and assume command of the *Erie,* a full-rigged, three-masted ship of nearly 477 tons. Built in Swansea, Massachusetts, in 1849 or 1850, at a length of only 122 feet,[6] the vessel would have been considered small for her class. Gordon's mandate from his employers was to sail the *Erie* to the Congo River on the west coast of Africa, exchange a cargo of whiskey for several hundred slaves, and deliver them to Cuba.

The *Erie* sailed from Liverpool with a load of coal and arrived in Havana on January 20 under the command of American captain and part-owner Gilbert A. Knudson. According to the story he told U.S. consul general Charles J. Helm, he had had extensive repair work—$4,000 worth—done to the ship's bottom before leaving England on the provision that he would send payment back to England after his arrival in Havana. Once in Cuba, however, he couldn't raise the money.

Knudson stayed in Havana for nearly two months, supposedly waiting for his partners in New York to authorize payment. Meanwhile, five men—one-third of his crew—deserted. Finally, on March 17, Knudson reported to Consul General Helm that he had chartered his vessel to "Messrs. Hamel & Co.," explaining that he was too old and sick to remain in Cuba, and had to return to his business in New York. Captain Nathaniel Gordon assumed command of the *Erie* under the Hamel charter. He would keep the true nature of his voyage a secret until the *Erie* was well out to sea; nonetheless, within four days of his appointment as captain, another six crewmen—five Europeans and an American—were discharged at their own request.[7]

Although these events appear convoluted, they are in fact an example of the procedures followed by slaving companies to maintain anonymity, to distance themselves from any legal connection with the enterprise. For decades, ships from New York, Baltimore, and numerous other ports sailed to Cuba, where their captains or owners would arrange the sale or charter—real or spurious—of their vessels. They would then report the transaction to the consul general, who would stamp the bill of sale or agreement, as well as any changes of crews and captains, thereby making it official. If an outbound vessel were stopped at sea by a naval patrol, its papers would declare it to be on a legitimate voyage, sanctioned by the U.S. government; if a "laden" vessel were stopped returning to Cuba with a cargo of slaves, there would be nothing to link the original owners to the slaving voyage.[8] Since Knudson's partners and his "business" were in New York, they probably either hired out the *Erie* to one of New York's "shadow" slaving companies or financed the voyage themselves. By chartering the ship to "Messrs. Hamel & Co.," they were breaking the chain of accountability. The Spanish customhouse referred to Messrs. Hamel and Co. as "merchants of this place," so it is highly likely that they were acting as agents for the slaving company.[9] Knudson's report to Helm was no more than a ploy to officially eliminate any connection between his company and Gordon.

Captain Gordon now had his course laid and his orders in hand. But first the ship had to be fitted out and provisioned. This entailed not only ensuring that everything needed to successfully operate the vessel—rope, sails, anchors, and the like—was in sufficient store and good condition, but that the needs of the crew and the "cargo" were addressed as well—food, water, medicine, clothing.

A slave ship's supplies—and the *Erie* was no exception—far exceeded the requirements of a crew of 15 to 18 men for a conventional voyage. In anticipation of the hundreds of captives soon to occupy the ship, there were tons of grain and huge boilers—"coppers"—for cooking it. Dockworkers also rolled aboard large barrels of salt pork and beef, and shouldered dozens of sacks of beans. Although it was not uncommon to bring pigs, chickens, and other animals aboard ships, there is no record that the *Erie* shipped any livestock. Slave ships also stored stacks of hoops and "shooks" (disassembled water casks), and large quantities of medicine and disinfectants.

The more dedicated slave traders went so far as to write their own medical manuals. Some ships smelled of pitch, with which the captains smoked their vessels to discourage the spread of smallpox among the slaves and crew.[10] The captain's cabin might hold a store of weapons—pistols, muskets, cutlasses—to keep order among the captives. An iron grating might cover the hold, to keep the captives secured below and to provide what little ventilation they would receive. The most obvious indication that a ship was bound on a slaving voyage was the presence of hundreds of feet of lumber, for the construction of a "slave deck" once the ship reached Africa. This was built approximately four feet below the main deck, running most of the ship's length, to accommodate hundreds of chained, recumbent captives.

Finally, slavers required trade goods. Some captains carried liquor, calico, beads, iron bars, guns, knives, cigars. (Gordon was one of those who carried only liquor for trade, and dozens of hogsheads of whiskey were rolled aboard and stowed in the *Erie*'s hold.)[11] If arrested, the captain of a slave ship could always claim that the extra merchandise was to be used in legitimate trade for palm oil, ivory, gold dust, gum copal, and peanuts.[12] The only items whose presence could not be explained away were shackles, which is why most slave traders, including Gordon, didn't carry them.

One federal prosecutor, describing his frustration in attempting to find clear-cut evidence aboard a suspected slave ship, wrote that the cargo would appear "scrupulously proper for the lawful trade," but that every item could just as well be applied to the slave trade and could "easily and instantly be so converted and applied."[13] Throughout the first six decades of the 1800s, in case after case, American courts were unable to prove complicity in the slave trade by pointing to the cargo or the manifest. Ironically, Britain and Spain had signed a treaty as far back as 1835 that included the "equipment articles." This stipulated that a ship's cargo list alone justified its seizure, and if the prosecution could prove that a single item from the list was on board, the vessel could be confiscated or condemned. The United States would not institute this policy until it signed its own treaty with Britain in 1862.[14]

Financing the fitting out of a slaving voyage was an expensive proposition, and one that most ships' captains could not, and would not, undertake alone. Behind nearly every venture was a well-organized "shadow" company that provided everything from food, water, ship's stores and crew to the ship itself. They solicited investors, generally from the ranks of respectable businessmen with an eye for huge returns. An agent company like "Messrs. Hamel" paid the merchants who supplied everything from the trade whiskey and rum to the food, medicine, and utensils necessary to maintain a human cargo from the coast of Africa to their eventual destination. Also to be paid were shipping agents, dockworkers, ship fitters, and customs officials—usually bribed to provide ship's clearance—as well as a force of skilled lawyers retained in the unlikely event the ship was captured. Often, the entire enterprise was underwritten by an insurance policy, with the loss of native lives merely representing a business expense. The slavers would purchase a policy on the captives, and if death occurred due to natural causes, the insurance company would pay the premium. If it could be proven, however, that negligence, abuse, or suicide was the cause, the slaver absorbed the loss. The slaver captain in *Sacred Hunger,* Barry Unsworth's well-researched novel of the slave trade, cautions two new officers,

> I have seen it happen. They become desperate when they see the ship putting out to sea. They will sometimes throw themselves over the side, chained as they are. And in their shackles, d'ye see, they cannot long

stay alive once they are in the water. They are gone before you can lower a boat for 'em. I have known 'em shout and laugh with the joy of cheating us. It is a dead loss to the owners, since we are not under-written for suicide.[15]

Once the fitting out was completed, Gordon's second order of busi-ness was to find a new crew. Twelve of the original crew had quit the *Erie*, leaving Gordon with three men; fifteen were required to sail the ship. This would not prove a problem, since Havana was filled with sailors looking for a berth. Gordon quickly signed aboard a dozen men. Among them were four Spaniards, to whom he assigned no spe-cific roles or functions. If detained at sea by a patrolling vessel, Gor-don could then present these gentlemen as the actual captain and mates of the *Erie,* thereby claiming the ship to be under foreign com-mand and declaring himself to be merely a passenger. This was a com-mon deception practiced by slaver captains.[16] And finally, Gordon had to obtain clearance for his voyage from the U.S. consul general. Prior to applying for their papers, captains were required to give notice to the consul general of the nature of their voyage. Gordon did so around March 21.

Slavers had been aided in the past by a series of negligent, uninter-ested, and occasionally dishonest U.S. consuls general in Cuba. Un-questionably the worst of these was Nicholas P. Trist, who served as U.S. consul general to Cuba in the 1830s and early 1840s. Trist was a deeply Anglophobic Virginian who believed slavery was good for the Africans. As a result, he would blithely sign clearance papers for slavers fitting out in Cuba, which entitled them to sail for Africa under the pro-tection of the American flag. So flagrant were Trist's violations of the slave-trade acts that he was openly attacked in newspapers on both sides of the Atlantic. The British despised him for constantly foiling their attempts to stop the slave traffic in and out of Cuba; the *New York Herald* called for his instant removal. John Quincy Adams, disgusted by the weight of the accusations against Trist, declared him "either guilty of the vilest treachery or the most culpable indifference to his duties."[17]

Although Trist stood out, most of the U.S. consuls general to Cuba saw themselves less as guardians of the law than as notary publics, act-ing on the requests of American citizens.[18] Finally, however, Havana saw a true anti-slave-trade activist in Thomas Savage. He had grown up in Havana's small American colony, and he knew both the language and the workings of the city. This made him the natural choice as assistant, or vice-consul, to a succession of consuls general. The position paid him $2,000 a year, but gave him virtually no control or authority. Thomas Savage hated the slave trade, but for years, he was powerless to do anything about it. Finally, in 1858, he got his chance. His superior, Consul General Andrew K. Blythe, resigned over a salary that he found "mean, contemptible, and unworthy of our government." Knowing that it would be several months before another consul general would arrive in Havana, Savage determined to move against the crop of American slavers in the bay. The number of Yankee slave ships in Cuba was increasing; around twenty had left Havana unimpeded for the Congo in the previous year alone.

For the next four months, Savage made the most of his opportunity. Ignoring his official instructions, he frequently refused to grant clearance to suspect vessels, thereby depriving them of the registration papers necessary to evade arrest at sea. He exceeded his authority on several occasions by seizing ships he recognized as slavers. When offered bribes by the local Spaniards who financed the voyages, he used the bribery notes and money as evidence that the ships under suspicion were, in fact, slavers. When Savage's customs officers approached the slaver *Nancy,* stevedores told them to leave the ship alone, because the Spanish governor, the chief of police, and the commandant of the revenue guards were all invested in the voyage. Savage immediately seized the ship and imprisoned her crew.[19] At one point, he wrote to his superior, Secretary of State Lewis Cass, that his actions against slavers to "stop . . . the prostitution of the American flag" had generated "considerable excitement and hostility" toward him, but that he would not be deterred.[20]

Eventually, a new consul general arrived in the person of Charles J. Helm. Where the slavers had failed to neutralize Savage in his campaign to drive them from Havana, Helm succeeded. When he stepped ashore, two confiscated slave ships, the *Ardennes* and the *Enterprise,* lay at anchor in the harbor. Savage had denied them clearance, and no amount of pleading or threats by their captains had moved him. Charles Helm immediately gave them their papers and cleared them from the harbor. Thomas Savage had diligently pursued an end to the American slave trade in Cuba, but without the letter, force, or support of American law behind him. The message from the State Department, as delivered through Charles Helm, was clear: the position of consul general existed merely to function as the United States' eyes and ears in Cuba, and to expedite the needs of Americans.

Had Gordon met with Thomas Savage, he probably never would have sailed out of Havana Harbor. Charles Helm, however, was of a totally different stripe. He was a proslavery politician, and as U.S. consul general, his main concern was to keep the consulate from interfering with slavers. He had come to Cuba from his post as consul of St. Thomas, Virgin Islands, where his record was unremarkable. As he saw it, his job was to observe and to report those observations to the appropriate superiors in Washington: his policy from the beginning was one of noninvolvement. Shortly after assuming his position in 1858, Helm wrote to Secretary of State Cass requesting clarification of his duties regarding American slave ships in Havana Bay. He received no reply and so, for the next two years, he took no action whatsoever.[21]

After reporting to Helm, Nathaniel Gordon obtained clearance from the Spanish customhouse.[22] He appeared before Helm again on April 7, and requested his papers. This should have been a mere formality. Yet something about Gordon inspired the consul general to take action for the first and only time during his tenure in Havana. For the third time in *his* career, Gordon found himself under the suspecting eye of a U.S. consul. Helm had no doubt as to the nature of Gordon's voyage; he was sure of it the first time Gordon appeared before him, and on April 11, he wrote to Secretary of State Cass. "Captain Gordon . . . gave me notice that he was loading his vessel with a *legal* cargo, for a *legal* voyage to the coast of Africa. . . . I then and still very strongly suspect her despatched for a cargo of slaves."[23]

Helm justified his suspicion with "the fact that *all vessels clearing from this port for the coast of Africa turn out slavers . . .*" He informed Cass that on March 25—shortly after Helm had received Gordon's notice of his voyage, and nearly two weeks before Gordon applied for his papers—he had written to Captain Moffitt of the U.S. Navy steamer *Crusader,* requesting him to come to Cuba for the express purpose of arresting Gordon. He'd received no response.

Helm then told Cass that although he'd detained the *Erie* for two days, since he had heard nothing from Captain Moffitt he had no choice but to sign Gordon's papers on April 9. Helm quoted the document in his letter:

I, Nathaniel Gordon, master of the ship *Erie,* of New York, do solemnly
swear that my said ship is chartered for a legal voyage to the coast of
Africa; that the cargo is legal and such as is described in the manifests,
that no cargo or article of any description had been taken on board of
said ship, except by special permits granted by the collector of customs
at this port, the contents of each article or package being described by
him, and by him described in his permit before being taken on board;
and I further swear that I will not during the voyage engage in any unlawful trade, or permit the said ship to be engaged in any trade which is
prohibited by, or contrary to, the laws of the United States of America.
I further state that the said ship has not been sold at this port to my
knowledge.[24]

Helm gave Cass his reason for releasing the *Erie* despite his suspicions: "Though I am morally convinced this vessel, if not taken, will
bring a cargo of African Negroes to Cuba . . . I am of opinion that I have
no right, under the law, to detain her, after being regularly cleared at
the custom house here, and complying with all the rules and regula-
tions of this port. . . ."[25]

Helm concluded his letter with the suggestion that the United States
be relieved "from all responsibility on account of the slave trade . . .
from Cuba, and throw the onus on the Spanish Government, where it
of right belongs. . . ."[26] He was requesting official approval to do what
he had been doing for two years—nothing.

A canny politician, if not a dedicated consul, Helm knew his rec-
ommendations for America's withdrawal from regulating the slave
trade were aimed at an administration of like thinking. Lewis Cass,
described by a contemporary as a "portly and pompous" man, had
long campaigned against any agreement that would allow for cooperation with Britain in combating the slave trade, first as minister to France
in the 1840s, and later as secretary of state. He was a Jacksonian Democrat who had fought in the War of 1812, and as a consequence harbored a cordial hatred of England. Cass was a lifelong proslavery
man, and consistently represented the slaveholding interest in foreign
policy.[27]

Secretary of State Cass and Attorney General Jeremiah S. Black supported Helm's proposal, and in late May, Spain was given formal notice that the U.S. consulate in Havana would henceforth refrain from
holding any American vessel that had been cleared by the Spanish

customhouse. America was officially out of the police business in Cuba.[28]

Helm received a communication on April 30 from Francisco Serrano y Dominguez, captain general of Cuba. (Helm was annoyed before he got past the address; Serrano had addressed him as "consul" rather than by his official title of "consul general.") The letter informed him that the Spanish customhouse had indeed given permission "of the said ship, *notwithstanding there is a suspicion that she may be going with the object of conveying an expedition of negroes.*" Serrano also stated that he had alerted the British consul general in Havana, "in order that the vessel aforesaid may be watched and pursued by a cruiser of her Britannic Majesty." First the Spanish cleared the *Erie* for an obvious slaving voyage, and then they alerted the Royal Navy to be on the look-out for her!

Annoyed as he had been at the slight to his title, Helm was furious that Serrano had bypassed him to communicate directly with the British. He fired back a response on May 5. In his letter, he quoted the slave-trade laws and reminded Serrano that the government of the United States had moved to suppress the African slave trade, and placed "the highest penal offence for her citizens to be engaged in the traffic." What Helm neglected to mention was that not a single person had been convicted under this law since its passage 40 years earlier. He wrote that "these penal laws have been enforced at all times with great vigor, in every ocean-bound State in the Union." Nothing could have been further from the truth. He then suggested to Serrano that if the Spanish government suspected Gordon of trafficking in slaves, it should have refused him clearance through customs, rather than attempt to close the door after the fact.

Helm confessed himself "at a loss" to understand Serrano's actions when the consul general surely had to have been aware that "the American government has a squadron on the coast of Africa and several vessels of war on the Cuban coast . . . for the express and only purpose of preventing the use of our flag in the slave trade." Once again, Helm was stretching the truth. The primary function of America's African Squadron was—and always had been—the protection of American shipping, mainly from just the type of interference that Helm had described. As an antislaver police force, the squadron was woefully inadequate. The likelihood of American patrol vessels actually apprehending a slaver was slim at best. Spain knew this, as did most nations at the time. Serrano's choice of Britain as watchdog was a logical one; for one thing, Spain and Britain had signed an anti-slave-trade treaty in 1835 (not that Spain had done much to enforce it); for another, the Royal Navy's record of seizures at sea was nothing short of brilliant.

Finally, Helm got to the crux of his complaint: England did not have—nor had they ever had—the right to interfere with American ships at sea, "nor does the government of the United States admit that the suspicion that an American vessel is, has been, or will be engaged in the African slave-trade, gives to any foreign vessel of war the right of visitation or search, and any such forcible visitation . . . would be regarded by the Government of the United States as an unfriendly act." It was the old issue of search and seizure once again. Better to let a slaver go than have a British presence on an American ship. In closing, Helm told Serrano, "I took it for granted that you entertained no suspicion, and that your clearance of this vessel was evidence that her cargo was intended for lawful trade; and was therefore greatly surprised when I received your Excellency's note, dated twenty days after I had delivered the papers to the master, and the *Erie* had sailed."[29]

Again Helm was being disingenuous. At the same time the Spanish were giving Gordon his sailing papers, Helm was trying to contact the U.S. Navy to warn them about the *Erie*. But Serrano's action made no more sense than Helm's, and was as unprecedented. Both men cleared Gordon for sailing, and then alerted the authorities. Why Gordon and no other? These officials had cleared dozens of slaver captains, and would clear more, without raising an alarm. Yet each found something in Nathaniel Gordon that inspired an out-of-character response. Could it have been his personality? Perhaps he was so caustic and arrogant that Helm and Serrano simply didn't like him. But slave-ship captains were a hardened, often brutal lot, and there is no indication that Gordon stood out. Besides, personal dislike seems an unlikely reason to alert two of the world's most powerful navies. It's also improbable that Gordon's reputation was the cause; if he had a known history as a slave trader, so had many of the captains who used Havana as a home port. The *Erie*'s cargo list seems in keeping with that of any vessel fitted out for the trade. And the crew, while composed partly of nonworking Europeans—a strong indication that the ship was bound for a slaving voyage—was interchangeable with those from any number of vessels.

Ultimately, it is impossible to know what Helm and Serrano were thinking, and their motives remain a mystery.

Helm, ever the opportunist, also sent Secretary of State Cass a copy
of this letter. Cass immediately forwarded Helm's letters of April 11 and
May 5 to Secretary of the Navy Isaac Toucey. Toucey was cut from the
same cloth as Cass. A former senator and attorney general, he was a
proslavery Connecticut Yankee whose voting record was so pro-
Southern that some members of his constituency hanged him in effigy,
with a note over the heart reading "Toucey, the traitor."[30]

Toucey received Helm's letters on May 30.[31] He then wrote two letters of his own—one a response to Helm, and the second to William
Inman, commander of the U.S. African Squadron. To Helm, Toucey
conveyed the government's official approval of the consul general's
recommendation not to interfere with American vessels in Cuba. However, his letter to Inman focused on Helm's concern that Captain Gordon was bound on a slaving expedition; Toucey advised Inman to be
on the lookout for the *Erie* and to do what he deemed necessary.[32]

And while this lively and unusual exchange of letters was taking
place, the *Erie* was sailing east to the African coast and the Congo River.
Gordon was unaware that he was a target of the State Department, the
Department of the Navy, and the African Squadron.

What exactly was the African Squadron? This ineffective little fleet,
whose name was much more impressive than the reality, was responsible for patrolling the ocean waters between Africa and the Americas
and the Caribbean in search of slave ships. It was born in 1842, when
the United States belatedly signed an agreement with Britain known as
the Webster-Ashburton Treaty. The treaty stipulated that both nations
would keep "a sufficient and adequate squadron" on the coast of
Africa, each squadron carrying a minimum of 80 guns. Each country
referred to its new force as the "African Squadron," to act independ-
ently, but in a spirit of "concert and cooperation." The treaty was made
after decades of debate, and it fell far short of the mark, never directly
addressing or resolving the real issue of search and seizure.[33]

Unfortunately, the treaty was specific only in regard to the number
of *guns,* whereas it would have made more sense to specify a suitable
number of *ships.* Instead, it vaguely stipulated a squadron of vessels "of

suitable numbers and descriptions" to enforce the laws of each of the two countries. The expectation of the signers of the agreement was that each navy would provide 15 fast ships, each carrying a small complement of guns. Speed was essential, since slave ships, such as the famed Baltimore clippers, were often built for speed. A slaver would run if given the opportunity, and a large, lumbering frigate would stand no chance to catch it. Just as vital, a force of 15 vessels could at least begin the task of patrolling the more than 3,000 miles of African coastline and countless thousands of miles of open ocean effectively.

The U.S. government, however, commissioned only four vessels, carrying a combined complement of 82 guns. The new African Squadron consisted of a frigate, two sloops of war, and a brig. The frigate *Macedonian* had been captured from the British during the War of 1812, and—as were all the ships of this tiny American fleet—it was old, slow, and poorly maintained. Until nearly the end of its service in 1861, the African Squadron numbered only from two to five ships. One young midshipman who had served aboard the squadron brig *Porpoise* in 1850 recalled, "She was so slow that we could hardly hope for a prize except by a fluke. Repeatedly we chased suspicious craft only to be out-sailed." The slave ships, on the other hand, "were generally small handy craft; fast, of course; usually schooner-rigged, and carrying flying topsails."[34] While the British introduced fast, powerful steam-powered warships in the late 1840s, it would not be until 1859—just two years before the demise of the Squadron—that the United States followed suit. The U.S. squadron was too small, and the ships too slow, to be effective—but that was assuming that chasing slavers was its primary objective.[35] It was not.

The mandate to reduce the slave trade took a poor second place to the orders to protect American merchant ships from foreign interference. Secretary of the Navy Abel Upshur, in 1843, set the tone for the priorities of the African Squadron in his initial instructions to Matthew Perry, squadron commander of the tiny fleet's first expedition: "You are charged with the protection of American Commerce . . . and with suppression of the Slave Trade, so far as the same may be carried on by American Citizens or under the American Flag." But, he specified, "While the United States sincerely desire the suppression of the Slave Trade . . . they do not regard the success of their efforts as their paramount interest."[36] Upshur had interpreted the vague terms of the treaty to apply only to American slavers, and had then made the squadron's first order of business the protection of American shipping, mainly from the nation with whom we were supposed to be partners. The hunt for slavers was not to interfere.

Upshur also envisioned American traders laying claim to a piece of the palm oil industry, which heretofore had been controlled by France and England; he saw the African Squadron as a means to help America achieve this goal. It was business, not slavers, that would determine the squadron's raison d'être for nearly its entire existence. Upshur was the first of nine secretaries under whom the African Squadron would serve; all but one were proslavery.[37]

To further complicate matters, the climate and conditions off the coast of Africa were not conducive to extended postings or visits. Matthew Perry selected Porto Praia on the Portuguese island of São Tiago in the Cape Verde Islands as a base for the squadron; after all, it had an American consul and supplies could be obtained relatively easily through the Portuguese customhouse. It was a disastrous choice. The port itself was inhospitable; the heat was oppressive; and every summer there was an outbreak of fever, which could sweep through a ship's crew like a scythe. Also, Porto Praia was a month's sail from the Congo River, which meant the squadron spent most of its time sailing to and from the slaving grounds.

Perry soon saw his mistake, but did nothing to correct it. He had hoped to set up a resupply system at sea, through the use of "floating storeships," so that the ships could stay on station, but the government refused to spend the money. The squadron came to loathe the base, the duty, and the coast, and would spend as little time on them as possible.[38]

There were no welcoming ports in which to enjoy shore leave near their fever-ridden base on Porto Praia, so the squadron would sail north to the island of Madeira. Called the "gem of the Atlantic," Madeira was a sailor's paradise—"beautiful, healthful, full of attractions for tired men in from the sea."[39] Presumably, this meant drink, a gentle northerly climate free of fevers, and the company of women. Unfortunately, there were no slavers anywhere nearby, so although Madeira quickly became a safe and seductive haven for the crews of the African Squadron, it also kept them from what minimal impact they might have had.[40] Only one or two—and sometimes, none—of the Squadron's four or five vessels were ever on active patrol at any given time. It cost the federal government $384,500 per year to maintain the African Squadron, which captured, on average, one slaver a year in its first seven years.[41]

As late as July 21, 1860, Commander Jenkins of the ship *Preble* wrote Squadron Commander Inman of his unwillingness to follow the patrolling schedule assigned him, because it would have "greatly hazard[ed] the health of the crew and officers" who were susceptible to "diseases of a febrile character."[42] Porto Praia would remain the African Squadron's base until 1859—two years before the dissolution of the squadron—when Secretary Toucey ordered it moved to St. Paul de Loanda (or Loango), a port city on Africa's west coast.[43]

All that was required to become commander of a navy squadron, including the African Squadron, were longevity and luck; achievement didn't factor at all. Until 1855, the navy operated on the seniority system, with no forced retirement and limited opportunities for advancement; junior officers could look to rise in the ranks only if their superiors resigned, voluntarily retired, or died. A junior officer usually had to wait at least 30 years to command a frigate, and 40 to become a squadron commander with the rank of captain. When he assumed his squadron command, he was given a bonus and the honorary title of "commodore." This title changed to "flag officer" in 1857. It was unusual for an officer at this point in his career to command a squadron for more than a two- or three-year tour of duty. They were old men, and in the words of one naval historian, "ready for permanent shore duty." The masters of the other ships in the squadron held the rank of commander, and no doubt looked to the time when they might command their own squadrons.[44]

As the first African Squadron commander, Matthew Perry set the precedent. He followed Navy Secretary Upshur's orders to the letter during the two years he commanded the African Squadron. During this time, he protected American vessels at sea from foreign interference, he burned the villages and executed the ringleaders of a gang of hostile native Africans who had killed the crew of an American trading schooner. And, in two years, he captured only one suspected slave ship, with no slaves aboard.[45] In September 1843, just prior to seizing the slaver, he reported to Upshur, "I cannot hear of any American vessels being engaged in the slave trade, nor do I believe that there has been one so engaged in years."[46]

There were eleven successive commanders of the squadron. The success or failure of its missions depended heavily on them, and they varied greatly in ability and dedication. Most squadron commanders, though, were like Matthew Perry—content to follow their orders to the letter, devoting their time and energies to the protection of American merchant ships, and taking the odd slaver only when the opportunity presented itself.[47]

Perry's successor was Commodore Charles W. Skinner. Under his command, the African Squadron captured six slavers, the largest of which, the *Pons,* carried a cargo of 913 Africans. But while Skinner averaged one captured slaver per year, during the same six-year period his British counterparts managed to capture 500 ships, with cargoes totaling nearly 40,000 natives.[48]

The worst commander of the lot was Commodore Thomas Conover. A relic with more than 45 years' service, he commanded the flag ship *Cumberland.* Conover took command of the squadron in 1857, and proceeded to spend the next two years lounging in Madeira, wintering in Porto Praia, and sailing far enough out to sea to safely avoid any contact with either slavers or the unwelcoming African coast. In August 1859, the *Cumberland* docked at Portsmouth, New Hampshire. After 26 months at sea, Conover had spent fewer than 26 days on active patrol of the Slave Coast.[49] He arrested but one slave ship, the *William G. Davis,* off the Congo River. (Her captain was later tried in federal court in Virginia, and acquitted.)[50]

The African Squadron's final commander was William Inman. He was a relic from the War of 1812, and had been previously declared unfit for duty and blackballed twice by navy boards. Inman published a pamphlet in his own defense entitled "Objections to the Finding of Naval Court of Inquiry No. 3, in the Case of Captain William Inman," and he appealed his case to President Buchanan. Secretary of the Navy Toucey determined that Inman was his man, applying the convoluted logic that anyone with such a driving need to restore his reputation would do an aggressive job.[51]

Such was not the case. Inman quickly discovered the delights of Madeira and remained there for his first two months of command. When he finally did weigh anchor and go to sea, it took him another two months to finally reach the Slave Coast. During this voyage, by sheer coincidence, the unladen slaver *Orion* was boarded, at various times, by all four ships in Inman's little squadron, including the flag-ship—and all four let her go. Unfortunately, none of them followed her. Had they done so, it might have been Inman's little fleet, and not the British warship *Pluto,* that ultimately captured the *Orion* (in late November 1859) with 874 slaves in her hold.[52] Even so, Inman did not hesitate to demand custody from the *Pluto*'s captain of the *Orion*'s captain and his two mates, whom the British officer cordially turned over. They were placed aboard an American ship to be returned to the United States for trial.[53]

Inman actually managed to capture a slaver, the *Delicia,* and promptly rewarded himself with several weeks of shore duty. Shortly thereafter, Inman wrote to Toucey that he would be taking on supplies and sailing to Madeira for a vacation, since months of hard work had "enfeebled" his men. He pointed out that the health of his "officers and men . . . will be strengthened by absence from Loanda, at the unhealthy [rainy] season, which exists during the months of March, April, May and June." It "strongly contrasts with the cool and bracing air we experience here." He further suggested that the sloop *Portsmouth* join him on holiday. He had, in essence, awarded himself and a large part of his force a four-month leave of absence.[54]

Although Conover had gotten away with a great deal worse, Inman's self-indulgence could not have been more ill-timed. The slave trade had been growing rapidly for the previous three years and had reached alarming proportions, with 25,000 Africans brought to Cuba in 1859 alone. In addition to the burgeoning traffic to Cuba and the Caribbean, some of the Southern states had been clamoring for a reopening of the slave trade as a means of helping their flagging economy.[55] Two years earlier, an economic crisis had plunged the United States into a severe depression; maritime commerce had slowed practically to a standstill. Thousands of ships lay empty and available, their captains and crews unemployed, in every seaport town on the East Coast. The slave trade offered an alluring and lucrative alternative. Slavers were now using larger, steam-powered vessels, with greater stowage capacity for cargo. Britain, in response, was pressuring Washington to do something about the escalating trade in and out of Cuba. They were also boarding and searching a growing number of suspected American slavers; since the Webster-Ashburton Treaty had not specifically given permission to either nation to board and search each other's ships, Britain's actions were technically illegal. As a result, the U.S. African Squadron was spending more time in addressing the complaints and protecting the rights of "violated" American vessels than it did in pursuing them. Letters bristling with indignation, such as that from the captain of the *Jehossee,* reached Inman's desk: "Now Sir—I look to you for that *protection* and *redress* that is due to *American Citizens* and their *Insulted Flag.*"[56] With the rest of the world's major nations actively working against the African slave trade, the U.S. claim that it was cleaning its own house was wearing transparently thin.

President James Buchanan and Congress, finally addressing the slaving issue, belatedly began to demand results. Feeling the pressure from above, Toucey canceled Inman's vacation and ordered him back to his post, declaring Madeira permanently off limits to the African Squadron. Inman was already at Madeira when Toucey's directives reached him— in fact, he had written his letters to Toucey *from* Madeira—and it took him another several months to return to Porto Praia. By now it was summer 1860.[57] Among Inman's orders from Toucey was a directive to be on the lookout for a ship called the *Erie,* which had left Havana the previous April heading for the African coast under the command of a Captain Nathaniel Gordon. The *Erie,* Inman was told, was more than likely on a slaving voyage, and was to be apprehended if possible.[58]

When Inman finally did start to take the patrol of the Slave Coast seriously, he drew up a plan to divide the cruising grounds among his three active vessels, with each ship assigned a specific area to patrol. Unfortunately, two of the three assigned sections were never sailed by slavers, and so only one of his ships would actually be patrolling the thousands of miles of the slaving grounds at any given time. Consequently, slave ships in great numbers were making the round-trip from Havana to the Congo in relative safety from American interference.

By May 1860, Toucey had had enough of William Inman's lack of effectiveness, and instructed him in no uncertain terms to "renew his exertions." Inman jumped to, with a letter to the commanders of his little fleet: "The Department has ordered . . . that *all the vessels of the squadron repair forthwith* to the cruising ground."[59]

Shortly thereafter, by sheer blind luck, Inman's cruisers finally showed results. While cruising together on the morning of August 8, 1860, two of Inman's steamships, *Mohican* and *San Jacinto,* sighted two vessels off the African coast, 50 miles from the mouth of the Congo

River, sailing in opposite directions. The *San Jacinto* pursued the *Storm King,* which was found to have 523 Africans aboard. The second slaver was the *Erie,* carrying 897 slaves.[60]

A week later, Inman wrote a "circular" to his officers, inspired by President Buchanan's newfound determination to curtail the trade. The message was simple: It had come to the president's attention that American ships cleared from Havana for a voyage to Africa "are very suspicious" and probably "destined for an illegal traffic . . ." The African Squadron was to pay special attention "in the examination of such vessels."[61]

In the unlikely event that a navy or Squadron vessel did capture a slaver and sail her and her crew back to the United States for trial, the odds favoring a conviction were slim. The *Orion,* the slaver released by Inman's ships and ultimately seized by the British, provides a good example.

By rights, the *Orion* should not have been on the sea in the first place. The previous year, the British ship HMS *Triton* had detained her up the Congo River under suspicion of being a slaver. Captain Burton of the *Triton* promptly sent word of the seizure to Captain Brent of the *Marion,* one of the African Squadron's recently acquired steam-powered sloops of war. Brent immediately searched the *Orion* and found a variety of goods suitable for the slave trade, including firearms, a large quantity of food, two sets of slave coppers, and—most telling—15,000 feet of lumber, for construction of a slave deck.[62]

A crew from the *Marion* sailed the *Orion* to New York for trial. On the way, the *Orion*'s captain, John Hanna, died (reportedly of a "broken heart"), but not before acknowledging that the *Orion* was indeed a slave ship. Once in New York, Captain Burton was vilified by the press and attacked by the State Department for violating American sovereignty. (So much for the Webster-Ashburton Treaty's "spirit of cooperation.") He was also blamed for the death of Captain Hanna. Nevertheless, Captain Brent of the *Marion* swore out the appropriate warrants, and the U.S. marshal's deputies duly arrested the *Orion*'s crew. The vessel itself was put under guard, and a "libel" prepared, requesting that the vessel be confiscated for violation of the slave trade acts.

The *Orion* crew was defended by Beebe, Dean, and Donahoe, the most prestigious and successful law firm of its type in New York. Founded and staffed by former judges, they specialized in defending accused slavers. In 1859–1860, as a result of the African Squadron's newfound sense of purpose, business was booming, and the firm's record of acquittals was extraordinary. The firm set about getting the *Orion* charges dismissed. According to Judge Samuel Betts and Justice Samuel Nelson, Hanna's deathbed confession did not constitute legal evidence, nor was the nature of the cargo sufficient to indicate it would be used for slaving. Commissioner Joseph Bridgham and District Attorney James J. Roosevelt both decided that there was not enough evidence to justify prosecution, and dropped the charges. Nor was any legal action taken against the ship's owner.

The *Orion,* however, remained in custody. Through a bizarre and often-used interpretation of the laws, exoneration of the captain and crew of a vessel did not necessarily impact the ship herself. Thus, a slave ship's crew might be cleared of all charges, as most of them were, while the vessel could be condemned as a slaver, confiscated, and either destroyed or sold at public auction. A loophole in the law allowed the owner of a libeled slave ship to post bond, thereby permitting him the use of the vessel until the trial. Upon posting bond, he would then sell his ship to another slaver, or perhaps secretly back to himself, and it would immediately set sail on another slaving voyage. This practice of bonding a ship and then selling it, or of simply skipping bond, was common among seized slavers. And this was exactly what the owner of the *Orion* did. Shortly after posting bond, he "sold" her to the late Captain Hanna's second-in-command; within a very short time, *Orion* was back at sea with more than 800 slaves in her hold. She was captured by a British warship for the second time. But this time, Judge Hall of the Circuit Court of the Southern District of New York declared the *Orion* a slaver, and as such, forfeit. He ordered her broken up.[63] The ship was destroyed as a slaver, while the captain and his two mates were each given a fine and a short sentence. The rest of the crew was released.[64]

Such convoluted legal procedures, played over and over again in courts both North and South, had a profoundly discouraging effect on the sailors and officers whose job it was to catch the slavers. Sailor Henry Eason, a former crewman on the *Marion,* heard about the release of the *Orion*'s crew, and his journal entry reflects his frustration.

We heard that our slavers we sent home had been acquitted because the Jury could not find substantial evidence to condemn them. The Orion came out on the coast as a trader the second time & the consequence was that the American Commodore detained her six days but could find nothing to condemn her & a short time after the English steamer Pluto captured her with 808 slaves on board & took her to St. Helena. This will make our people at home open their eyes at an American ship capturing slavers and sending them home for triall [sic] & get honorably acquitted then come & load up with slaves three months after. The Orion had everything that is needed on board of slavers.[65]

If this perpetual game of catch and release was a source of frustration to the sailors aboard the warships, there was yet another wrinkle, devised by the slavers and their lawyers, that genuinely terrified the navy and squadron commanders. It first occurred in 1846, when USS *Boxer* seized the *Malaga,* a ship fitted out with all the obvious goods and accoutrements for slaving and chartered to a known Brazilian slave trader. A New England judge ruled that there was nothing illegal about selling goods to a slaver, the charges were dropped, and the *Malaga* immediately left port on another slaving voyage. But after the ship was released, her owners charged the *Boxer's* commander with false arrest and sued him personally for more than $10,000 in damages. A similar suit was brought against another navy commander by the cleared slaver *Casket.*

It took the Department of the Navy three years to get around to defending her officers. They were both eventually acquitted, but the damage had been done. When the suits were first brought, the African Squadron's commodore George C. Read alerted his superiors that the officers "dread the trouble and expense to which they are liable to be put, and they will hereafter be so very cautious as to what they seize that I have reason to doubt the probability of your hearing of a capture." He was correct. In the words of slave-trade historian Warren S. Howard, for the next three years, America entered into "one of the most inglorious episodes in American naval history: a mass shirking of assigned duties, carefully concealed from the American public."[66] If the U.S. Navy had been lax before in the pursuit of slavers, now it became totally inactive. From the time of the initial damage suits until their resolution three years later, not a single slaver was captured. Nor did the fear of legal action ever completely dissipate. As late as 1860, a ship's commander, in the process of making a capture, defended his actions to U.S. district attorney James J. Roosevelt (the same man who advocated the dismissal of the charges against the *Orion*), but added,

> should my expectations not be realized, I most earnestly hope the Court will find the cause of suspicion sufficiently strong to relieve me from all claims for damage, &., that terror of all our naval officers who strive for conscientious discharge of their duties on this station.[67]

When it formed the African Squadron, the government had specified that each slave ship taken and ultimately condemned would be considered a "prize." As such, half the proceeds from her sale at auction, as well as a bounty of $25 for every recaptured slave, would be divided among the crew that captured it.[68] This amounted to a considerable sum for an officer or a crewman; now, however, with the threat of litigation looming over every officer on patrol, not even the lure of prize money could induce federal ships to attempt seizure at sea. Within the year, Massachusetts senator Henry Wilson proposed legislation that would ban suits against naval officers. Once again, Congress did nothing.[69]

Finally, with the sting of Secretary Toucey's orders driving Captain Inman, the year 1860 proved the most productive for the African Squadron. With the addition of a few steam-powered sloops-of-war to patrol both the African coast and the waters off Cuba, the Squadron now consisted of eight vessels. It captured seven slavers, carrying a total of 4,300 Africans.[70] Initially, no one had the slightest idea what to do with them. While Britain was sending the slaves it liberated either to their colonial plantations in Cuba, Brazil, and the Caribbean, or to the British free Black colony in Sierra Leone, the United States had made no provisions, since there had been little expectation of liberating them in such large numbers. The government had not provided funds for medical aid, food, or accommodations. When the slaver *Echo* was seized, it was carrying 450 slaves. They were shipped to Charleston pending disposition; 300 survived the voyage. Within a short time ashore, another 30 perished.[71] After a few such debacles, Congress remembered Liberia.

The idea of an African colony for the "repatriation" of both freeborn and manumitted African Americans had begun some 40 years earlier.

The nation's free African Americans had increased, mainly through natural population growth, from 59,467 to 186,446 between 1790 and 1810; many Southerners saw this as a disaster in the making. The successful 1791 slave revolt in Haiti, combined with two slave rebellions in Virginia and one in Louisiana between 1800 and 1816, motivated several Southern luminaries to seek a solution. On December 21, 1816, a number of prominent statesmen met in Washington, D.C., and created the American Colonization Society (ACS). Numbered among the "colonizationists," as they were known, were President James Monroe, former presidents James Madison and Thomas Jefferson, future president Andrew Jackson, Henry Clay, and Chief Justice John Marshall. Marshall had written, "The removal of our colour population is I think, a common object by no means confined to the slave states." President Monroe, who had been governor of Virginia at the time of the 1800 Prosser Rebellion, observed, "Unhappily, while this class of people exists among us, we can never count with certainty on its tranquil submission." Thomas Jefferson, himself the father of several children by a slave woman, was clear—if ironic—in his views: "Their amalgamation with other colors produces a degradation to which no lover of this country, no lover of excellence in human character, can consent." And James Madison wanted "the free blacks . . . permanently removed beyond the region occupied by or allotted to a white population." Henry Clay wrote, "Of all classes of our population, the most vicious is that of the free colored. . . . If the principle of colonization should be confined to them, if a colony can be firmly established and successfully continued in Africa . . . much good will be done." And Francis Scott Key, author of our national anthem, felt that "any scheme of emancipation without colonization [is] productive of nothing but evil."[72]

The membership didn't consist solely of slave-owning Southerners. Daniel Webster was a founding member, and Northern abolitionists saw in the ACS an opportunity to provide free Blacks with an opportunity to build an existence far from America's tainted racial culture. But the slaveholders were by far the dominant group in the ACS.[73]

While some African Americans welcomed the opportunity, others clearly did not. The ACS had to confront the likelihood that many free African Americans might not want to leave their homes to colonize a piece of Africa. Most of these free Blacks and manumitted slaves were American-born, and viewed themselves as such. In the words of Frederick Douglass, "[We] claim no affinity with Africa. This is our home . . . the land of our forefathers. [We] do not trace our ancestry to Africa alone. . . . The best blood of Virginia courses through our veins." Fearing that volunteers might be scarce, the ACS made a deal with several slave owners, whereby all their slaves who were to be freed would be obliged to subscribe to the Liberian program immediately upon manumission, or be sold back into slavery.[74]

Using as its model the small British free Black colony of Sierra Leone, the ACS launched a venture in 1818 to find comparable land for a colony of transported American Blacks. The land 200 miles south of Sierra Leone seemed suitable; the following year, Congress allotted $100,000, to be combined with money raised by selling memberships to the ACS, to finance the venture. The ACS's charter was also extended, in response to the recent battery of slave-trade laws, to include those Africans—"recaptures"—who were liberated from slavers. The colony would now welcome and provide for not only free Blacks from America, but also the human cargoes of the slave ships. The fact that the recaptures came from homes nowhere near this part of Africa seemed of no consequence; after all, neither did the American-born free Blacks and former slaves who would make up the majority of the transplanted population of the colony.

In 1820, the *Elizabeth* sailed from New York for Africa, filled with tools, guns, supplies, 88 free Blacks, and 3 ACS agents. Within three weeks of landing in Africa, 22 immigrants and all 3 agents died of fever, and the survivors were evacuated to Freetown, the capital of Sierra Leone. A second group sent the following year resulted in the establishment of the first colony. The settlement was called Liberia—literally, "Land of Freedom"—with Monrovia, named for the president, as its capital.[75]

The ACS provided Liberia's original settlers with housing and food for six months, giving them an opportunity to build houses of their own and to put in their crops. Most of the provisions soon ran out, and the letters home—many to the writers' former masters—were filled with requests for food, tools, clothes, guns, powder, and shot. They also document the settlers' battles with local natives, disease, and the land itself.

The colonists immediately set about basing their new home on systems and customs from their old home—America, not Africa—and referred to themselves as Americo-Liberians. Their constitution (drafted by the ACS for the colonists) mirrored that of the United States; their flag was a one-starred variation of the Stars and Stripes. They gave their colonies names like Virginia, Maryland, and Providence, and created a model of Capitol Hill. They set about establishing a government and a society based—sadly—on caste, oppression, and slavery.

No one had given much thought to the fact that the land to be colonized by the ACS was already occupied. It hadn't troubled the U.S. government in the settlement of the American West, and it certainly didn't trouble them here. As the colony grew, Congress repeatedly sent warships and men to back up the colonists' bids for more land and control. After several attempts by the natives to drive them out, Liberia's colonists, with the help of the U.S. Navy, subjugated the indigenous population. The former inhabitants were forced to work on the new owners' plantations, or were sold as slaves to other African countries. And so by sponsoring the Liberian colony of free Blacks, America was tacitly approving the institution of slavery. Ironically, many of the native tribes themselves had been—and continued to be—involved in the slave trade. The U.S. government knew this when it acquired the land from the local chiefs, and it allowed them to continue their slaving activities as part of the agreement. The ACS, while "clothing their intentions in a garment of philanthropy," was promoting a system whereby freed slaves were coming into the country at the same time newly made slaves were being shipped out. It was, as one historian puts it, a "recipe for disaster."[76]

The native Africans were forbidden to attend the new schools and churches, go to the best hospitals, or intermarry with the new residents. The Americo-Liberians mimicked in the worst possible ways the practices of their former masters. Eventually these restrictions were lifted, but the bitterness remained, and remains to this day. According to present-day Liberian community leader Mary Brunell, "As for America—we could have taken the best from them. We took the worst. We could have risen above slavery, but we didn't, and that is the crux of our problems."[77]

Four distinct classes emerged in Liberia. At the top were the mulattos—free Blacks and manumitted slaves who could prove White ancestry. Although the ACS initially kept a White governor in office, the mulattos ultimately ran the government, owned the major businesses, and controlled the country. Those from Virginia placed themselves at the top of this caste. Next came those of West Indian or pure African descent. Third on the list were the recaptured Africans brought to Liberia from the slave ships. They were known as "Congos." Occupying the bottom rung were the native Africans—those who were living there when the colonizing experiment began and now lived under the thumb of the new planter class, or who inhabited the regions surrounding Liberia.[78]

The ACS supported the colony for more than 20 years, until it became too costly. With the ACS's encouragement, Liberia declared its independence in 1847. By 1867, more than 13,000 people had emigrated from America to Liberia, joining thousands of others liberated from slave ships during what would be the African Squadron's brief run of success from 1860 until its end the following year.[79]

For the first time in its brief, pitiful history, the African Squadron was actually showing results. Unfortunately for Captain Inman, it was a case of too little effort made too late in the game. When his tour ended, despite the new Union navy's need for capable officers, he was put back on the undesirable list and was never again allowed to hold command. Ironically, the demise of the African Squadron would be brought about by the first president to be truly and actively committed to ending the slave trade. Soon after Abraham Lincoln took office in 1861, the Civil War commenced. One of the North's first priorities was the creation of a large and effective navy, and Lincoln needed all the ships he could find. Under these circumstances, he had no choice but to recall the African Squadron, leaving only one ship on active patrol, and request that the British government send ships to patrol Cuba and arrest slavers. The British reminded the president that no amount of patrolling would be effective without the long-debated right of search. Lincoln eventually authorized his secretary of state, William Seward, to sign a treaty with Britain's Lord Lyons that provided for the mutual right of search and for trial by "mixed courts" composed of American and British judges in specially provided venues in New York, Capetown, and Sierra Leone. The provisions of the law were impressive. And again, the results were pathetic: in fact, not a single case ever found its way into any of the three Anglo-American mixed-court offices.[80]

Nonetheless, the treaty signaled the beginning of the end of the American slave trade. Although a few slavers continued to chance the voyage, Cuba was now under close surveillance, Brazil had ended its importation of slaves, and the Union was systematically blockading the Confederate ports. With a disappearing market and government-sanctioned interference from the Royal Navy, there was nowhere for a slave ship to go.

(*above*) TYPICAL OF MID-NINETEENTH-CENTURY SLAVERS, THE *WILDFIRE* LEFT THE AFRICAN COAST IN 1860 WITH A CARGO OF 650 SLAVES. WHEN SHE WAS CAPTURED, MORE THAN 100 HAD DIED.

(*right*) EARLY-NINETEENTH-CENTURY DIAGRAM OF THE BRITISH SLAVE SHIP *BROOKS.* WEIGHING ONLY 297 TONS, THIS SMALL VESSEL CRAMMED IN AS MANY AS 740 CAPTIVES THROUGH THE USE OF A SPECIAL SLAVE DECK. THE MORE SLAVES A SHIP COULD ACCOMMODATE, THE HIGHER THE MORTALITY, BUT THE GREATER THE PROFITS.

# CHAPTER III

# ONE DOLLAR A HEAD

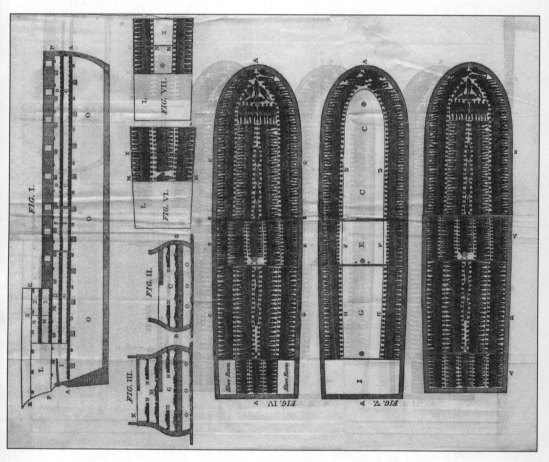

The commerce of the world in 1860 moved chiefly by water. A ship at sea operated under the direction of the captain and his two mates, and included a cook, a carpenter, and a boatswain, who oversaw the maintenance of the vessel. But the everyday work of taking a ship downriver or across the ocean rested with the sailors. Herman Melville, himself an experienced seaman, wrote, "There are classes of men in the world who bear the same relation to society . . . that the wheels do to a coach, and are just as indispensable. . . . Sailors form one of these wheels."

Whether the vessel was a China clipper, a Hudson River sloop, or a slaver en route to Africa, the sailor's responsibilities were the same. He had to have a thorough knowledge of the workings of his ship, which included an understanding of the complicated arrangement of sails and spars as well as the impossibly complex cobwebs of the ropes— "sheets"—that connected to the sails and controlled the ship. The more experienced, or "able," seamen were also adept at weaving and splicing rope, and forging hooks, rings, and a variety of other metal parts. The captain set the course, but it was the sailors who stood at the helm to steer, and at the bow or aloft to watch for land, other ships, and changes in the weather. When storms arose, two men were often required to hold the wheel and keep the ship on course and out of danger. And in all weathers, the sailors were ordered to climb into the rigging to work on the sails. This was frightening enough in calm seas; in storms and icy seas, it was deadly, and many sailors perished from a fall to the deck or into the sea.

When the sailors' work wasn't dangerous, it was monotonous. Every day, the crew was ordered to scrub the deck with sandstone, and wash it down with seawater drawn in huge tubs. They had to rub down the wooden masts with heavy grease—"slush"—made from rendered animal fat to keep them from drying out. On occasion, they were lowered over the side to chip rust from the anchor. The chores seemed endless.

But there was music aboard—sometimes when the sailors were enjoying a quiet moment, but more often when they were at work, to relieve the tedium. Many jobs, such as hoisting and lowering sails and raising the anchor, required the coordinated effort of most of the crew; a crew member, designated the "shantyman," would lead the singing or chanting, establishing a cadence. The words to many of the songs made little sense, but they maintained the rhythm needed to get the job done.

Shantyman: O, they calls me Hangin' Johnny
Crew: Away, boys, away!
Shantyman: They says I hangs for money.
Crew: Hang, boys, hang!

Ships functioned on a daily series of four "watches," of four hours each. When a sailor wasn't on watch or attending to daily chores, he was free to amuse himself as best he could. The options were few. Some carved in wood. Whaler men often etched, or "scrimmed," images and designs into the teeth of sperm whales. Occasionally, a man with some education would read a novel or the Bible. But most frequently the sailor would simply go to his bunk or hammock in the forecastle and sleep for an hour or two. The space was close, and reeked of stale tobacco and the sweat of unwashed men, but it offered rest.[1]

Perhaps they were between watches, and bored or curious. Or they might have finally grown suspicious about the true nature of their voyage. Perhaps they were simply sent below for provisions. The reason isn't known. But about a month after Nathaniel Gordon set sail on the *Erie,* four or five members of his crew had occasion to take a good look in the hold. There they saw the 150 hogsheads of whiskey; tons of rice, beans, and farina; barrels of beef and pork; and 250 bundles of disassembled water casks that had been loaded in Havana. A year and a half later, in a New York courtroom, various crew members would testify that when they signed aboard, they had believed the *Erie* "to be bound upon a legitimate voyage, and that, when at sea, they suspected, from the nature of the cargo, that all was not right, which suspicion they mentioned to the Captain, . . . who satisfied them by saying that he was on a lawful voyage, that they had shipped as sailors, and would do better to return to their duties than to talk to him."[2] A Yankee captain—especially one on a slaving expedition—was not a man to entertain a democratic exchange of ideas with his crew; there would be no further confrontations.

As April 1860 gave way to May, and then June, and the *Erie* continued to sail eastward to the Congo River, arrest and punishment were far from Captain Gordon's mind. The most recent law prohibiting his trade was a forty-year-old toothless relic that had gone unenforced for its entire existence. The only military power in any position to apprehend him was a tiny naval force whose primary purpose was the protection of American vessels from foreign interference. The courts—North *and* South—were ruled by judges sympathetic to the slavers and abetted by corrupt officials. And presiding over them all was President James Buchanan, who had gone on public record to say he would never hang a slaver. All things considered, Nathaniel Gordon had every right and reason to feel secure in his venture.

When the *Erie* reached the Congo River in early July, Gordon sailed upriver 45 miles, to a depot where he could safely refit his ship, meet the African slave traders, and offload his cargo. The Congo was vast here, more than three miles across. While there were legitimate places along the river where a captain might buy or trade for goods such as palm oil, depots such as this were set up by the local slavers and existed solely for the human trade. Often it was the home of the local slave trader, and depending upon accommodations and the inclination of the owner, the captain and his officers might be kept as guests in the slaver's house for the length of their stay. The crew stayed on board, and the slaves themselves were kept downriver; the ships would pick them up on their way out.

Why didn't the ships of the world's various navies simply station themselves at the mouth of the Congo River and await the exit of laden slavers? Not all slave traders did business from isolated outposts, nor was the commerce exclusive to the Congo River. It was merely one of numerous market sites that dotted the coastline. For example, slave trading was a major part of the economy of Dahomey, a coastal nation along the Bight of Benin. There were similar port cities as well as native villages and trading depots ranging the thousands of miles of African coastline, east and west. It was impossible to patrol them all. When slave ships were caught, it was almost always at sea, and usually by luck.[3]

After throwing anchor on the Congo, Gordon immediately assembled his entire crew and confirmed what they almost certainly suspected—that they had indeed "shipped up a slaver."[4] He then offered each man "one dollar a head" for every slave delivered alive to Cuba. The response was mixed. Some accepted readily, while one man had the temerity to ask for more; Gordon refused. The others had no recourse but to agree. Nineteen years earlier, six sailors on the slaver brig *Sophia* had been abandoned on the coast of Africa, possibly for refusing to participate in a similar enterprise; five of them died. It was not a forgiving place, and death could come in short order from any one of a number of directions: hostile natives, brigands, starvation, thirst, or, most probably, disease such as malaria and yellow fever. There was no way to know when another ship might come along; besides, most

American ships on the river were slavers, so the prospects of a ride home on a legal vessel were slim.

Over the next few weeks, Gordon set about the business of negotiating with the local trader and refitting the ship. After making his deal, he had the whiskey off-loaded, along with the 250 packets of shooks and hoops; these were assembled into hogsheads, filled with river water, and stowed in the hold. At least one of the crew, William Martin, fell ill with fever and remained aboard the *Erie;* Gordon put him to work making and repairing sails. When all was in readiness, he sailed downriver to pick up his cargo.

On August 7, he anchored off Sharks Point, within a few miles of the Congo's mouth. It was one of a number of makeshift ports with names like Snake's Head and Black Point that had been set up specifically as pickup sites for slaves. Bound or chained in slave caravans often led by Arab traders, captives were brought from the interior, where slavery was a common practice. The long trek was harsh, and many died of thirst, hunger, or beatings along the way. The slavers saw the march as a rendering process; the weak died, while the strong proved themselves to be sound stock.

The slaves represented many tribes, and had been enslaved in any of a number of ways. Most were captured in the numerous intertribal wars that raged across the continent. Sometimes bands of brigands swept down on villages and trade caravans, seizing captives for the slave market. Some were enslaved as a sentence for crimes or witchcraft. Often, their own parents or tribal leaders would sell them for weapons, trinkets, or drink, or as tribute to a greater ruler.[5] The African Squadron brig *Porpoise* in 1850 took a Spanish slaver containing 354 men, women, and children. Young midshipman J. Taylor Wood wanted to know where they had come from.

I was anxious to learn their story. After a good deal of questioning [through an interpreter], I learned that they were from a long distance in the interior, some having been one and some two moons on the way, traveling partly by land and partly by river until they reached the coast. They had been sold by their kings or by their parents to the Arab trader for firearms or rum. Once at the depots near the coast, they were sold by the Arabs to other traders to the slave captains for from twenty-five to fifty dollars a head.[6]

Once delivered to the traders on the river or the coast, they were confined in crude "barracoons," or slave barracks, until inspected, sold, and loaded aboard ship.

Gordon's whiskey bought him 897 Africans. Approximately half were children, the youngest six months of age. The rest were divided fairly evenly between men and women, the oldest around forty.[7] As was the case with all slaver captains, Gordon could select his cargo. While males brought the most money and children the least, he could accommodate more slaves—and therefore make more money—with a strong complement of children. Sometimes, however, a captain simply had to take what was available. Gordon's was not the largest cargo of slaves ever shipped; some slavers sailed with more than 1,000 people belowdecks. The steamer *Nightingale,* a 1,066-ton behemoth, was captured with 961 slaves aboard.[8] But Gordon's *Erie,* at less than half the *Nightingale*'s weight, shipped nearly as many Africans.

They were loaded onto launches by the Spaniards who had sailed from Havana on the *Erie* and rowed to the ship's side. Gordon stood on deck holding a knife, and as they came aboard, he cut off and threw overboard whatever skimpy rags some of them were still wearing. Taking each by an arm, he shoved the men in one direction, the women in another. This procedure was not unusual. As the slaver Captain Canot recalled, "[A]s they touch the deck, they are entirely stripped, so that women as well as men go out of Africa as they came into it—*naked.* This precaution . . . is indispensable; for perfect nudity . . . is the only means of securing cleanliness and health."[9]

Prior to accepting them, Gordon would have closely inspected his charges. Again, this assumption is substantiated by Captain Canot's first experience with a slave master, named Mongo John.

> Mongo John . . . as each negro was brought before him, examined the subject, without regard to sex, from head to foot. A careful manipulation of the chief muscles, joints, arm-pits and groins was made to assure soundness. The mouth, too, was inspected, and if a tooth was missing, it was noted as a defect liable to deduction. Eyes, voice, lungs, fingers and toes were not forgotten; so that when the negro passed from the Mongo's hands without censure, he might readily have been adopted as a good "life" by an insurance company.[10]

Boarding the Africans on the *Erie* went quickly. The *New York Times* would later report that "the entire operation of launching and unloading nearly 900 negroes, occupied but *three-quarters of an hour,* or less time than a sensible man would require for his dinner. It was also shown, by one and all the witnesses, that the packing of the Negroes was wonderfully close, that their sufferings were really agonizing, and that the stench arising from their unchecked filthiness was absolutely startling."[11]

In his memoirs of life as a slave, Joseph Wright, a Nigerian, tells of being taken from his village by rival tribesmen and marched to the Congo River to be sold to a slaver. In later life, he recalled the feelings he and his people experienced upon reaching the coast: "[W]e were all naked, both men and women; so that we hardly had any rest in the night for we were very cold. Next day, early in the morning, we were all brought down close to salt water to be put in canoes. We were all heavy and sorrowful in heart, because we were going to leave our land for another which we never knew; and not only so, but when we saw the waves of the salt water on which we were just to enter, it discouraged us the more. . . . Many of the slaves had died for want of water."[12]

Some of the Spaniards left the *Erie* at this point, and eight or ten more came aboard. Some worked as sailors with the crew, while the others stayed among the officers. At no time did they attempt to order or direct the members of the *Erie*'s original crew. These men composed a "phantom" crew, deliberately placed on board in the event of search by a patrolling ship. It was a common deception, and one in which the U.S. government, by refusing foreign naval access to American slavers, was unwittingly complicitous. The way it worked was really quite simple. If the captain of an American slaver suspected that a pursuing vessel were British, he would immediately hoist the American flag; this was usually enough to ward off interference, since the British didn't have the right to board and search American vessels. If, by some slim chance, the warship were American, the slaver captain would hoist a foreign flag, generally Spanish or Portuguese. If challenged and boarded, he would introduce a foreign national as captain, and present to the American officer a complete—though spurious—set of foreign registration papers. He would then claim that he had merely shipped as a passenger and was uninvolved in the commerce of the vessel. American naval vessels had no legal right to interfere with foreign vessels manned by foreign crews. Transparent though this farce now appears, it usually worked. If the American captain and his mates were arrested at all, the charges were generally dismissed in court.[13]

Gordon sailed the *Erie* out of the mouth of the Congo River the morning after loading the Africans and headed north with all sails set, bound once again for Havana. As day broke, with only a few hours of ocean behind her, she sighted a large steamer in hot pursuit. Glass in hand, Gordon stood on the forecastle deck and studied the fast-moving vessel, concluding that she was a British warship. This would prove a costly mistake. The ship was the USS *Mohican,* one of the African Squadron's new steam-powered sloops of war. She was also rigged as a bark, so she could move quickly under either steam or sail. She carried six guns—four "long thirty-twos" and two large eleven-inch pivot guns.[14] The *Mohican* sailed under the command of Sylvanus W. Godon, a battle-seasoned career officer who had joined the navy as a ten-year-old midshipman, and would leave it in 1871 as a rear admiral and a war hero. His patrolling vessel had happened upon the *Erie* by sheer chance. "Lucky Nat's" luck had just run out.

Later that day, Commander Godon would write to Secretary of the Navy Toucey:

> I have the honor to inform the Department that this morning at daylight, I discovered a sail 30 miles at sea off the mouth of the Congo. Hauling up for her—and finding I drew near without her showing any flag, I fired a gun, when she showed American Colors. And on boarding her she proved to be the Ship "Erie" of New York, with nine hundred and ninety seven (997) slaves from the Congo. [In fact, there were 897][15] And a large number of persons on board claiming to be passengers and indeed most of them were foreigners. As there was no acknowledged Captain or mate, and no Ships papers to be found, I could obtain no information that I could rely upon. A clearance from Havana, dated 20th Jany 1860, named Nathl. Gordon as Captain then. He says he sold the vessel up the Congo, and is now a passenger on board, I send him and two persons believed to be mates.

According to navy law, the *Erie* was now the *Mohican*'s prize. Gordon selected a small prize crew from among the men and placed them aboard the *Erie* under Lieutenant John W. Dunnington and passed midshipman Henry Davis Todd. He ordered them to sail to Monrovia—a voyage of 1,500 miles—where they were to discharge their cargo to John Seys, the government agent in Liberia. He had no actual proof that Gordon was still captain, but his strong suspicions led him to leave

Gordon and his two mates aboard under arrest. He gave orders that Dunnington and Todd, after leaving Liberia, "proceed to New York . . . and hand the vessel over to the judge of the U.S. District Court" and surrender Gordon and his two officers to the law. They were to immediately wire news of their arrival to Toucey and rejoin their ship at the first opportunity.

Godon then sailed the *Mohican* to the African Squadron's new base on Loanda, where he discharged the *Erie*'s Spanish crewmen. Loanda was a Portuguese port, and they would have no trouble finding passage home. The Squadron ship *Marion* was in port making preparations for her trip home; her crew's tour was nearing completion, and she was sailing to the naval base in Portsmouth, New Hampshire. Godon placed four sailors from the *Erie*—"such of the crew as I believe to be Americans"—aboard her, with orders to turn them over to the U.S. marshal when she docked.[16]

Commander Godon's concise account of the taking of the *Erie* does not begin to describe the misery his two officers found when they boarded the slaver. The captives had been "packed wonderfully close" belowdeck, with the hatches locked, in the summer heat. They had been allowed no food or water, and "in their hunger and thirst, they had become clamorous for relief. . . . Their sufferings were really agonizing, and . . . the stench from the hold was fearful." While both Dunnington and Todd were competent and dedicated officers, neither had been with the African Squadron very long, having both served aboard the *Mohican* less than a year. Young Midshipman Todd, new to this type of situation and reeling from it, asked the *Erie*'s seasoned first mate, William Warren, for advice.[17] Warren would later testify:

> Lieut. [sic] Todd . . . came to me and asked me what to do with the Negroes to keep them quiet; I told him he ought to give them something to eat and drink, as they had had nothing since the evening before; they wanted some water; I told him to pass it down; he began to do it, and they spilled it as fast as it was passed down, and he said that would not do; I told him he had better let some of them come on deck; he said he durst not, and I told him I had nothing more to say; finally, he came and asked if I thought it was safe; I told him I thought it was perfectly, and he put the steps down to the lower deck, and they began to rush up; he said he durst not let these men come up, and he must keep them down; I said he could let the women and children come up, and he did so; he

said what shall I do with all these people? I said let them down, and you will have room to work the ship; "How?" said he; "Why," said I, "let one down, and the rest will follow." [18]

When the captives were allowed up, they so crowded the main deck, said Todd, that "one could scarcely put his foot down without stepping on them. The . . . filth and dirt upon their persons [was] indescribably offensive." [19] This was Todd's euphemistic way of saying that many of them had vomited and soiled themselves from fever, seasickness, and terror. The slaves themselves "had corn cobs and cotton in their nose[s] to keep the stench away." [20] They had been at sea only a matter of hours; another two weeks lay ahead, and it would get worse.

Once the Africans had been fed, Todd discovered that they had been "packed so closely that the United States officers could not replace them," and Gordon's advice was sought. Gordon, without hesitation, demonstrated to the officers how a slaver's cargo was arranged, "by spreading the limbs of the creatures apart and sitting them so close together that even a foot [of a passing sailor] could not be put upon the deck." [21]

Other than to note their sufferings, the officers on board the *Erie* left no physical description of the captives themselves. However, Midshipman Wood of the brig *Porpoise* left extensive descriptions of his experience in 1850. His words could easily have applied to the captives aboard the *Erie*—or, for that matter, to any one of hundreds of slave ships. Misery was the common denominator.

From the time we first got on board we heard moans, cries, and rumblings coming from below, and as soon as the captain and crew were removed, the hatches had been taken off, when there arose a hot blast as from a charnel house, sickening and overpowering. In the hold there were three or four hundred human beings, gasping, struggling for breath, dying; their bodies, limbs, faces, all expressing terrible suffering. In their agonizing fight for life, some had torn or wounded themselves or their neighbors dreadfully; some were stiffened in the most unnatural positions. . . . For an hour or more we were all hard at work lifting and helping the poor creatures on deck, where they were laid out in rows. A little water and stimulant revived most of them; some, however, were dead or too far gone to be resuscitated. The doctor worked earnestly over each one, but seventeen were beyond human skill. As fast as he pronounced them dead they were quickly dropped overboard. Night closed in with our decks covered so thickly with the ebony bodies that with difficulty we could move about.

My charges were all of a deep black; from fifteen to twenty-five years of age, and, with few exceptions, nude, unless copper or brass rings on their ankles or necklaces of cowries can be described as articles of dress. All were slashed, or had scars of branding on their foreheads and cheeks; these marks were the distinguishing features of different tribes or families. The men's hair had been cut short, and their heads looked in some cases as if they had been shaven. The women, on the contrary, wore their hair "a la pompadour"; the coarse kinky locks were sometimes a foot or more above their heads, and trained square or round like a box-wood bush. Their features were of the pronounced African type, but notwithstanding this disfigurement, were not unpleasing in appearance. The figures of all were very good, straight, well developed, some of the young men having bodies that would have graced a Mercury or an Apollo. Their hands were small, showing no evidences of work, only the cruel marks of shackles. These in some cases had worn deep furrows on their wrists or ankles.[22]

Despite the fact that the *Erie* was now in the hands of the African Squadron, the plight of the slaves would not—in fact, could not—improve. The sheer numbers rendered any form of proper care impossible. Todd eventually managed to feed his charges, but their suffering rapidly increased. As the *New York Times* would later report, "the entire voyage they appeared to be in great agony. The details are sickening, but . . . we will but mention that running sores and coetaneous [sic] diseases of the most painful as well as contagious character infected the entire load. . . . Decency was unthought of, privacy was simply impossible—nastiness and wretchedness reigned supreme."[23] According to Todd, "Some of them fell sick and died very rapidly."[24] Over the next 15 days, between 30 and 37 Africans would die, their bodies thrown overboard. Horrific as this is, had Gordon pursued his original course to Cuba, a two- to three-month journey, the number certainly would have been far greater. With an average captive mortality rate aboard slavers of 17.5 percent, a likely death toll on board the *Erie* would have been around 157 Africans; Gordon's record on previous voyages was even higher.[25]

Though there is no detailed account of the *Erie*'s hellish sail to Monrovia, once again, Taylor Wood's log tells of a similar voyage, of the routine of feeding and watering his "charges" and the method of bathing them:

> Every morning after breakfast we would rig the force pump, screw on the hose and drench them all. They appeared to enjoy this . . . for be it remembered that we were close under the equator, the thermometer dancing about 90 deg[rees]. As the water was sluiced over them they would rub and scrub each other. Only the girls would try not to get their hair wet, for they were at all times particular about their headdress.

Wood slept on deck, since the captain's cabin "was a veritable arsenal, with racks of muskets and cutlasses on two sides." After 14 days, he could see the palms at the entrance to Monrovia Harbor. "When the anchor dropped from the bows and the chain ran through the hawse pipe, it was sweet music to my ears; for the strain had been great, and I felt years older than when I parted from my messmates. A great responsibility seemed lifted from my shoulders, and I enjoyed a long and refreshing sleep for the first time in a fortnight."

No doubt, Midshipman Todd and Lieutenant Dunnington felt the same sense of relief after their fifteen-day trip on the *Erie*. The officers and their charges were met at the Monrovia docks by the Reverend John Seys, who, as U.S. agent for Liberia, was responsible for the settlement and survival of all newcomers to the little republic.

A Methodist missionary with decades of service among the Mohawks of the American Northeast, as well as the Liberian colonists, Seys was something of an anomaly. He was born in St. Croix in 1799 to an aristocratic White family, but when he became a missionary, his family disinherited him. He and his wife had lost children to the "African fever," but he maintained an unshakably positive attitude, and in letter after letter written by the Liberian settlers, he is praised for improving the quality of their lives. In February 1857, colonist William Douglass, writing to the executor of the plantation from which he had recently sailed, wrote with optimism of the land in which he had settled, singling out Seys for praise: "[W]e are all provided for by the Rev. John Seys, our excellent Agent. . . . And we think could find no better man for that experiment, no how in the world." [26] One month later, his optimism was tempered by the deaths of several of his friends and family by "the fever." In this letter, Douglass lists the names of the sick and the dead, beseeches his former masters to send supplies, and still manages to praise the Reverend. "Mr. John Seys is continually thinking of some thing to increase our comforts and happiness."[27]

Seys was fighting a hard, often impossible battle. Funds were woefully slow in coming, and his charges were constantly writing to the ACS—and to former masters—to send them provisions and materials for survival and commerce. Yet when he was called upon to receive the thousands of recaptured slaves taken from the various ships during the African Squadron's last spasmodic efforts, he did so with enthusiasm. In his November 1860 report to Secretary of State Lewis Cass, he writes:

> I have the honor to inform you that the latest and most unprecedented success has attended the efforts, during the last two months, of the U.S. Squadron, Stationed on this Coast for the Suppression of the Slave trade. On the 21st of August last the Brigadier "Storm King" captured by the U.S. Steam Brigade "San Jacinto" with 616 recaptured Africans arrived in this port under the command of Lieutenant A.K. Hughes. The very next day the ship "Erie" with 867 more of these victims to the merciless rapacity of the white-man, followed under the command of Lieutenant J.W. Dunnington, having been captured off the Congo River by the U.S. Steamer "Mohican." This large addition so unexpectedly made to our small population here, and of such character, poor, nude, emaciated, enfeebled and dying creatures, hundreds of them, Boys and Girls, caused no small stir among the people of Liberia. So soon as I received officially information of the arrival of the first prize, I addressed His Excellency [Liberian] President Benson and most respectfully requested permission to land said Africans, making immediate preparation so to do without waiting for a reply.

Struggling with a crippling economic depression, President Stephen A. Benson told Seys that the "Congos" would be admitted on the condition that the United States pay a per capita charge to the Liberian government. When Seys tactfully reminded the president that the United States had already contracted to "make provisions for their support" in the original charter of the colony, President Benson allowed the landing of the Africans. And they kept coming, wrote Seys.

> On Sunday evening Oct. 14, the Barque "Cora" under command of Master John W. Eastman arrived with 694 more captured by the Flag Ship

"Constellation," and on Saturday evening the 27th, the Hermaphrodite
Brig "Bonita" commanded by Lieutenant Foster, came into port with 616
more, a prize to the U.S.S. "San Jacinto," thus up to date no less than 2793
Africans, snatched from endless bondage and oppression have been re-
moved by the U.S. Squadron and brought within the Liberian Territory.
Add to this, the Prize ships "Castilian," "Star of the Union," and "South
Shore" have all arrived from Key West with 823 more making a total of
3616, three thousand six hundred and sixteen.

Given the previously lackluster record of the African Squadron, this
was a massive and unexpected number of people to drop onto the little
country. The citizens of Monrovia were unprepared, lacking sufficient
provisions and money to adequately accommodate their new charges.
Nonetheless, Seys responded with alacrity, forming an advisory committee to help him assign the Congos to "reliable and responsible applicants for them" throughout the Republic. He wrote:

To provide for their immediate wants and necessities was the first consideration, and to do this required no small amount of care and anxiety.
. . . I ventured to assume the responsibility of making some provision for
them until I received definite instructions from the U. States. I engaged to
furnish each with a country blanket which I obtained hundreds at $80, to
give each two suits of clothes, or materials to make them, each suite [sic]
by strict economy not exceeding $50 . . . and to pay for each African
taken into the interior or rural settlements 50 cents per week, and 75 for
such as remain with the citizens of Monrovia. . . . The applicants for Congos, on the part of the people of Liberia have been more numerous than
could be supplied though quite possible that some are actuated by more
mercenary motives.

The Americo-Liberians had just been given a windfall of cheap labor
to work their farms and businesses. There had been strong suspicion in
the States that some of the recaptures from various slave ships had
been sold into slavery by the Liberian colonists. Earlier, a New York
newspaper had printed an article charging that some of the Africans
from the slaver *Echo* had been sold by the local citizenry, taken to the
Congo River, re-shipped, and "re-recaptured." At this point in his letter,
Seys defends the colonists against these allegations, going to great
lengths to account for all the *Echo*'s survivors, and pointing out that the

1,500-mile voyage from Liberia to the Congo River made it too inaccessible for a slaving voyage Besides, "slavery is declared Piracy by the laws of Liberia. . . . It would not pay." Seys might have been right, or he might have been naïve and overly optimistic. The settlers had been intermittently at war with the natives for 40 years, and many of them saw the liberated captives as just so many more barbarians to be dealt with. One way of dealing with them, as with the hostile natives, might have been to sell them to the slave traders.

Seys admits to Cass that his resources are taxed beyond their limit due to the lack of money and materials from the United States and pleads with him to send "a certain amount of U.S. coined money in half and quarter eagles" for "temporary relief." Seys had gone to President Benson to urge the printing of promissory notes, to be redeemed when adequate funds were sent, but Benson had refused Seys's request. The situation was growing desperate, and the Reverend looked ahead to the possibility of even more freed slaves being introduced into Liberia:

> As the very efficient squadron now on this Coast . . . seems destined by the wise and overruling Providence to accomplish much more in the breaking up of this infamous traffic in human beings, it is not impossible that Liberia may yet be the asylum of thousands more of these liberated Africans. . . . I would most respectfully suggest whether some way cannot be devised by the U.S. Government which may render the work easier and more generally satisfactory.

Seys concludes with his conviction that Liberia "is the only safe and secure home where they can find refuge from the cruelty of the oppressor. Here they are free and no where else and here they become civilized, blessed with the Teachings . . . of Christianity and finally saved."[28] John Seys was a true believer.

While the *Mohican*'s officers were sailing the *Erie*'s recaptured Africans to their new home in Monrovia, the recent successes of Inman's little fleet were reflected in the letters, logs, and journals of the ships of the Squadron. On August 10, two days after the seizure of the *Erie,* the journal of Seaman Henry Eason of the Squadron ship *Marion* records the rendezvous with her sister ships in port:

This morning the Constellation came in & was soon followed by the U.S. Steamer Mohican. . . . She had the good fortune to capture a ship called the Erie of New York. . . . The Erie's captain took the Mohican for an English Steamer & showed the American ensign. She was immediately sent to Monrovia to land the Slaves & then proceed to the U.S. for Trial.[29]

Later that day, the crew of the *Marion,* under Commander Thomas W. Brent, received the order to convey four crewmen from the *Erie* to Portsmouth, New Hampshire, for trial: seamen Thomas Nelson, Samuel Sleeper, Thomas Savage, and John McCafferty.[30] Commander Godon of the *Mohican* confirmed to Secretary of the Navy Isaac Toucey that "I have sent by order of the Commander-in Chief four prisoners who call themselves Americans, to the United States in the 'Marion,' to be handed over to the U.S. Marshal of the District in which Portsmouth, N.H. is situated. These four men formed part of the crew of the Slaver 'Erie' captured by me . . . with a cargo of slaves on board."[31]

Flag Officer Inman, ever ready to tout his successes, also wrote a report to Toucey on August 14 "to inform the Department, of the capture of the 'Erie', on the 8th instant, off the river Congo, by the U.S. Steamer 'Mohican,' commander S.W. Godon—Whose report to the Navy Department, was sent home in the prize." Inman goes on to list the captures of the *Triton* ("suspected as a slaver"), and the *Storm King* ("taken without colors or papers, having on board 619 Slaves"). Inman, clearly offended by Toucey's earlier letter encouraging stronger action, goes on to justify his conduct.

The clause that the "Department renews its wish that every exertion may be made to intercept and capture all vessels engaged in [the slave] traffic"—is noted. I respectfully remark, that the exertion thus ordered, is, and has been constantly made, since I assumed this command—I have never spared myself nor those under my orders, from the utmost activity of mind and body, to meet the views of the Department, on that and every other point of duty. The vessels are constantly at sea. . . . Eight captures of Vessels with over 1600 Slaves, have been made. . . . The African Squadron, under my command, has performed its whole duty. I must be permitted to say, that this has been done, in the face of positive discouragement, from the Department. . . . I have been rebuked. . . . No Commander-in-Chief, should be placed in such a position, nor the Flag of his Country, thus discredited in his person, and I respectfully state that

... I am constrained to protect myself ... by aid of my Representatives in the National Legislature."[32]

His pride bruised, Inman was threatening to write his congressmen.

On August 29, the *Erie* sailed for New York.[33] No account exists of Nathaniel Gordon's voyage as a prisoner; however, nearly eight months earlier, Flag Officer Inman wrote a letter to Commander Benjamin J. Totten of the Squadron ship *Vincennes,* instructing him as to the treatment of the officers of the recently captured slaver *Orion*. It can safely be assumed that his instructions concerning Gordon and his mates would have varied little, if at all.

> You will provide suitably for the safety of those persons, as prisoners, on their way to the U.S. for trial, as pirates, according to our laws. You will have such care taken for their sustenance and health as humanity demands. When at Sea, you will permit them to take exercise, under supervision of some responsible person, but they will always be separately and closely confined at night, and when your Vessel is in the neighborhood of land, in irons, more especially in any port, until they are given into the charge of the Civil Authority.

> On your arrival ... you will anchor ... and remain there until you deliver to the U.S. Marshal ... those prisoners, and the names and condition of the Witnesses, [and] the letter and papers you receive herewith, for which [you will] ask for and obtain a receipt. It will probably be advisable to have these prisoners under the especial charge of the Officer Commanding the Marine Guard, from the time you approach land, until after their delivery to the Marshal, which you will cause the Marine Officer, with a proper Guard, to do.[34]

The *Marion* arrived in Portsmouth with its prisoners on October 3, 1860.[35] The same day, Gordon and his mates arrived in New York City for indictment and trial. Given its history as the nation's single largest center for the financing and fitting out of slaving voyages, New York probably seemed to Gordon the closest thing to a snug harbor that his present circumstances would allow.

THE CAPTAIN IN THIS ILLUSTRATION IS CONTENT TO STAND AT THE MAST AS THE CAPTIVES ARE BROUGHT ON BOARD; GORDON WAS BUSY AT THE *ERIE*'S RAIL, STRIPPING HIS "CARGO" OF THEIR RAGS, THEN SENDING THE MEN IN ONE DIRECTION AND THE WOMEN AND CHILDREN IN ANOTHER.

THIS WAS THE METHOD USED BY CAPTAIN GORDON TO "STOW" HIS CARGO.

# CHAPTER IV

# NEW YORK AND PRISON

When the *Erie* sailed past Governors Island into the East River and New York Harbor in early October of 1860, it left the relative quiet of the sea for a world of sights and sounds that reflected the seaport's standing as America's most vital maritime center. Boats of every size and description were plying their trade in an "ever-changing pattern of vessels anchored or passing by." Some were steam-powered: side-wheeler tugs, hauling barges and pulling the big ships into the harbor; ferries crisscrossing from Brooklyn, Queens, Harlem Village, New Jersey, Staten Island; huge commercial and navy steamers—all belching smoke from their tall black stacks.

Despite the number and variety of steamers in the harbor, they were still vastly outnumbered by sailing ships. The era of the steamship was rapidly approaching, but for now, sail still ruled the water. The graceful forms of the Hudson River and Long Island Sound sloops, looking like seaborne gulls, glided up and down the harbor, as two-masted pilot boats sailed out of the harbor mouth in search of large incoming ships to guide safely to port. Oceangoing sailing ships of every type could be seen entering or leaving the seaport, lying at their moorings, or docked at the piers, their long graceful bowsprits thrust upward over the walkways. Most common were the packets—stout three-masters that made regularly scheduled round-trips to San Francisco, Liverpool, Paris, Le Havre. They sat at the dock with banners in their rigging advertising their names and destinations, and on their masts flew the ensigns of their various companies. A forest of masts grew straight up from the docks, as far up and down the seaport as one could see.

South Street, known as the "Street of Ships," was the heart of the seaport. It ran the port's length, from the Battery north. At all hours, it was a hopeless confusion of traffic with wheelbarrows; horse-drawn wagons, drays, and carriages; and pedestrians all vying noisily for passage.

Along South Street's cobblestones tradesmen piled barrels, bales, casks, and crates of tea, molasses, tobacco, spices, and wool, along with sail canvas, lumber, and seemingly endless coils of cable. Dwarfing all were the shipyards, where huge vessels towered in various stages of completion. The entire scene was one of constant activity; one foreign visitor commented that "everything was in motion." The noise could be deafening, combining shipwrights' hammers and saws from a dozen yards; the clanging of the iron and brass foundries; the shouts of the wagon drivers, hawkers, and food vendors; and the shriek of the steam whistles. A confusion of smells assaulted the nose—oysters and fish for sale in carts and stalls, food and coffee from the cheap eateries, freshly sawn wood, the fruit vendors' produce, the ever-present stench of hot tar used in the yards for calking—and, pervading all, the smell of salt water. New York Harbor was alive with the business of shipping.[1]

This was the *Erie*'s home port, to which she had ignominiously returned. When Lieutenant John W. Dunnington docked, he placed Nathaniel Gordon and his two mates in the custody of U.S. Marshal Isaiah Rynders. Although New York was the location of the country's most prominent federal court, it was nonetheless an ironic choice of location to which to bring a slaver. New York had been a slaveholding city from its inception as a small Dutch settlement. The West India Company delivered eleven Brazilian natives to tiny New Amsterdam in 1626; they were given slave names, such as Simon Congo, Anthony Portuguese, and John Francisco.[2] New York saw its first slave revolt in 1712, when an armed group of slaves murdered nine Whites. Retribution was swift and savage: the gallows claimed thirteen, while three were burned at the stake, one was broken at the wheel, one was starved to death, and another was cooked over a slow fire for an entire day. Twenty-nine years later, New York's slaves again attempted to rebel. Instigated by a White tavern owner, they allegedly planned to burn the city and rob and kill its White inhabitants. The plot was discovered before any damage was done; the government's response dwarfed what had occurred earlier. Four Whites and 18 slaves were hanged, 13 more slaves were burned at the stake, and an additional 70 were sent in chains to the Caribbean. There would be no further uprisings.[3] By 1800, one out of every five New York families were slave owners—many keeping slaves "under conditions that were disorienting, brutal and cruel."[4]

Whether in the Caribbean, West African, or Madagascar trade, there were always New York slave ships, financed by New York capital.[5] The slave traders were well known to the city's business community; some ranked among the city's most prominent members of society, frequently meeting at such places as the Astor House hotel to plan their voyages. The money behind their expeditions was provided secretly by many of New York's most respected merchants.[6] By the time Gordon was captured and returned for trial, New York City "had become notorious as the place where more slave-trade voyages were being organized, financed, and fitted out than anywhere else in the world."[7]

As late as 1857 the *New York Journal of Commerce* wrote, "Few of our readers are aware . . . of the extent to which this infernal traffic is carried on, by vessels clearing from New York, and in close allegiance with our legitimate trade; and that down-town merchants of wealth and respectability are extensively engaged in buying and selling African Negroes, and have been, with comparative little interruption, for an indefinite number of years."[8]

In the year and a half ending in August 1860—the month of Nathaniel Gordon's arrest—New York City sent out nearly 100 slaving expeditions. Many of these ships were New York–built steamers, whose cargo capacity far exceeded that of the earlier sailing ships. Although it was generally known that many of the city's wealthier merchants had put a lot of money into the trade, there was no way to prove it. Whenever an attempt was made to effect stronger controls over the traffic, New York's businessmen were among the most vocal opponents. In May 1860, a resolution condemning the slave trade was shouted down at a meeting of the American Tract Society of New York. Why make waves, these men of commerce reasoned, "simply because somebody takes a few niggers from the jungles of Africa to Cuba?"[9]

Upon its return to New York, the *Erie* was seized, and Nathaniel Gordon and his two mates faced indictment. By law, such cases went immediately to federal circuit court. At this time in our history the circuit court bench was shared by a U.S. Supreme Court Justice and a district court judge. On October 16, William Davis Shipman, district judge for the Circuit Court of the Southern District of New York, summoned a grand jury to appear on October 25. On that day, Samuel Nelson— who in addition to being a circuit judge was also associate justice of the Supreme Court of the United States—swore a panel of 20 men to the grand jury, with George Briggs named as foreman. The two key witnesses were Officers Dunnington and Todd. Four days later the jury returned indictments against Gordon, William Warren, and David Hall for violation of the Act of 1800—"voluntarily serving on board a vessel engaged in [the] slave trade," an offense punishable by a fine and two years' imprisonment. The three men were also indicted under the 1820 act. If convicted, the defendants would face death by hanging. This should have been a source of great concern to the slavers, but they were well aware that in the 40 years in which this law had been on the books only one man had ever been convicted.

As captain of the brig *Julia Moulton,* James Smith had sailed from Africa to Cuba with a cargo of slaves, 150 of whom died on the voyage. There was no question that he was a slaver. He neither denied it nor apologized for it. When Smith was tried in November 1854, the jury took one hour to bring in a guilty verdict. Smith's lawyer, however, challenged the verdict on a technicality, and the judge overturned the conviction. Smith's prosecutor, sensing the futility of pursuing another trial, allowed Smith to plead to a violation of the less severe law of 1800. He was given a short sentence and a fine. Ultimately, Smith received a pardon from President James Buchanan, a longtime Southern sympathizer who still occupied the White House when Gordon was indicted.[10] The justice in the Smith case was the same Samuel Nelson who would preside over Gordon's indictments. For years he had built a reputation for his elastic and forgiving interpretations of the slave laws. The Piracy Act of 1820, for all intents and purposes, was a dead letter, and everyone—including Nathaniel Gordon—knew it.

For his defense, Gordon hired Philip J. Joachimsen, an attorney well versed in the legal aspects of the slave trade.[11] Only a few years earlier, he had served as assistant U.S. district attorney under John McKeon, and had been active in the prosecution of accused slavers. On November 23, Joachimsen moved to quash the capital indictment against Gordon, Warren, and Hall, on various technical grounds relating to the wording of the charges. The motion also included the claim that the supposed offense was committed "in the River Congo, on the coast of Africa," outside United States jurisdiction. Judge Shipman denied the defense's motion.[12]

Next day, the *New York Evening Post* printed an editorial under the heading "The African Slave Trade at New York" condemning the increase in the slaving business out of New York Harbor and listing the various vessels that had recently been seized.

> Some of them have been bonded and allowed to proceed on their voyages, while others have been detained, awaiting trial or the decision of the judges of the United States Court. As yet no conviction has been rendered against vessels so seized. In the matter of bonding vessels, there is no absolute security given when they are allowed to depart that they will not bring back cargoes of slaves. The owners can well afford to forfeit the amounts given as security in consideration of the profits of the voyage. . . . There are other vessels fitting out at this port, to which suspicions attach, but as judgments are not readily obtained against this class of slavers, it is probable that they will be allowed to depart unmolested. We can only hope for the suppression of this trade under a new administration.[13]

Among the various slavers listed was the *Erie,* and she had, in fact, been libeled on November 14, 1860, and condemned to be sold at auction, along with "her tackle, apparel and furniture." The sale took place on February 5, 1861, and the *Erie* brought a respectable price of $7,823.25 before expenses. No record exists of her buyer's name, or her fate.[14]

James J. Roosevelt, the U.S. attorney in the Gordon case, had been a member of the state assembly in 1835 and 1840; a congressman from 1841 to 1843; justice of the New York Supreme Court from 1851 to 1859; and recently appointed U.S. district attorney for the southern district of New York. Sixty-five years old at the time of Gordon's arrest, he was of a conservative, old-school turn of mind. He indicted Gordon, Warren, and Hall, but no one—Roosevelt least of all—seemed to have the slightest intention of hanging them. In fact, Roosevelt had publicly stated that "if they are tried and found not guilty (which is highly probable) of piracy; or if they are found guilty, such an outside pressure would be brought to bear upon the President as would compel him to pardon him. In either case he would go scot-free."[15]

President James Buchanan personally detested slavery; nonetheless, he was, in the parlance of the time, a "Hardshell" Democrat, maintaining that slavery was an issue to be decided by the states themselves. His position obviously endeared him to Southerners. His closest friend, congressional colleague, and roommate for more than 20 years had been William Rufus King, vice president under Franklin Pierce, senator from Alabama, and slaveholder. Perennial bachelor Buchanan and the consumptive King were an acknowledged couple at Washington balls and functions, and were so close that King was often referred to as "Mrs. Buchanan," and "Old Buck's wife." [16]

In 1853, before he was president, Buchanan was sent to London as Franklin Pierce's ambassador to the Court of St. James's. "Old Buck" was a veteran of the War of 1812, and he was not especially fond of the British. One of his responsibilities was to promote America's desire to acquire Cuba. In a meeting with two other American diplomats in Ostend, Belgium, he overreached his position, co-orchestrating a policy paper stating that it was the United States' right to take Cuba by whatever means necessary, peaceful or otherwise. According to the plan, Cuba's farms would be added to America's slave-owning plantations, providing additional land and political support to the South. Buchanan was surprised to find that most European nations as well as a large section of the American public took offense at the "Ostend Manifesto." Even President Pierce, who might have responded otherwise in different times, disavowed the document. The South, however, felt that it had gained a firm friend. [17]

Buchanan attained the presidency in 1856. Though an imposing figure—over six feet tall and crowned with a white mane—by this time Buchanan was an old man of 65, cranky and set in his ways. For 140 years, scholars have debated whether there might have been a diplomatic course around the coming Civil War; if so, James Buchanan was the absolute wrong man to navigate it. Under his influence, the Supreme Court handed down a clearly pro-Southern decision in the Dred Scott case, which denied even former slaves the right to sue for their freedom. He advocated a proslavery constitution for Kansas, which Kansas soundly thrashed, resulting in an embarrassing defeat for the president that painted him as an ineffectual leader. It was an accurate portrayal. [18]

The presidential campaign of 1860 reflected the widening gulf between the forces within the party. Two Democratic hopefuls—Stephen Douglas and John Breckinridge—sought the office, and the party split along regional lines. Buchanan witnessed the fall of the Democrats and the victory of a relatively unknown Abraham Lincoln, spearheading the nearly untried Republican Party. By the end of his one term as president, Buchanan craved nothing more than to go home to Pennsylvania and live in obscurity. The last thing he wanted, as his final weeks in office wound down, was to be known as the only president in American history to countenance the execution of a man for trafficking in slaves.

Back in New York, District Attorney Roosevelt offered Gordon a plea bargain: if Gordon gave up the identities of his backers, the government would drop the piracy charge and allow him to plead to the lesser count, with its maximum sentence of two years' imprisonment and $2,000 fine. Roosevelt's rationale was clear: "this city [is] the head and front of the slave trade." If defendants could be persuaded to reveal the names of the men behind it, "they could be of much more use to the government than by hanging them."[19]

Justice Nelson went on record to say that he didn't consider himself responsible for Roosevelt's actions, he knew nothing about the case, had no opinion about it, but would follow Roosevelt's lead, with "confidence . . . in the judgment and priority of the . . . District Attorney."[20] Certain of either an acquittal or a pardon if convicted, Gordon and his attorney refused the deal.

The day after Gordon's indictment, Henry Raymond, editor of the *New York Times*, responded to the U.S. attorney's offer in a blistering editorial—sarcastically entitled "Punishment for the Slave Trade to Be Abolished"—aimed at Roosevelt, Nelson, Buchanan, and the entire ineffectual system that would allow a man to walk away from so heinous a crime. In the case of Gordon and his mates, 'a clearer case could not well be conceived by the common mind." Yet Roosevelt, far from aggressively pursuing a conviction for piracy, seemed to be buying in to the defense's "two Spaniards" tale: "This is the old, old story—These Spaniards being invariably the alleged Captains, whenever the Captain's neck is in danger, but relapsing into the character of perfectly innocent passengers, bound for Havana, if any attempt be made to hold them responsible in their assumed capacity.'

What detonated Raymond's outrage was Roosevelt's comment that this crime no longer merited the charge of piracy in the opinion of the public, and that "the President would 'probably pardon' the guilty man or men. We confess to a . . . stunning of all the moral senses." The district attorney wasn't speaking on his own, said Raymond. "He is fresh from the President's hand, bound to him by social ties, and the official representative of his views upon this point. Let us ask him, then . . . whether the President considers that a possibility of imprisonment for two years should be the highest penalty held out to deter bad and desperate men from engaging in a traffic which returns a net profit of four or five hundred per cent?"

The editor found the plea bargain absurd: "As to the suggestion that the Captain and mate of the *Erie* might, if leniently dealt with, give evidence against their employers, long experience has only too clearly proved that all such promises are illusory." Besides, the prisoners hadn't even promised to cooperate; their counsel said only that they would *"probably* be glad to avoid trial for their lives."

"Let us have done with this farce of pretending to punish persons engaged in the Slave-trade," Raymond concluded, "if the officers charged with and paid for the execution of the laws can make no better semblance of a desire to discharge their duties," especially when the president himself declared that the death sentence would not apply " 'even upon conviction.' "

The Slave-trade is not, unhappily, a plant of such weak growth in our midst that it requires to be watered with these tear-drops of Executive clemency. Rather it is a spreading and poisonous weed, requiring vigorous arms, unflinching industry and the most unyielding discharge of every duty on the part of our law officers charged with its repression. If MR. BUCHANAN desired to signal the last days of his unhappy term by giving assurance of impunity to this crime, he could not have chosen a better means than the declarations made by Judge ROOSEVELT.[21]

The district attorney was quick to fold. In an article entitled "District Attorney Roosevelt Repents," the *New York Evening Post* quoted the prosecutor as saying, "in the present excited condition of the public mind on the African question" he had decided to "leave the prisoners to plead guilty or not guilty on both or either of the charges against them

. . . without any understanding or commitment on the part of the authorities either here or at Washington."[22] By November 2, Gordon and his attorney had reconsidered Roosevelt's offer, but it was too late; with the local press crying "Shame!" at his feeble efforts, the district attorney had rescinded it. Joachimsen, taken aback by Roosevelt's reversal, requested a few days to determine his clients' course. When they returned to court, Gordon and his mates pleaded not guilty to the charges.

While awaiting trial, Gordon was lodged in the Eldridge Street Jail, a minimal-security institution where the government often housed witnesses who lacked the funds for a proper hotel. He roamed the building freely, receiving friends and family, and was "dined and wined to an almost unlimited extent." For a fee—more correctly, a bribe—of $50 sterling per night paid to his jailer, Gordon was allowed to leave Eldridge Street and go on the town "on his parole," provided he return the next morning. As U.S. Marshal Robert Murray later wrote, Gordon considered himself "not as a felon, but a gentleman temporarily out of his latitude."[23]

In fact, Gordon had no reason to be apprehensive. His position differed little from that of other slaving captains who had actually been indicted, few though they were. He had engaged one of New York City's top attorneys to defend him before a court with an impossibly poor record of slaving convictions. He would be prosecuted by a district attorney with no stomach for a capital verdict, and tried by a judge who had reversed the jury in the only piracy conviction on record. In the highly unlikely event of a conviction, the president of the United States stood ready to pardon the offender. If all this was not enough to assuage Gordon's concerns, he had only to consider the venue: he was being tried in New York City—the largest and most notorious center for the promotion of slaving expeditions, North or South, in the United States.[24]

It was commonly assumed that there was no legal problem relating to the slave trade that could not be resolved by a payment to the appropriate New York official. Sometimes this payment took the form of an outright bribe, and sometimes, as in the case of one Captain Cornelius F. Driscoll, former master of the slaver brig *Hope,* it took the form of $1,000 bail. Driscoll was arrested in New York in 1844, after having delivered a cargo of 600 Africans to Brazil. Along with his release on bail, Driscoll requested—and *received*—permission from Circuit Court

Judge Samuel Betts to sail to Rio de Janeiro on his own recognizance, so that he might procure evidence for his defense! The captain fulfilled the first half of his bargain; he sailed to Brazil. Driscoll was, however, disinclined to return to New York, and no extradition agreement existed between the United States and Brazil to pressure him to do so. In a saloon in Rio, Captain Driscoll addressed his friends:

> Well, boys, you don't have to worry about facing trial in New York City. Let the cruisers take you, if they will; I can get any man off in New York for $1000. All you have to do is get some straw bail, and you'll be free as the birds. Look at me. . . . Made myself a pirate, they say. . . . The marshal caught up with me in New York and put me in jail. Pretty soon they had me up before old Betts and were talking of hanging me. But here I am, and I'll never go back.[25]

Driscoll did go slaving again; understandably, he never returned to New York.

The men actually responsible for sending out the slave ships acted as an "investment firm" for enterprising, anonymous New York businessmen. They were members of a shadow company that financed, fitted out, and oversaw the slaving voyages from New York to Cuba to the Congo, and back again. Beginning around 1852, what had once been a group of individual slave traders became a loose conglomerate. This business had no official name, since the law, after all, did prohibit slaving. It was generally referred to, however, as the "Portuguese Company" since its membership was largely—but not exclusively—Portuguese. The company had offices located along lower Manhattan's waterfront, among the shops and shipyards of the Seaport. The signs over the office doors touted the names of such experienced and highly successful slavers as José daCosta Lima Viana, John Machado, and the firm of Figaniere, Reis, and Company, the senior partner of which was the Portuguese consul general in New York. These companies would build or buy ships as legitimate businessmen, then register, crew, and send them out under puppet companies or individuals.[26]

The Portuguese Company's New York City base was a natural choice, due to the vast amount of shipping that left this port. It was relatively simple to purchase ships and launch a few slavers a month by hiding them in the midst of hundreds of legitimate outward-bound vessels. Ships were a glut on the market, and could be purchased cheaply after the devastating Panic of 1857. This, combined with the increasingly high selling price of slaves, provided a strong inducement to many captains and tradesmen who had had no previous dealings with the slave trade. Business flourished accordingly. Horace Greeley called New York "the nest of slave pirates." [27]

Another, much larger shadow company, loosely dubbed the "Spanish Company," arose in 1857. It absorbed the old Portuguese Company, expanded it to include several Spanish and American "businessmen," and ushered in what would be the African slave trade's last big boom. [28] The insidious presence of the new conglomerate was felt across the world, as vessels were purchased and fitted out in the ports of the United States, Spain, Mexico, Venezuela, Denmark, Haiti, Portugal— even Great Britain. The two ports of choice, however, remained Havana and New York City. [29]

If a slave ship's papers could not be acquired through legitimate channels, or a slaver was in danger of seizure, outright bribery was employed. Within a month of Gordon's indictment, the case of the slave bark *Kate* was tried in New York district court. The vessel had been seized in New York Harbor by a federal revenue cutter shortly after having been approved for sailing by the customhouse. The question was put as to how the *Kate,* obviously a slaver, had been cleared. As reported in the *New York Evening Post.*

Henry C. Smith, a Custom-house broker, and Mr. James De Graw, clearance clerk in the Custom-house, were called as witnesses. Mr. Smith swore to the legality and honesty of the proceedings in obtaining the clearance of the bark Kate. Mr. De Graw testified, in substance, that after the clearance of the Josephine [another slaver, whose captain jumped bail earlier in the year] Mr. Smith came to him, and putting a twenty dollar gold piece on the table, asked him why he was reporting these vessels, and told him a similar sum would be paid in each case, if he made no trouble in future.

At this point, Smith stood and approached Mr. de Graw as he was leaving the witness stand, and threatened to "spoil his face so that his mother would not know him."[30] The charges against the *Kate* were sustained, and she was confiscated.

On May 1, 1860, the court seized and libeled the proven slaver *Storm King*. She was due to weigh anchor the next day, on another slaving expedition. Two deputy marshals were dispatched to the ship with orders to prevent her from sailing. One of the deputies, who also happened to be the nephew of U.S. marshal Isaiah Rynders, was offered a $1,000 bribe; he refused—and held out for $1,500. The captain paid up and immediately set sail. The deputy, not known for his keen mind, had the poor judgment to return to the marshal's office and brag about his shrewdness in the transaction. He was arrested and indicted for "willfully and unlawfully obstructing the due administration of justice," a charge that carried a maximum penalty of a $500 fine and six months in jail. He was never brought to trial.[31] The *Storm King* pursued its course to the coast of Africa and was one of two "laden" ships sighted, pursued, and captured by the African Squadron on August 8. The other was Nathaniel Gordon's ship, *Erie*.

If any one man reflected the chicanery, bigotry, racism, corruption, and violence that represented New York City politics in the mid-1800s, it was U.S. marshal Isaiah Rynders. Born in Virginia, he became a gambler and pistol- and knife-fighter on the Mississippi. Reputedly run out of Vicksburg by vigilantes in 1835, he shortly thereafter made his way to New York. At some point, he styled himself "Captain" and was so known for the rest of his life. Within a short time of his arrival in New York, he became boss of the city's notorious, gang-ridden Sixth Ward. Rynders was the main "fixer" for the corrupt Democratic political machine known as the "Tammany Ring." Elections were sometimes bought but almost always "directed" by the presence at the polls of Rynders's force of gang-based "head bangers," "shoulder hitters," and "repeaters."[32]

Isaiah Rynders and his gangs served three-time mayor Fernando Wood. "Fernandy," as he was known, born a Philadelphia Quaker in 1812, started life as a cigar maker. He served a term in Congress, during which he was accused, but not convicted, of fraud. He won his first term as New York's mayor in 1854, garnering 400 more votes in the Sixth Ward alone than there were voters. Corrupt to the bone, Wood strong-armed the police for bribes, sold public offices for tens of thousands of dollars, and arranged for the immediate naturalization of immigrants—conditional on their voting for him at election time. With the help of the Dead Rabbit Gang's ballot-box–smashing, arm-twisting tactics, Wood carried the election by 9,651 votes. It was later claimed by his opponents that 10,000 of his votes were fraudulent.[33]

An article in *Harper's Weekly* in the 1850s asserted that New York under Wood was "a huge semi-barbarous metropolis . . . not well-governed nor ill-governed, but simply not governed at all—with filthy and unlighted streets—no practical or efficient security for either life or property—a police not worthy of the name—and expenses steadily and enormously increasing."[34] Theodore Roosevelt later referred to Fernando Wood as "an unscrupulous and cunning demagogue, whose financial honesty was more than doubtful," and to Rynders as a "brutal rowdy" who, with Wood, "ruled by force and fraud, and were hand in glove with the disorderly and semi-criminal classes."[35] Throughout his remarkably self-serving career, no one questioned that Fernandy Wood owed much of his success to the machinations—congenial and otherwise—of Isaiah Rynders.

Rynders was clearly a man of strong opinions. He shared his boss's opposition to the liberation of African Americans, declaring them racially inferior and viewing slavery as a "divine institution."[36] With the help of his thugs, he broke up meetings of reform groups and speeches by the likes of abolitionist William Lloyd Garrison.

In fact, Southern sympathy in antebellum New York was widespread. The editor of the *New York Evening Post* wrote that "New York belongs almost as much to the South as to the North."[37] The city was the South's major supplier of factory-made cheap clothing and other articles for the outfitting and maintenance of its slaves. In his 1858 campaign, Fernando Wood stated that "the South is our best customer. She pays the best prices, and pays promptly."[38] Wood's appeal to New York's Southern sympathizers, interlaced with his racist fearmongering, won him the vote from the city's gentry and businessmen who benefited from the slave industry, and from its working class who feared free Blacks would take their jobs.[39] After his election, Mayor Wood declared that "the profits, luxuries, the necessities—nay, even the physical existence [of New York City] depend upon . . . continuance of slave labor and the prosperity of the slave master!"[40]

During the 1860 presidential campaign of Republican Abraham Lincoln, Mayor Wood's brother Benjamin, editor of the hate-mongering

*New York Daily News* (which younger brother Fernandy had purchased for him), wrote one editorial after another, railing that "if Lincoln is elected you will have to compete with the labor of four million emancipated Negroes," and "we shall find Negroes among us thicker than blackberries. . . ."[41] Slavery was clearly the issue, and fear the weapon. New York was then, as now, a city dedicated to business, and much of its business was with the cotton growers of the South. And if the South depended upon slavery to generate the product, then so be it. As a New Orleans editor put it, without slavery, New York's "ships would rot at her docks; grass would grow in Wall Street and Broadway, and the glory of New York, like that of Babylon and Rome, would be numbered with the things of the past."[42] The prospect struck terror in the hearts of New York's businessmen.

But Abraham Lincoln was elected president on November 6, 1860, and the Southern states' threats to secede were becoming a reality. On December 15, more than 2,000 frightened New York businessmen gathered to make known their support of the South, and their willingness to let the Southern states leave if they so chose. "If ever a conflict arises between the races," they announced, "the people of the city of New York will stand by their brethren, the white race."[43] These men, and thousands of New Yorkers like them, owed their livelihood to the cotton commerce with the South, and they feared the economic consequences that a separation would bring upon them.

On December 20, the South Carolina legislature declared the dissolution of union between South Carolina and the United States. Two weeks later (while Nathaniel Gordon was still under indictment and comfortably awaiting his first trial), Mayor Wood sent a message to his common council, recommending that New York City follow South Carolina's example, secede from the Union, and become an independent commonwealth called the Free City of Tri-insula, after Long, Staten, and Manhattan islands. As such, it would "make common cause with the South" and refuse to allow passage of Union troops through the city. Better this, reasoned Wood, than jeopardize the strong business relations between New York and the South. The council, whose habitual chicanery had earned them the epithet "The Forty Thieves," actually approved the plan—but reversed themselves after the attack on Fort Sumter three months later would have made their actions treasonous.[44]

While most rational New Yorkers condemned the mayor's proposal

and his actions, there were many who subscribed to his personal and
political philosophy. In a very literal sense, it can be said to have struck
a sympathetic chord. The first public presentation of New York min-
strel, composer, and blackface performer Dan Emmett's song "I Wish I
Was in Dixie's Land" was given in New York City's Mechanics Hall in
April 1859. Within two years, it would find acceptance as the national
anthem of the Confederacy.[45]

Though New York City on the brink of Civil War was home to an
alarming number of Southern sympathizers; had a near-traitorous
mayor; a crooked, proslavery U.S. marshal; a thoroughly corrupt administration; a less-than-aggressive district attorney; and a level of
slave-trade activity that had reached alarming proportions, Nathaniel
Gordon still might have had a reason to be concerned. There was, after
all, the matter of a trial in *federal* court for a capital offense. But as his
attorneys doubtless had informed him, there was little reason for worry
on that score, either. Juries were often either bought or intimidated into
delivering the "appropriate" verdicts; if that ploy was not effective, the
judges could almost always be counted on to lean in favor of the defendant in a slave case.

Two of the most notorious were Judge Samuel Betts and Justice
Samuel Nelson, who had reversed the verdict in Captain Smith's piracy
trial. At nearly 75 years of age, Betts was one of the oldest sitting federal
judges, having occupied the bench since his appointment by President
John Quincy Adams in 1826. Nelson had served on the circuit court
since 1845. During their time of service, they provided continuous support and encouragement to New York's slavers.[46] They effectively took
practically all likelihood of conviction out of the slave-trade laws of
1794 and 1818 by making it nearly impossible to prove a case against
the defendant. Through their interpretation of the laws regarding outfitting a slaver, crews, tradesmen, financiers, even customs officials became exempt from charges; according to their rulings, only captains,
owners, or supercargoes could be convicted of slaving, and then only if
it could be clearly proven that they had had total control over the voyage.[47] Such hard evidence rarely if ever existed. The judges then went
on to reduce the 1807 act to a mere fineable offense, with no possibility
of imprisonment, and little likelihood of conviction.[48]

Through their clearly biased readings of the statutes, in case after
case they managed to shield the violators from punishment. Betts

demonstrated his inclinations in the case of the schooner *Mary Ann.* Sensing that the captain was planning to turn their voyage to the African coast into a slaving expedition, the crew had taken over the ship and put the captain ashore. Refusing to relinquish the vessel to a British man-of-war, they searched for an American naval ship to which to surrender the *Mary Ann.* Unsuccessful in their quest, they then sailed to New York, both to return the ship to her owner and to seek their due wages for the length of the trip. The ship was immediately seized and libeled, as was appropriate. However, in circuit court, Judge Betts officially saw the crew's action as "a naked aggression upon the rights of the owner," and released the libeled vessel. Adding insult to injury, he then denied the crew its wages.[49]

In the case of the slaver *Horatio,* the registered owner was arrested with an incriminating note in his pocket, clearly indicating that the owner himself had helped in outfitting the vessel—a punishable offense under the 1818 law. The jury was therefore baffled to receive a charge from Judge Betts, explaining to them that the defendant was guilty only if he had been in charge of the actual voyage. Nowhere does the law say this, and the jury, understandably confused, questioned Betts. He responded that they would either find accordingly or he would declare a mistrial and impanel a jury that could follow orders. They found the defendant not guilty. As a result, it was no longer possible to find anyone guilty of "aiding and abetting" in fitting out a vessel.[50]

When Captain Isaac Morris and Captain Frederick Peterson, of the slavers *Butterfly* and *Catherine,* respectively, appeared before Judge Betts and Justice Smith Thompson, Betts made a ruling that summarily dismissed the whole concept of intent. According to Betts, a slaving voyage could not be determined as such until and unless there were actually captive Africans aboard. It was, therefore, perfectly legal for a backer to finance a slaving expedition, for an owner to outfit it, a captain to prepare a slave deck and store manacles, to sail to the very barracoons in which the slaves were held, and to carry and off-load whiskey, rum, and other trade goods for their purchase; it only became a slaving enterprise when the slaves were boarded. To crown his argument, Betts referred erroneously to a previous Supreme Court ruling as precedent.

Justice Thompson was outraged. In the event of a disagreement between two members of the bench, an appeal to the Supreme Court was allowed. Thompson did just that. The higher court promptly rebuked Betts and reversed his opinion. Captains Morris and Peterson, who had been so encouraged by Betts's earlier judgment that they elected to stay around for their trials, quickly changed their minds, jumped bail, and were not heard from again. Morris's ship, the *Butterfly,* which came before Betts for libel proceedings, was declared forfeit, since Morris was not around to explain the nature of her business. Nonetheless, Betts took advantage of the moment to rule that no cargo in itself could be judged incriminating; this effectively removed from the naval patrol vessels the right to seize a suspected slaver on the basis of its provisions, even if they included chains and coppers.

When the absent Peterson's ship, the *Catherine,* came before Betts, it was shown that the vessel had contained two large sacks of handcuffs, 1,500 feet of wood for a slave deck, 7,000 gallons of water, 570 spoons, a large quantity of trade rum, and a crew of about 25 Spanish and Portuguese sailors—along with a document in Spanish instructing them as to their responsibilities when they took over the ship from the handful of American sailors on board. Additionally, there was a letter from the owners, taken from Captain Peterson by force, directing him in the event of boarding by a patrol ship: "Always stick to the same story, take all command with your American sailors . . . ; and all the others are to be passengers." The supercargo, on his return to New York for trial, killed himself.

Betts knew all this, yet he found that the actual "business arrangements" for the voyage were within legal parameters. It was claimed by the defense that the ship had been purchased in Havana, and was to be delivered to her new owner on the African coast. It was a shopworn defense that presumed that there was nothing peculiar in sailing a ship hundreds of miles to the fever-ridden mouth of the Congo simply for an exchange of ownership papers. This line of defense was preposterous. In case after case, however, the defense's claim went unchallenged, as it did in the case of the *Catherine.* Betts determined that there was nothing suspect or illegal in the transaction. He dismissed the libel against the vessel and returned her to her owners.[51]

What Betts seemed to miss continually was the essence of the law, and of the Supreme Court's ruling: a vessel was a slaver the moment she was *intended* for the trade, regardless of changes in ownership, destination, and fittings. The decision was appealed, reversed, and the

vessel confiscated. Nevertheless, Betts's original decision was successfully referenced over and over in future cases to secure the release of
captured slave ships. Again and again, the American right of property
outweighed the legal and moral directive to make an impact on the
slave trade.[52]

One of the most outrageous cases to come before Betts was that of
Captain Philip Van Vechten, of the brig *Ellen*. As he was about to set off
on a slaving expedition in 1859, he mentioned to his brother—a customhouse official—the nature of his voyage. The brother, horrified, immediately reported Philip to the authorities. He sailed anyway, but was
quickly overtaken by a government revenue cutter.[53] It seems he had
also discussed his intentions with the captain of the cutter before he
sailed. No one could have accused Captain Van Vechten of an over-
abundance of good sense.

The case came before Judge Betts, whose clerk, acting as a U.S. commissioner, simply released Van Vechten. This left the libel suit against
the vessel itself. Betts once again misquoted the Supreme Court, and,
finding nothing to "justify the presumption that the admissions or asser-
tions of Van Vechten were made with the knowledge or approval of the
owner," dismissed the libel and released the *Ellen*. The captain might
declare to the world at large that his ship was on a slaving voyage, Betts
reasoned, but that did not mean that the owner was aware of it. The
district attorney appealed the decision, this time to Justice Samuel Nelson. But in Nelson, Betts had found the ally he had lacked in Justice
Thompson; Nelson supported Betts's decision, as he would do whenever called upon to render such a judgment.[54] Between the two, they
had ravaged the slave-trade acts and rendered inadmissible or incon-
clusive the following: confessions by slaver captains—even when
made to captains of patrol boats; fitting out by anyone other than captains, owners, and supercargoes—and then only if they could be
proven to be in control of the expedition; slaving voyages at any point
other than the actual transport of slaves; documents clearly incriminating slavers; and cargoes of any kind, so long as they were "properly"
manifested.[55]

Horace Greeley's *New York Tribune* fumed,

The impunity . . . with which the slave trade is carried on from this port
of New York has arisen from the construction which Judges Betts and

Nelson have seen fit to put upon the laws for the suppression of the slave trade. There is a singular but very natural contrast between the spirit of good will with which these two learned judges apply themselves to the enforcement of the Fugitive Slave Act [i.e., returning slaves to their owners], and the severe spirit of strict construction with which they seem to be seized whenever the slave trade suppression acts are before them. Property . . . is a much greater thing than the freedom . . . of any number of niggers. But this same maxim, which appears to be the beginning and end of the law with these two learned Judges, when applied to the slave-trade suppression acts, leads to a totally different system of construction. . . . Property is not to be interfered with . . . and though invented for the purpose of the slave-trade, it still remains highly sacred.[56]

Betts and Nelson, the editorial states, "strain every nerve" to "nullify the slave-trade laws."[57]

Had Nathaniel Gordon suspected that his case would differ in any way from all those that had preceded it, there is little doubt that he would have fled prior to his trial. Despite the fact that he stood indicted of a capital crime and therefore was not entitled to bail (although his attorney actually did present an unsuccessful motion to obtain it), he certainly had the opportunity to flee. Gordon's liberal terms of incarceration at the Eldridge Street facility gave him ample chance to run.

Why, then did he choose to stay and go through the embarrassment of a court procedure? Clearly, the answer is arrogance. Hubris. Gordon and his lawyers were so sure of themselves that they chose to play it out. The slaver's attorney knew the legal aspects of the slaving game extremely well, having played it for years. His client's personal needs were being attended to, and all the familiar players were in place.

The players, however, would not remain the same for much longer. Within a week of Gordon's indictment, a new federal administration was voted into office. If Gordon had followed the presidential election of 1860, one of the planks of the victorious Republicans' campaign platform might have given him some anxious moments:

[Resolved:] That we brand the recent reopening of the African slave trade, under the cover of our national flag, aided by perversions of judicial power, as a crime against humanity, a burning shame to our country and age, and we call upon Congress to take prompt and efficient measures for the total and final suppression of that execrable traffic.[58]

The Republicans would soon replace many of New York City's Democratic officeholders and politicians, including U.S. Attorney Roosevelt and U.S. Marshal Rynders. Still, there was time for Roosevelt to bring Gordon to trial. None of the political changes would take effect before spring of the new year, leaving the prosecutor ample opportunity to dispose of the case of *United States v. Nathaniel Gordon.*

What no one anticipated was the unwillingness of District Attorney Roosevelt to prosecute. Perhaps he was merely slow in preparing his case. Or perhaps he sensed a shift in the wind. After all, the New York papers were running more and more vitriolic editorials attacking the slave trade and New York's pathetic legal efforts to curtail it. Just prior to leaving office in April 1861, Roosevelt stated that he was "preparing the case for his successor to carry on," and explained the delays as being caused partly by the illness of a key witness.[59] More likely, the case had simply become too hot for the lame duck district attorney to handle. By expediting the trial, he would gain nothing except the enmity of his party if he pushed for the death penalty, and the anger of a growing number of the populace if he didn't. Either way, he stood to lose.

His successor, staunch Republican Edward Delafield Smith, would take a harsher view of Roosevelt's foot shuffling. In a letter written the following year to his superior, Secretary of the Interior Caleb B. Smith, the new district attorney lambasted his predecessor:

On my appointment, in April last, I found that Capt. Gordon, of the slaver "Erie," had been in custody for a long period of time, with no apparent effort to prepare the case for trial. Indeed, my eminent predecessor had declared, in open court, last winter, that in his judgment, public opinion would not justify a capital conviction.[60]

Gordon would have to wait until mid-June 1861, after Roosevelt left office, to have his day in court. Ironically, the four sailors arrested along with Gordon and his mates had faced a district judge in New Hampshire's circuit court seven months earlier, on November 22. All four were convicted of voluntarily serving aboard the *Erie,* "knowing the same to be engaged in the African slave trade."[61] The men were not tried under the Piracy Act of 1820 until May of 1861—one month before Gordon's first trial. The jury returned a verdict of not guilty.[62] When sentence was passed on the charge of voluntarily serving aboard a slaver, each man was fined one dollar and sentenced to prison until the following September. Including time already served, they would spend less than a year in jail. There can be little doubt that Gordon's attorney gave him the results of these trials, and that the slaver drew a measure of comfort from them.

However, once the broom of the new Republican administration swept Marshal Rynders out of office, things changed radically for the accused slaver. Rynders's replacement, Robert Murray, a balding, impressive-looking man of strong character, was described by a contemporary as resembling "an admiral on his quarterdeck," with a reputation as a "detective of fair and excellent repute."[63] Soon after assuming his new role in April 1861, Marshal Murray determined that the Gordon case was significant enough to require considerably stronger security; he had Gordon and his two mates placed in the New York City Hall of Justice. Here, Gordon would spend the last ten months of his life, and here, he would learn the true meaning of "prison."

When Charles Dickens first saw New York City's prison in the 1860s, it struck him as a "dismal-fronted pile of bastard Egyptian, like an enchanter's palace in a melodrama!"[64] Finished in 1838 at a then-enormous cost of $430,000, it was, indeed, built to resemble the common council's conception of an Egyptian temple. Although officially named the Hall of Justice, the forbidding structure immediately earned for itself the epithet "the Tombs."

Ironically, the site chosen for the construction of what would soon be considered one of the nation's worst penal institutions was, at one time, a clear, spring-fed pool. Long before the Dutch settled Manhattan Island, the local Native American residents fished for trout in its waters. Named Collect Pond by the English settlers, it ran 50 feet deep, was surrounded by low hills, and flooded during heavy rains, bisecting lower Manhattan. From the pond ran two clear streams that flowed into a 90-acre marsh and then into both the Hudson and East Rivers. The pond was indeed a lovely spot.[65]

Its loveliness faded quickly after the arrival of European settlers, who dumped their garbage and waste in it. The island's tanners located their mills along its banks in 1745, followed two years later by a powder works. A constant soup of tannin, arsenic, sulphur, saltpeter, and a variety of the other by-products of these factories killed off the plants and wildlife, and turned Collect Pond into a cesspool. In 1787, a committee assigned to lay out streets for lower Manhattan reported the pond to be in a "filthy condition, owing to the practice of throwing refuse in it."[66] By the early 1800s, Collect Pond sat in the middle of the Five Points, New York's most depressed neighborhood—and, reputedly, the worst slum in the world. According to one guidebook of the period, "From Canal Street to Chatham Street there is not the slightest sign of cleanliness or comfort."[67] Herds of pigs and wild dogs ranged the crooked, muddy streets, overshadowed by sagging, overcrowded houses. The district was rife with theft, prostitution, and murder. By the first decade of the nineteenth century, the once-idyllic Collect Pond had become a foul-smelling eyesore.

In 1808, the common council provided jobs for several of New York City's unemployed citizens, and set them to work tearing down the surrounding hills, using the land to fill in Collect Pond. Eighteen years later, the site was chosen for the new city prison, and construction was begun. Not surprisingly, just below the topsoil, the crew struck water. The quick-thinking contractor, rather than lose the job or wait for the drawn-out selection of another site, sank pilings and ordered a massive hemlock raft constructed to serve as a floating foundation. Two years later, the Tombs was finished; it immediately began to insinuate itself into the mud, settling several inches in six months. Cell walls warped, pipes backed up, hinges groaned constantly, and a seemingly endless parade of locksmiths, carpenters, and stonemasons serviced the prison for its remaining 59 years, when it was finally condemned by a grand jury as being "unhealthy and unfit for its purposes."

The Tombs was irregularly rectangular in shape, and ran 253 feet by 200 feet. The main entrance was on Centre Street (originally named "Rynders Street" after the notorious Isaiah), and featured a broad, oppressive portico, supported by four stout columns. It appeared to be a one-story structure, but the building actually contained four tiers, or "galleries," of cells lining its walls. Prisoners were designated to tiers based on the severity of their offenses. The top tier, containing the smallest cells, held those charged with the mildest offenses. Below them were prisoners charged with burglary and grand larceny. The next gallery accommodated accused murderers and arsonists, while the bottom level was reserved for those already convicted or under sentence of death. This tier was referred to as "Murderers' Row," and was the most severely afflicted with dampness, foul air, and flooding.

The Tombs contained 200 cells, each designed to accommodate a single prisoner. From the time the prison opened, however, the population often ranged between 500 and 600 inmates, with two or three to a cramped cell. Each cell had a small iron door that Dickens described as "furnace-doors, but . . . cold and black, as though the fires within had all gone out." The author asked that a cell be opened. "The fastenings jar and rattle, and one of the doors turned slowly on its hinges. Let us look in. A small bare cell, into which the light enters through a high chink in the wall. There is a rude means of washing, a table, and a bedstead."

Despite the fact that it was only a detention center from which prisoners would either be released, sent to state institutions, or executed, the Tombs accommodated a large number of men, women, and children in the most depressing of circumstances. Dickens was outraged. "Do men and women, against whom no crime is proved, lie here all night in perfect darkness, surrounded by the noisome vapours . . . and breathing this filthy and offensive stench! Why, such indecent and disgusting dungeons as these cells, would bring disgrace upon the most despotic empire in the world!"[58]

Corruption among the police and the staff was widespread. Warden Malachi Fallon, who served during the 1840s and 1850s, was particularly resourceful. He started the tradition of providing Phineas T. Barnum with the death masks and clothes of notorious murderers and pirates for display in Barnum's Museum of Curiosities on lower Broadway. Barnum generally compensated the warden with cash, and the prisoner with such creature comforts as cigars. Future wardens kept this tradition alive.[69]

The women were incarcerated in the outer shell of the prison, while the men's cells were located in a separate building in the center of the complex. Between the facilities was a narrow courtyard, which served as the hanging ground. A span connecting the two structures was known as the "Bridge of Sighs," since condemned prisoners generally had to cross it in order to descend to the courtyard, and their deaths. The Tombs hosted the hanging of 50 men before its long-overdue destruction in 1897.

Gordon's trial date was set for June 18, 1861; meanwhile, he languished in his cold, dank cell on Murderers' Row. Warden Charles Sutton, who would later write a history of the Tombs, recorded the reactions of Gordon and his mates to their new situation: "They had hitherto felt but little concern at their arrest and imprisonment—there never having been as yet anyone hanged for their offence. When they found that the new administration was disposed to view the case in all its enormity, and to treat the criminals accordingly, they became greatly alarmed at their position." [70]

Once and sometimes twice a day, nearly every day, Elizabeth Gordon took the ferry across the East River from Williamsburg, Brooklyn, and made her way to this foul-smelling place to visit her husband. She and their four-year-old son were staying at the home of Gordon's friends, Captain and Mrs. David Woodside, and it was they whom Gordon later thanked for caring for his family during his long months of imprisonment. Elizabeth was 22, and she had come to New York from Portland to be near Nathaniel. She loved and depended upon him, and the circumstances of his arrest and trial were devastating to her. Of all the players involved in the trials of Captain Gordon, Elizabeth is clearly the most tragic.

Marshal Murray had made provision for her to visit her husband in his cell, which greatly comforted Gordon. The effect it had on Elizabeth can only be conjectured. Meanwhile, her financial situation was growing ever more precarious. Whatever money her husband might have had was fast disappearing, absorbed in legal fees, payment for prison privileges, and the daily cost of providing decent food and amenities for himself and his two penniless mates. Shortly after Gordon's indictment, the *New York Times* interviewed the former steward of the *Erie,* who reported that the supercargo had managed to smuggle off the vessel a hidden cache of $40,000 in gold Spanish doubloons. [71] The story may have been apocryphal, but even if it were true, certainly none of the gold found its way to the accused slaver. There was nothing coming in, and Gordon watched helplessly as his family's financial circumstances grew increasingly strained. The *Springfield Daily Republican* wrote that Gordon "when arrested was worth $80,000, but every cent has been expended in legal proceedings. His wife was so destitute that she has been obliged to beg for money enough to cross the ferry."[72]

The original Tombs, New York City's prison, as depicted in a stereoscope card of the period. Its massive Egyptian columns and facade—along with the awful conditions within—earned the building its nickname.

## CHAPTER V

## FIRST TRIAL

The eight-month period from October 1860 to June 1861 during which Nathaniel Gordon sat in his cell—first at Eldridge Street and then the Tombs—awaiting trial was one of stunning changes in New York City, and in the country at large. It saw New York adapting to the new—and, to Gotham's majority, unwelcome—administration. Here was a city that had never been overly enthusiastic about either Abraham Lincoln or the Republican Party. In May 1860, George Templeton Strong, native New Yorker, successful attorney, and astute observer of his times, recorded in his diary New York's acerbic impression of Lincoln: "He is unknown here. The Tribune and other papers commend him to popular favor as having had but six months' schooling in his whole life; and because he cut a great many rails, and worked on a flatboat in early youth; all which is somehow presumptive evidence of his statesmanship."[1]

Lincoln had surprised and impressed many New Yorkers with the moderate and intelligent tone of his Cooper Union Address, given during his campaigning days. Nonetheless, in a campaign that called up the demons of poverty, racism, and fear, New York gave 62 percent of its votes to Lincoln's opponents. On the national front, the country had literally come apart. Southerners rightly saw the November 6 Republican victory as a major blow to the expansion of slavery into the territories. The main issue on the minds of all Americans became the right of an individual state to secede. Senator James W. Grimes of Iowa stated the Northern case succinctly: "The issue now before us is, whether we have a country, whether or not this is a nation. . . . I could agree to no compromise until the right to secede was fully renounced, because it would be a recognition of the right of one or more States to break up the Government at their will." The president-elect had made his feelings on secession very clear: "Plainly, the idea of secession, is the essence of anarchy."[2]

The South didn't see it that way. In the minds of most Southerners, the freedom to maintain a slave system was instrumental to the preservation of their social, political, and economic way of life. The only way to meet forced restriction on a federal level was through separation and, if necessary, force of arms. Six years earlier, Greeley's *Tribune* had predicted the coming rift in tones that would become more credible as the situation worsened: "We are not one people. We are two peoples. We are a people of Freedom, and a people of Slavery. Between the two, conflict is inevitable."[3] By late 1860, few in America would have disagreed.

In his final message to Congress on December 4, 1860, James Buchanan made one last feeble effort to find a middle ground by speaking against Northern interference in Southern policy, while at the same time declaring that the South had no right to separate from the Union. He left no one satisfied. Nor was compromise any longer a possibility, if ever it had been. Buchanan was in an untenable position. He did not want war, and had "spent the secession crisis hoping that the deluge might not descend until he was out of office." But while the administration was playing a waiting game, events in the South were moving very quickly.[4] George Templeton Strong wrote in his diary on December 24, "That termagant little South Carolina has declared itself out of the Union, and resolved to run away. . . . This proceeding surprises nobody. . . . It's a grave event, and may well bring tremendous calamity upon the country."[5]

A number of Southern states followed South Carolina in short order. By February 1, 1861, it had been joined by Florida, Alabama, Georgia, Mississippi, Texas, and Louisiana. During that same week, a group of compromise-minded statesmen, under the leadership of ex-president John Tyler, met in Washington. This peace commission, representing twenty-one states (but none from the lower South), addressed the issue of slavery in the territories, and recommended the removal of all congressional control over slavery in the states. Their proposals failed dismally. Affairs had progressed too far by now for talk. Less than two months later, soldiers of the newly formed Confederate army fired on Fort Sumter, catapulting the country into four years of war. As Virginia, North Carolina, Tennessee, and Arkansas seceded, tens of thousands of men on both sides scrambled to enlist.

The North desperately needed ships and crews, both to combat Confederate warships and to establish blockades of Southern ports. Lincoln ordered all but one of the African Squadron's eight vessels to abandon their patrols and return for assignment to wartime duty. It was an ironic twist that saw the first administration to show promise of ending the slave trade actually having to cripple its own resources for doing so. With the British still prohibited from the search and seizure of American vessels, and the African Squadron disbanded, the slave trade continued virtually unimpeded. And despite Great Britain's declared intention to remain neutral, she effectively recognized the Confederacy as a separate country—from which England hoped to continue to buy cotton.

Immediately after the formation of the Confederate States of America in early February, the greatest fear of New York's merchants became a reality. As one of its first orders of business, the South repudiated all debts owed to the North, and, most specifically, to Manhattan. The numbers were in the hundreds of millions of dollars. While the North had seen the relationship with the South's cotton growers as mutually beneficial, it appears that the South perceived New Yorkers as avaricious opportunists. The *Vicksburg Daily Whig* summed up the Southern viewpoint dramatically: New York "sends out her long arms to the extreme South; and with avidity rarely equaled, grasps our gains and transfers them to herself—taxing us at every step and depleting us as extensively as possible without actually destroying us."[6]

There was some truth to the charge. The New York merchants, by charging for credit, shipping, storage, and insurance, did in fact take 40 cents of every dollar on Southern cotton sold to European markets. By refusing to pay their debts, the South was firing a salvo directly at Wall Street. The effects were severe: panic struck New York City. Northern creditors went out of business as debts went unpaid. Goods that had been bound for the South either rotted in the warehouses or were sold in the North at a fraction of their worth. Orders for all types of merchandise, from clothing to carriages, dried up, and there was fear that the citizens would be driven "into panic for bread[,] and violence toward capital and order."[7]

Delegations of both Republicans and Democrats descended on Washington between January and March 1861 to plead with the lame-duck president to effect some sort of accommodation with the South. One such group carried with it a petition signed by 40,000 New York merchants. All efforts failed, and the crisis worsened, until, according to an estimate by the *Tribune,* the losses reached $478 million.[8] It was not surprising that when President-elect Lincoln visited New York on the way to his inauguration, he did not receive the warmest of receptions. When wealthy industrialist William E. Dodge asked Lincoln whether he would consider yielding to what Dodge considered the South's just demands, or whether the grass, as the South had predicted, would grow in the streets of the Northern cities, Lincoln answered that the Constitution must be "respected, obeyed, enforced, and defended, let the grass grow where it may."[9]

Predictably, the economic crisis and fear for the future initially inclined many Northerners toward reconciliation with the South. However, after the attack upon Fort Sumter, there was a radical shift in attitude. Nowhere was this more profoundly felt than in New York. In his 1910 history of the city, Theodore Roosevelt recalled New York's near-treasonous attempt to secede, authored by the mayor but supported by a huge bastion of pro-Southern Democrats.

> But when Sumter was fired on [in April 1861] the whole current changed like magic. There were many more good men than bad in New York; but they had been supine, or selfish, or indifferent, or undecided. . . . The thunder of Sumter's guns waked the heart of the people to passionate loyalty. The bulk of the Democrats joined with the Republicans to show by word and act their fervent and patriotic devotion to the Union. Huge mass-meetings were held, and regiment after regiment was organized and sent to the front. Shifty Fernando Wood, true to his nature, went with the stream, and was loudest in proclaiming his horror of rebellion.[10]

Suddenly, the city that had proposed legislation forbidding Union troops from crossing its borders was raising its own regiments and lining Broadway, cheering its ranks of marching men. Every park and square was used to bivouac soldiers, as the city's women made garments and food for the troops and volunteered by the score as nurses.[11] George Templeton Strong, initially moderate in his views, became one of the North's staunchest Unionists. In the one-month period between the attack on Fort Sumter and the response to Lincoln's call to arms, there was a marked change in his tone. As Sumter was being shelled on April 13, he had grieved in his diary,

> [T]his is a time of sad humiliation for the country. Every citizen of what has heretofore been called the Great Republic of America, every man,

woman, and child, from Maine to Texas, from Massachusetts to California, stands lower among the inhabitants of this earth than in March, 1860.
We are a weak, divided, disgraced people, unable to maintain our national existence. . . . The country of George Washington and Andrew
Jackson . . . is decomposing. . . . I should be ashamed to show my nose
in the meanest corner of Europe. . . . All my right, title, and interest in the
Fourth of July and the American Eagle and the Model Republic can be
bought at a "low figure." It's a pity we ever renounced our allegiance to
the British Crown.[12]

Only one month later, he wrote the following:

Events multiply. The President is out with a proclamation calling for
75,000 volunteers and an extra session of Congress July 4th. It is said
200,000 more will be called within a few days. Every man of them will be
wanted before this game is lost or won. Change in public feeling
marked, and a thing to thank God for.[13]

Strong would eventually become Lincoln's treasurer of the U.S. Sani-
tary Commission, which was founded at the outbreak of the war to improve military hygiene. He sacrificed his law practice and devoted
himself to raising and disbursing $5 million for care and equipment.
Strong became closely acquainted with most of the key figures in the
hierarchy of power during the next four years, and his contribution to
the Union was enormous.[14]

Even the city's merchants jumped on the Union bandwagon. Reasoning that if there was to be a concerted New York war effort, it
should be controlled and guided by the city's businessmen, the leading
merchants established the Union Defense Committee (UDC), consisting
of 12 Republicans and 13 Democrats. Lincoln was so impressed by their
commitment that he transferred $2 million to the Committee, to buy
weapons, steamships, and equipment, as well as to pay the new re-
cruits. The opportunistic Mayor Fernando Wood, his plan of secession
all but forgotten, authorized a loan of another $1.5 million from several
of the city's various banks and finance houses. The UDC actually did an
extraordinary job. It assembled and sent off to war 66 New York regiments by the end of 1861, in addition to financially aiding the depend-
ents of 12,000 volunteers.[15]

Few Northerners equated Unionism with abolitionism. At this phase, it was still too early for most people to view the war as a means of ending slavery. The racism and hatred that infested New York, and the country in general, was in no way ameliorated by the advent of civil conflict. If anything, it would grow to terrifying and, more than occasionally, violent proportions as the war ran its course and the issue of emancipation became an inextricable element of its resolution. But for now, the primary concern of the North—and of New Yorkers—was the swift and decisive termination of the conflict.

The first flush of patriotic fervor that imbued New York would wane with the growing awareness that the war would not be quickly or easily won. Then, as the growing need for soldiers took a new and provocative twist, the city would witness a fervor of an entirely different and darker kind. But that lay two years in the future. Now, a pro-Union, righteous determination lay upon New York, and it was in this venue that Nathaniel Gordon would go on trial for his life.

A reporter from the French publication *Courier des Etats Unis* entered the Tombs on June 17, 1861—the day before Nathaniel Gordon's trial was to begin. He had come to interview a fellow countryman, a sailor from the slaver *Bonita*. A few days later, the interview made its way into the *New York Times*. The sailor, Charles Blaus, claimed to have been stranded in New York the previous July, without work and in debt, when he signed aboard the schooner *Bonita*. He claimed he had no idea she was a slaver.

The *Bonita* sailed to the Congo River, where the captain took on a Spanish crew. "We could not get ashore," said Blaus, "that would have been death for us—and we had no chance to make the least remonstrance." On October 9, 1860, the captain boarded a cargo of 765 slaves and set sail. Next day, the *Bonita* was sighted and pursued by the new American Squadron steamship *San Jacinto,* in what became the "longest successful chase of a laden slaver ever made by an American cruiser." [16] The *Bonita* was small—only 277 tons—and fast; for a while, it looked as though she would outrun the patrol ship. But the *San Jacinto,* after a pursuit of more than three and a half hours, steamed within cannon range, and fired two warning shots just behind the *Bonita*'s stern. The slaver lowered sail. The captain and crew were arrested and sent to New York for trial. [17]

The *Bonita* shares several parallels with the case of the *Erie*. As with Gordon's ship, the *Bonita* was sighted by chance and in daylight, which was generally the only way to find and run a slaver down; there were no searchlights in 1860. And she was sighted by the *San Jacinto,* a new type of naval cruiser—well-armed and capable of attaining sufficient speed, by either sail or steam, to overtake a slave ship. Slavers were chosen for their speed as well as their storage capacity, and it required a vessel of impressive standards to overtake them. Blaus and his companions were brought to New York in December 1860, while Isaiah Rynders was still U.S. marshal. He placed them in the Eldridge Street facility, as he had Captain Gordon and presumably all the other accused slavers the squadron sent him. However, after Robert Murray assumed the marshal's post, the *Bonita*'s crew joined Gordon in the Tombs.[18]

It is interesting—and not a little alarming—to note that the 277-ton *Bonita* managed to stow more than 765 Africans on board. The *Erie,* at 500 tons, boarded 897 captives in such impossibly tight circumstances that only Gordon himself was able to "arrange" them. At roughly half the *Erie*'s weight, the *Bonita* carried only 132 persons fewer than Gordon had loaded.[19]

The case against the entire crew of the *Bonita* was nol-prossed— dropped—the following November.[20] Blaus may indeed have been innocent of "aiding and abetting" a slaving expedition. But innocent or not, his defense was the one most commonly used by accused slavers: "I just happened to be in the wrong place at the wrong time, and I had no idea what was transpiring around me." It was used with almost predictable success. In one day, it would be Nathaniel Gordon's turn to try this line on a federal jury.

The *Herald* of June 17, 1861, ran an interesting pair of articles. The first, entitled "Our Monrovia Correspondence," was dated the month before and delivers a stinging attack upon the United States' African Squadron. It attributes the navy's pitiful record in the capture of slavers to inactivity born of greed:

> Several vessels of a suspicious nature are closely watched, and many others that are known to be in the trade are permitted to remain unseized, as the capture of an empty vessel rarely brings with it any prize money in the United States service. But when captured with Africans on board your government allows $25 for each one, to be divided equally between all on board of the lucky vessel. This is the reason why so many

Africans are annually shipped from these shores. The men-of-war give to slavers every opportunity to ship their cargo, and then run the risk of capturing them.[21]

An empty slaver, the writer charges, is worth nothing to an American crew. He uses as example the *Nightingale*. The ship was a known slaver, yet allowed to fit out in New York and embark on another voyage. When the article was written, the *Nightingale* was still at large. By the time the report was published, however, the ship, with 950 Africans aboard, had been captured by the USS *Saratoga* and returned to New York; her captain and mates were arrested and placed in the Tombs.

This gave the editor of the *Herald* the opportunity to answer the "Monrovian correspondent's" charges. In the second article, he lists by name the various officers of the *Saratoga,* pointing out that most of them were Southerners without "even the smell of abolition on [their] garments, and yet they are all as eager to suppress the slave trade, and their hearts feel as deeply for the real sufferings of poor negro humanity as even [Horace] Greeley and [Senator Charles] Sumner. . . . Let not the hope of prize money be imputed to them as a motive." The editor was no doubt taking some license; the lure of prize money was certainly as much a motivation as the Southerners' supposed compassion for the "sufferings of poor negro humanity."

Why was the *Nightingale* not seized sooner? The editor refers to the crews' fear of legal action, as discussed in chapter 2:

> The *Nightingale* would have been taken before she took her negroes, for all were sure she was "after no good" here, but the fear was that, without the negroes on board, evidence could not be produced to convict her . . . before a New York or Boston jury, and *commanders of naval vessels here do not wish to make themselves personally liable for damages to wealthy slave traders, when their own government will not protect them in the discharge of their duty from such risks. . . . Let the law be amended so as to protect officers . . . from legal action for damages, and slavers will be taken much faster, without slaves on board, than they ever have before with them* [italics added].[22]

This was clearly an oversimplification, but it nonetheless points to a fear that was increasingly plaguing the minds of U.S. naval officers.

The next issue of the *Herald* announces the commencement of

*United States v. Nathaniel Gordon,* and gives a cursory description of the case. Philip J. Joachimsen had stood beside Gordon at his indictment and would represent him throughout the trial. Joachimsen was a practicing Jew, in a time and place where this would not have endeared him to many New Yorkers. But he had built quite a reputation for himself by this point in his career. He had come to America from Germany at the age of 14, and by 23 he was assistant corporation counsel for New York City. He was appointed assistant U.S. attorney in the early 1850s, and it was the team of Joachimsen and U.S. Attorney John McKeon whose efforts were responsible for the conviction of Captain James Smith of the *Julia Moulton* on the piracy charge in 1854. They brought the slaver captain to within sweating distance of the gallows before Justice Nelson reversed the verdict on a technicality. Ironically, Joachimsen was now in the private sector, defending a slaver against the same capital charge he'd previously prosecuted. Such a shift was not unusual. Upon leaving office in 1858, McKeon also entered the private sector and took on notorious slavers as his clients. And Captain Smith's defense attorney during his trial had held the U.S. district attorney's position prior to McKeon. It appears that the U.S. Attorney's Office provided lawyers with a veritable springboard for the future lucrative defense of slavers.

The prosecutor newly named to replace James Roosevelt was E. Delafield Smith. (His first name was Edward, but he tended not to use it.) An impressive-looking man with a full beard and a prominent nose, Smith was born in Rochester, New York, on May 8, 1826. He graduated from the University of the City of New York on May 8, 1846, was admitted to the bar in 1848, and appointed U.S. district attorney for the Southern District of New York in 1861. A staunch Republican, he had a strong friend and supporter in William H. Seward, President Lincoln's new secretary of state. He was, in fact, so devoted to his mentor that Gideon Welles, Lincoln's secretary of the navy, referred to Smith in his diary as a "pet of Seward."[23] By the time of Gordon's trial, Smith had risen to chairman of the New York Republican Central Committee. Greeley's *Tribune* had written of him: "[He] is still one of the youngest members of his profession, and has not achieved its highest distinctions; but he has talents and a spotless reputation."[24] He also had ambition, and he picked his battles carefully. The Gordon case was Smith's first opportunity to make an impact on both the slave trade and his own reputation, and he intended to take full advantage of it. In this, he would be assisted by Assistant District Attorneys M. V. B. Wilcoxson and Ethan Allen.

Delafield Smith reported to Caleb B. Smith, Lincoln's secretary of the interior. Until the Republican victory, a number of government officials—the attorney general, the various U.S. marshals, district attorneys, and the Departments of State, the Navy, and the Treasury—shared the responsibility for suppressing the slave trade. As a result, procedures were often conflicting or confusing, if they existed at all. Lincoln simplified matters. In an executive order dated May 2, 1861, he gave the responsibility for suppression of the slave trade to the Department of the Interior. Thus Caleb Smith was charged with "execution of the Act approved March 3, 1819, and all subsequent Acts for the suppression of the African slave trade."[25]

The slave trade would soon end, but for the short time remaining, there seemed to be a promise of accountability and consistency. Apparently for the first time, district attorneys and marshals would have an easier time enforcing the old slave-trade laws. However, the only law "subsequent" to 1819 was the Piracy Act. According to Lincoln's order, none of the earlier legislation was to be included—not the 1800 act, forbidding serving aboard a slaver; nor the act of 1794, which allowed for forfeiture; nor the 1818 statute, forbidding fitting out in home ports.

Warren S. Howard, in *American Slavers and the Federal Law,* argues that the new arrangement was essentially old wine in new bottles. Neither marshals nor prosecutors, he claims, delivered regular reports, nor did they keep Secretary Smith aware of their slaving cases. They approached the Washington office only when they needed money. When it came to suppression of the slave trade, the Department of the Interior's primary function was the reimbursement of expenses. The new arrangement under Lincoln was merely a political dodge, affected to convey the impression that the Republicans were a party for dramatic and progressive change.[26] Delafield Smith did, however, maintain a tight line of communication with the secretary throughout the Gordon case, keeping him apprised of every significant development.

It would be satisfying to think of Delafield Smith, appointed by President Lincoln to this vital post at such a crucial time, as a man strongly opposed to slavery. Not so. Smith was, by his own admission, at most a moderate on the slavery issue. The abolitionist views of such men as Horace Greeley and the progressive views of his own party were, to him, "peculiar." He believed that the controversial Fugitive Slave Act, reaffirmed by the *Dred Scott* decision years earlier, was to be observed and enforced. Smith drew the old distinction between the institution of slavery and the slave trade, which he considered "against humanity, unjust and impolitic."[27] It was also illegal. And although Smith was no antislavery crusader, his fervor was for the law. The statute that Nathaniel Gordon stood accused of breaking had gathered dust for 41 years, and now it fell to Delafield Smith to prosecute his case with zeal. This he was resolved to do.

The presiding judge at Gordon's trial was William Davis Shipman. Born and raised in Connecticut, he was admitted to the bar at thirty-one. Shipman swiftly rose from private practice to judge of probate for East Haddam, then to U.S. attorney for the district of Connecticut. Reappointed in 1856, he held the position until 1860, when he was named U.S. district judge for the district of Connecticut. As district judge, he would occasionally hold regular terms for the Circuit Court of the Southern District of the City of New York. It was in this capacity that he would hear arguments concerning Nathaniel Gordon. Sharing the bench would be Justice Samuel Nelson.

Although the Gordon trial would be the first slave-trade case Shipman would preside over, he had had an experience as a Connecticut prosecutor involving an accused slaver in 1859. Eleven years earlier, the whaling bark *Laurens* had been seized, libeled, and condemned in the New York District Court, so she shouldn't have been sailing at all; and yet, there she was, libeled once again, with over a decade of activity behind her. When taken, she was fitted out more for a slaving voyage than a whaling expedition. Shipman prosecuted the case before federal judge Charles H. Ingersoll, who determined that no significant proof had been offered to convince him that the *Laurens* was a slave ship, and that the case was weak. Shipman wrote, "I am in great doubt whether to appeal this case. The Judge's opinion is so decided, not to say fervid, in vindication of the ship, that it is calculated to inspire me with distrust of my own opinion."[28] The whaler was released. Now that Shipman's turn had come to preside over a slaving case, he most likely remembered the *Laurens*.

The federal government's attempts to enforce the Piracy Act of 1820 had suffered 41 years of prosecutorial failure. What, exactly, would it take for the prosecution to bring about a conviction, and then to actually hang a slaver? A "chain of five circumstances" had to exist. First, and most difficult to fulfill, the arrest had to be made by an officer of the United States, at sea, with slaves actually found on board. As was demonstrated in the history of the African Squadron, this hardly ever occurred.

Second, a slaver had to be held long enough to stand trial. Escape was remarkably easy, and took the form of a long rope over a wall and a waiting boat in the harbor (with a bribed jailer looking the other way), or, more often, a walk out the front door on bail, which was immediately forfeited when the defendant left town.

The third provision, assuming that the culprit lingered in jail long enough to face judgment by his peers, was that the jury actually had to be willing to convict him. Many jurors, if not in sympathy with the crime, at least displayed a certain compassion for the accused. Why should a man hang for following the orders of his employers, they reasoned, when these entrepreneurs were themselves outside the reaches of the law? Besides, why hang an American for bringing Africans from one foreign country to another? After all, it had no practical impact on the United States, and no Americans were hurt in the transaction. Should such a man be punished to the fullest extent of the law, when it was perfectly legal for an American in, say, Kentucky to sell his slaves "down the river" to Louisiana or Mississippi? Even if the jurors were disgusted by the slave trade itself, the idea of calling a man a pirate and hanging him accordingly was one that was rejected consistently for over four decades.

Fourth, a man who had been fairly caught, held, and brought to trial might still get off if he could prove either that he was foreign born or that his ship was foreign owned. The latter was a relatively easy task to accomplish. If appropriate documentation could be presented in court, an acquittal was a virtual certainty.[29]

Finally, the accused could claim that he was on board merely as a passenger, or that he had shipped for a legal voyage and had been coerced into helping the slavers.

How do these five qualifications apply to the case of Nathaniel Gordon? He had, in fact, been captured by Americans at sea, with slaves belowdeck, and he had remained in jail—initially by his own choice, ultimately by the walls and bars of the Tombs. His lawyers could attempt a defense by addressing Gordon's citizenship, the ownership of the *Erie,* and the defendant's status on board; was he master or passenger? As to the jury's willingness to convict and hang, only time would tell.

• • •

When court convened on June 18, 1861, the courtroom was quiet and nearly empty. To the observer, there was nothing to distinguish this trial from any of the other slave-trade farces played out in circuit court. But Delafield Smith was determined to make this a landmark case. He had elected to drop the minor charge of serving on board a slaver and to prosecute on the piracy indictment alone. His opening statement to the jury was a powerful one. He spoke of the passage of the Piracy Act of 1820, recounting how it was universally praised, but "rarely executed." The one conviction, said Smith, was overturned on a technicality, although it was clear that the man was guilty. The same was true of the earlier slave-trade laws; while highly lauded, there was "very little regard paid to their execution." It was common knowledge, said Smith, that the flourishing slave trade was the "most profitable traffic . . . ever carried on in this country or in the world." It had enriched hundreds but convicted few. The reason, he explained, was that people of all social classes confused slavery with the slave trade; to condemn the crime of slave trading, and to convict the slavers, one need not oppose slavery: "A crime . . . arising from the slave traffic has no connection whatever with slavery as it presently exists in the Southern States." The 1820 statute was, in fact, "drawn up by Southern hands, perfected by Southern statesmen, and passed by Southern votes, as well as by votes of Northern men."

Smith then did a peculiar thing. He presented his case in the form of two questions: Should the slave trade with all its "inhumanity . . . and heinous outrages" be allowed to continue, and if so, should it be "further permitted . . . to crowd the virgin soil . . . and Territories of the country . . . with negroes to the exclusion of the white man[?]"

Clearly, Smith had digressed from the legal aspects of the case to play upon the jury's fears and bigotry. His second question is irrelevant. As he himself had pointed out earlier, expansion of slavery into the territories had nothing to do with the case. Nor did the slave trade at this time impact the slave population of the South; slaves were being conveyed mainly from the Congo to Cuba, not to Richmond or Charleston. Yet he paints a picture of imported Africans who, by sheer force of numbers, would crowd White Americans out of their own country, and its holdings as well. It was a strange and devious card to play.

He concluded his address by explaining the need for Gordon's execution: the prescribed death penalty for the offense "is intended as an example to deter" others, and the "crimes and cruelties which characterize the slave traffic" call for the harshest of punishments.[30] He then began the case for the prosecution.

The first issue to be addressed was that of Nathaniel Gordon's citizenship. In *his* opening statement, Gordon's attorney, Philip J. Joachimsen, had claimed that Gordon's mother had often accompanied her husband on his voyages; he asserted that the defendant had been born at sea, in foreign waters, and could therefore claim foreign citizenship. Delafield Smith had brought to New York an old Portland sea captain named Richard Crockett, whom he called to refute Joachimsen's claim. Crockett testified that he knew Gordon, as well as his parents and siblings, and had watched him grow from a boy of two or three to a grown man. Crockett couldn't swear to the father's citizenship, but he had known him as a fellow seafaring man, and "always supposed he was an American."

Joachimsen, on cross-examination, got Crockett to acknowledge that Gordon's mother often went to sea with his father, but he lost ground when the witness stated that he had "never heard that Gordon was born anywhere but in Portland till to-day I heard he was born in the Mediterranean." Crockett was of the opinion "from frequent conversations with the prisoners, that they were Americans."[31] Nothing had been proven by either side.

The next issue to be determined was the nationality of the *Erie*. With Gordon's citizenship in question, proof that the *Erie* was an American-owned ship would clear the prosecution's way for a conviction. Smith's witness was Mason Barney, a shipwright from Swansea, Massachusetts, who had built the *Erie,* but testified that he had not seen the ship since he finished her in 1849 and sold her to New York businessman Ralph Post. And though he had had a financial interest in her until seven or eight years previous, he "didn't know who owned her in August, 1860."[32] What no one involved in the trial seemed aware of—except perhaps Gordon—was that Ralph Post was one of the partners of Captain Knudson, who had turned over the *Erie* to Gordon in Havana.

Joachimsen claimed that the *Erie* had been sold to foreigners in Havana or on the Congo, but without any records or bill of sale, he couldn't prove it. But then, neither could Smith prove that it hadn't. Again, neither side scored a point.

Thus far, the trial's course was predictable. The questions raised as to Gordon's citizenship and the *Erie*'s country of registration were formulaic. But now the testimony would become more dramatic as the details of the arrest at sea and the condition of the Africans were brought out.

Lieutenant John W. Dunnington was the ranking officer who boarded the *Erie,* arrested Gordon and his crew, and ultimately commanded the *Erie* on the trip to Monrovia. However, when the Civil War commenced, Dunnington resigned his commission to return to his home in Kentucky and serve in the Confederate navy. Smith offered to pay Dunnington's expenses out of his own pocket if he would return to New York to testify, but clearly the lieutenant had better things to do than collaborate in the hanging of a slaver. A June 18 editorial in the *Tribune* stressed Dunnington's importance to the case, and predicted that his absence "will render a conviction quite difficult."[33]

This left Smith with Henry Davis Todd. Since leaving the *Mohican* for service on the sloop of war *Cumberland,* Todd had been promoted from passed midshipman to lieutenant. He was an excellent witness, and for the few listeners in the courtroom, the sea chase must have made for an exciting story. Todd told of the *Erie*'s pursuit and capture, and of the "number and position of the slaves." He testified that Dunnington had been the first to board the *Erie* and confront Gordon, his mates, and the *Erie*'s cargo of captives. Todd was not actually present at the arrest; he went aboard only "after Lieut. Dunnington came back from her, to get ready to take her home." The witness stated that Gordon and his two mates had been initially taken aboard the *Mohican,* but that they were returned to the *Erie* for the trip to Monrovia, and thence to the United States. Todd then described the misery that confronted them regarding the captives. The *New York Times* reported: "The negroes appeared to have been on board but a short time; the coppers were not up to cook for them and for the first day or two they were fed on biscuits and water. Neither Dunnington nor witness knew how to manage the negroes, and Gordon and another showed them how to manage about their feeding, etc." Todd told the court of the difficult time he and Dunnington had in providing food and water for the slaves, and of rearranging them on deck. He spoke of his appeal to Gordon, and of the slaver's help in "stacking" the captives.[34] He further testified, according to the *Times,* that "[First Mate] Warren was seen tampering with the negroes, and lest they should get up a revolt he was confined in one part of the cabin in irons, and Gordon was confined in his room and kept so till they got to Monrovia; [Todd] had talked with Gordon after they discharged the negroes at Monrovia."[35]

According to Todd, Gordon claimed that he had not sailed the *Erie* from Britain to Havana, but had assumed command only a few hours before she sailed to Africa. Gordon's claim of a last-minute command was preposterous; he had submitted documents requesting clearance weeks before the *Erie* sailed to Africa. Whether Gordon had awaited the ship's arrival by prearrangement with a slaving company or had been contracted after she had anchored in Havana Harbor, there is no doubt that he had been hired as her captain early in the enterprise. He had no other reason to be in Cuba.

Todd said they found a chart of the Atlantic in Gordon's cabin, with the *Erie*'s course laid down. Despite the slaver's claim that he had no responsibilities on the return voyage, Todd "understood [Gordon] was responsible for the ship; he spake of Portland, Maine, as being his home; he said the *Erie* got ashore at the mouth of the Congo when he came out with her from Havana; he always spoke of her as if he was master of her."[36] After Todd's testimony, court was adjourned.

The following day, Smith "gave some further evidence as to the parentage of Gordon"; the accounts don't specify what the evidence was.[37] Still, the prosecutor had provided no actual proof of Gordon's citizenship, nor of the *Erie*'s country of ownership. The strength of his case lay with Todd's testimony. Todd hadn't actually been the arresting officer, but technically that shouldn't have mattered. The prosecution rested.

When it was Joachimsen's turn, he raised a jurisdictional issue: if it could be proven that the section of the river where the Africans were taken aboard the *Erie* was within Portuguese territory, then Gordon would not be liable under American law. If no ocean water flowed into the river, it was technically the property of Portugal all the way past its mouth. Therefore, claimed Joachimsen, if Gordon boarded his slaves at any point on the Congo, he was outside American jurisdiction. Joachimsen called Sylvanus Spencer, a native of New York State, to provide the appropriate testimony. "I am a seafaring man," Spencer testified. "I have been on the Coast of Africa as first officer of the *Chimberazo,* belonging to London. It is always an ebb tide at the mouth of the Congo River."[38] It was an interesting and creative ploy.

For his last argument, Joachimsen dragged out the old "Spanish captain" story—one so commonly used in slaver cases that it had become an expected defense. Gordon was not involved in the enterprise at all, Joachimsen argued, but was merely seeking passage home from the Congo River. Through Spencer, he presented testimony that the coast of Africa "was an unhealthy place . . . and that it was difficult for anyone to get away from there except by means of slavers."[39] According to Joachimsen, Gordon found a berth on the *Erie* thanks to the kindness of its new Spanish captain.

To support this transparent fabrication, Joachimsen called his next witness—none other than William Warren, first mate of the *Erie*. Warren was an interesting choice, since he himself was under indictment for violation of the Piracy Act. But the attorney needed his testimony. Warren swore that "before the negroes were taken on board, a Spanish captain [came aboard] with Spanish officers and about the same number of sailors as before; and that after the negroes were shipped, the vessel went to sea under the direction of the Spanish captain, and that he did not see Captain Gordon do anything after the negroes were taken aboard,—which was the day before the capture."[40] Warren was clearly lying for reasons that should have been clear to everyone: if Gordon was acquitted, Warren would also go free. Conversely, if Gordon was convicted, Warren stood to face the gallows along with his captain. Ironically, by calling Warren to the stand, Joachimsen was placing his client's fate in the hands of a highly dubious witness. This was the very man who had shown Midshipman Todd how to feed and water the slaves, and who had to be chained and confined to his cabin for attempting to foment a rebellion among the captive Africans.

After the defense concluded its case, both attorneys delivered their summations, which unfortunately have not survived. We can assume that each attorney stressed the points which he felt most forcefully made his case. In reality, on most of the issues—citizenship, vessel ownership, jurisdiction—neither attorney had scored a major victory, and Warren's testimony was simply incredible. The only strong, indisputable evidence for the jury to consider was Todd's statement; it should have been enough.

After the summations, Judge Shipman adjourned once again. The next morning, he charged the jury. His own feelings regarding Gordon's guilt are clearly reflected in his words. The defense, through First Mate Warren, had claimed that Gordon had turned the ship over to a Spanish captain. Shipman appealed to the jurors' common sense:

"Now, gentlemen, the law addresses itself to the plain sense of plain men, and you are as competent to pass upon this question as I am." The only evidence that the *Erie* had changed hands was the word of First Mate Warren, "a person who is indicted as an accomplice in this same offense. . . . There is no other evidence to show that the national character of this vessel was changed but his statement," so "give such weight to his testimony as it seems to carry. The testimony of accomplices is to be scrutinized in the light of the circumstances."

Shipman then places the burden upon the defense to prove that the ship had been sold to a foreigner.

> You must look at this and say whether . . . there is any evidence of a sale of the ship. Are there any papers produced? Where is the owner of the ship? Who authorized Gordon to deliver her? . . . What circumstances are shown that ordinarily characterizes a sale of property, except the delivery of it sworn to by an accomplice? Why was the Congo River chosen as the place for this transaction? Captain Gordon was a resident of Portland, Maine. Why was it that this vessel sailed from Havana and went to Africa, forty miles up the Congo River, and there these witnesses were called on to witness their handing over of authority? If this was a *bona fide* sale, why were men employed to go over to this unhealthy place to transfer their ship—a place where, according to the claim of the defendant, a man would be probably compelled, if he wanted to get away from it, to embark on a vessel in the Slave-trade, involving the perils of that trade, and the horrors of a passage through tropical seas upon such a vessel? . . . Is that an ordinary transaction? Do the shipping merchants of New-York, or any other place, do their business in that way?

Shipman didn't even attempt to conceal his incredulity over the defense's claims: "It is for you to say whether that was a sale . . ."

He then points out to the jury that if they determine that the ship is American owned, they needn't bother with the question of Gordon's citizenship; under the law, foreigners serving aboard American slavers were as guilty as Americans. All the jury need do was determine whether Gordon had forcibly detained the Africans. "If he was the master-spirit of the enterprise, directing the putting them on board or detaining them after they were put on board, and if he did this himself or through his men, if the Spanish Captain was only a cover and the defendant was really the man," he was guilty as charged.

Shipman, by implication, dismisses as absurd the defense's claim that Gordon was "merely an idle spectator." The jury must determine, he said, whether Gordon commanded the vessel all the way to the Congo, delivered the whiskey, and stood by as slavers "packed these unfortunate beings on board, and [had] nothing to do with it. . . . The evidence is, that these 897 negroes were brought on board and stowed in an hour; and they must have been stowed with some skill, for the navy officers were unable to do it, and were compelled to call upon Gordon to show them how it was done. It is for you to say whether it could have been done so rapidly without force of the most violent kind. . . . The vessel started for Havana within an hour after they came on board. You must say whether the intent was to make them slaves." Even if Gordon was acting as a member of the crew, and not as the captain, he was liable. If the *Erie* was not owned by Gordon, "but only hired . . . and navigated by him," he was still liable. Again, Shipman left no room for doubt as to his opinion.

If the jury decided that the *Erie* was a foreign ship, then it would be necessary to determine whether Gordon was an American citizen, and whether the ship was actually involved in the slave trade. "I can only refer you to the fact that she took on board 897 negroes and started for Havana. It is for you to say whether that is the Slave-trade." An American serving aboard a foreign slaver was as guilty under the law as a foreigner serving aboard an American vessel.

Shipman then deals with the issue of Gordon's nationality: "Witnesses have told you that they knew Gordon's father and mother at Portland before he was born, and never knew anything but that they were citizens. Evidence is given that his mother sometimes accompanied his father on voyages to sea, but if his father was an American citizen, he would be [as well], even though born abroad." He then adds, "It is fair for you to infer from the fact that no evidence is given on the part of the defendant to show anything to the contrary that he has no such evidence." Gordon, in the judge's eyes, was an American citizen.

Shipman dismisses the jurisdiction argument in a single sentence: "[I]f you find on the evidence that these negroes were confined on board this vessel on the Congo River, at or near its mouth, it being an open river, three miles wide twenty miles above, then I charge you that it is within the jurisdiction of the United States." In closing, Shipman delivered the obligatory qualifier: "The presumption, of course, is in favor of his innocence. Every man is deemed innocent until he is proved guilty, and he must be proved guilty beyond a reasonable doubt, not beyond all possible doubt, but beyond a reasonable doubt. . . . If on considering this case, you can say that you feel an abiding conviction to a moral certainty that the charge is proved, it will be your duty to bring in a verdict of guilty. If you have a reasonable doubt, you will find the accused not guilty."[41]

It is difficult to imagine how any honest, intelligent juror could have harbored a reasonable doubt after that address. Despite his direction that "the presumption . . . is in favor of his innocence," Judge Shipman all but lit the jury's path to a conviction. Referring to First Mate Warren as Gordon's "accomplice," he didn't even bother with the legal nicety of adding "alleged." He all but told the jury to take Warren's testimony with a grain of salt. Every question he presented to the jury had, by its very phrasing, a rhetorical tone, with a predetermined answer. He undermined the claim that Gordon was merely a passenger, dismissed the argument that Gordon was foreign born, brought to serious question the likelihood that a sale of the *Erie* had taken place—especially in so unlikely a place as the coast of Africa and under such shadowy circumstances—and rendered preposterous the idea that the ship could have been on the Congo River for any purpose other than a slaving voyage. Finally, Shipman told the jury that they need only address *reasonable* doubt, not "all possible doubt," in order to make its determination. Throughout his entire charge, there is a controlled but recurrent disgust for the slavers.

The jury retired to consider its verdict. They were out for 20 hours, and came into court the following morning hopelessly deadlocked. They stood seven to five for conviction, with no hope of a unanimous verdict.[42] Judge Shipman was furious.

"How long have you served on this jury?" he asked.

"Since the first of April," replied the foreman.

"You have served quite too long! I discharge the panel."[43] He declared a mistrial, on June 21, and dismissed the jury.

Predictably, both the *Times* and the *Tribune* fumed. Here, finally, was a case in which all the elements had come together, and still the jury had failed to convict. The *Times* blasted them: "With those who failed to agree with the majority in that case, just fault is found. . . . It is certainly to be regretted and wondered at, that a jury could fail to agree in a case involving such evidence of turpitude."[44]

Horace Greeley's *Tribune* was a good deal more caustic in its condemnation of the jury's finding.

From the clear evidence in the case, and the careful and lucid charge of Judge Shipman, the failure of the jury to agree is disgraceful, especially to themselves. . . .

It is a remarkable fact that the slave-traders in this city have matured their arrangements so thoroughly that they almost invariably manage to elude the meshes of the law. Now they bribe a jury, another time their counsel or agents spirit away a vital witness; oftener the principal is apprised of an impending libel upon his outfitting slave vessel, for his coming arrest, before the Marshal receives his papers—before he knows anything about the matter at all. . . . The truth is, the United States offices in Chambers Street, under the influences which have been brought to bear here, have become thoroughly corrupt. Fortunately, however, a new class of men now have the direction of affairs, and a stop will be put to this iniquitous complicity with crime. The Government is determined to break up the African slave-trade, and it will accomplish it. To effect this it will be necessary to purge the Courts and offices of these pimps of piracy, who are well known, and at the proper time will receive their just deserts.[45]

Were members of the jury bribed, as the *Tribune* implied? There is no way to know with any degree of certainty. However, the judge, the district attorney, and the marshal had made a crucial mistake; whenever a recess or an adjournment was called, they let the jurors go their separate ways. The court had made it easy for Gordon's supporters to approach the individual jurors, if such was their intent. It was a mistake Delafield Smith and Marshal Murray would not make a second time.

When Judge Shipman declared a mistrial, it was left to the discretion of the U.S. attorney to decide whether to pursue a second trial or to drop the charges. Immediately following Judge Shipman's dismissal, District Attorney Smith announced that he would "try the prisoner again at as early a day as practicable" on the same piracy charge.[46] Nathaniel Gordon's troubles were far from over.

The Slaver Erie
or
The Career of Nathaniel Gordon
The Slaver Captain.

## Part I.
### Official History.

#### Introduction.

Possibly no case was tried *that has been* before a United States
Tribunal *ever* awakened more interest among the professional classes, or produced more anxious excitement among the slave dealers than the prosecution
and condemnation of Nathaniel Gordon, Captain
of the Slaver Erie.

The following history of the case has been
compiled from official correspondence, newspaper *)
extracts and personal experience, and, if possessing
no other merit, has at least that advantage of correctness
and authenticity.

#### Chap. I.

Letter from U. S. Consul General Helm at Havana
to the Secretary of State. Washington.
First suspicions of the Erie. Change of Captain and
ownership. Gordon appears on the scene. All vessels leaving Cuba, turn out slavers. Gordon's
affidavit as to the legality of the voyage. Spanish
Government fosters the Slave Trade. Consul
asks power to detain suspected vessels. Refers
to unanswered despatch, three years old. Spiteful
slap at England.

Con          eneral of the United States of America

For a brief moment, Nathaniel Gordon breathed a sigh of relief. History had shown that in the event of a hung jury in a slave-trade case, the prosecutor's office either attempted to convict the defendant of a lesser charge or simply let matters drop. But with District Attorney E. Delafield Smith's announced intention to pursue a second trial, Gordon understood for the first time that he was facing a prosecutor who would settle for nothing less than a capital conviction.

The months of incarceration had taken a severe toll on the slaver. A small man to begin with, he had lost considerable weight, and had developed a jailhouse pallor that contrasted sharply with his black hair and beard. The *New York Evening Post* noted a marked change in "Captain Gordon's personal appearance and presence. . . . At the close of his first trial, visitors who saw him in the Tombs could not fail to contrast the lurking sense of fear which he harbored, notwithstanding his assumed indifference, with the air of easy confidence which had formerly distinguished him. Still, he had apparently a firm conviction that, whatever might be the result of his trial, he would not be executed."[1]

Determined though he was to try Gordon again, Delafield Smith had his own reason for concern. Immediately following the close of the first trial, the defense retained the Wall Street firm of Beebe, Dean, and

*(left, inset)* U.S. MARSHAL ROBERT MURRAY. MURRAY WAS AN HONEST MAN OF STRONG CONVICTIONS. VEHEMENTLY OPPOSED TO THE SLAVE TRADE, HE WAS INSTRUMENTAL IN PROCURING A CONVICTION IN GORDON'S SECOND TRIAL.

*(left)* FIRST PAGE OF MARSHAL MURRAY'S HANDWRITTEN *THE CAREER OF NATHANIEL GORDON, THE SLAVER CAPTAIN*. IT PROVIDES THE MOST COMPLETE ACCOUNT OF THE GORDON CASE.

Donahoe to work with Philip J. Joachimsen. They were, without question, the foremost attorneys specializing in the defense of accused slavers. Normally, BD&D did not come cheap, but this time, they offered their services pro bono, either from a sense of compassion or from the concern that a man hanged for slave trading would impact badly on business. Gilbert Dean, the principal who would represent the defendant, would comment after the case was concluded that Gordon had used what funds he had to pay the board of his penniless mates and himself in prison, until the money ran out. Apparently, the shadow company and the merchants behind Gordon's voyage gave nothing; Dean stated that, despite rumors of their financial support, he "had not received $1 in the matter, and whatever labor had been done or expense incurred, whether in going to Washington or otherwise, had been done voluntarily, without reward or the hope thereof. . . . The vessel was owned by parties . . . who entirely deserted them, and left them to their own resources."[2]

Gilbert Dean was a highly respected member of the bar with a stellar record. A graduate of Yale, Dean had successfully practiced criminal law in Poughkeepsie, New York, for 11 years before moving his practice to New York City. He was twice elected to terms in Congress, and appointed a justice of the Supreme Court of New York in 1854 while still in his thirties. The press and his colleagues still referred to him as Judge Dean. He was widely read, with a strong interest in science and literature, and wrote several "caustic, criticizing" articles for professional periodicals. He was handsome, aggressive, ambitious, and accustomed to winning. When he was hired to represent Gordon, Gilbert Dean was 41 years old, and at the top of his game. With both Dean and Joachimsen beside him, the slaver had a veritable legal "dream team" working on his behalf.[3]

The Gordon case was called again for trial on July 2; Gilbert Dean would take the helm for the defense. The first thing he and Joachimsen did was to apply for a postponement. Two reasons were given: a witness necessary to Gordon's defense was absent, and Dean had been asked to give a Fourth of July oration in Chatham Four Corners, New York, 130 miles north. Prosecutor Smith opposed the postponement, and Judge William Davis Shipman denied the motion.

Dean then challenged the court on several technicalities relating to the jury selection. Both sides debated the issue, and court adjourned until Shipman decided on the matter. The *Times* wryly commented that, despite Judge Shipman's refusal to grant a postponement, "It would seem probable that Judge Dean will be able to deliver his Fourth of July oration."[4]

Judge Shipman rescheduled the trial for the week of July 16, but now it was Delafield Smith's turn to request a postponement. Lieutenant Todd, who was as crucial to the second case as he had been to the first, had been assigned to blockade duty aboard the frigate *Cumberland,* and Smith needed time to arrange for his appearance. Predictably, Philip J. Joachimsen opposed the delay, stating that Todd's testimony could be read from the judge's minutes of the previous trial. However, since this was a capital case, Judge Shipman feared that denying the presence of a vital witness might provide grounds for a motion for a new trial, so he allowed the postponement.[5]

Shipman allowed Smith extraordinary latitude in preparing his case, and the delay would be considerably longer than anyone had anticipated; Nathaniel Gordon would not face another jury for four months. It would take that long to arrange leave for Lieutenant Todd, but Smith had other plans as well. This time, he was determined to go into court armed with as much damning evidence as he could find. First, he wrote to Captain Robert W. Shufeldt, the new American consul general in Havana, requesting a complete list of the *Erie*'s crew. "Upon receiving it," he later recalled, "I gave copies to detectives, with instructions to watch arrivals here and at Boston and if possible to discover the seamen." To this end, Smith also employed U.S. Marshal Robert Murray and his deputies. They first found three Spaniards from the false crew taken aboard on the Congo River, but these would not do for Smith; he described them as "desperate creatures in appearance and speech." Worse yet, they were already in custody, having been captured once again, this time aboard the slaver *Bonita.* Smith examined only one of the three, and "he rather damaged the case than otherwise."[6]

However, four of the "more civilized of the crew" were found in Boston, and would provide Smith with the information and the credibility he sought. He questioned each man separately, and found that their stories matched. Smith recorded each account verbatim, "thus, no appearance of a concerted sailor's yarn was created." He finally had the witnesses he needed—presentable, well-spoken American seamen, with the added weight of having been reluctant members of Gordon's own crew.[7] Along with Todd, Smith's witness list was complete.

Nathaniel Gordon's second trial would not commence until November. During the months in which the attorneys on both sides were busy preparing their respective cases, real battles were raging outside the courtroom as the Civil War gained momentum. Missouri, soon to become one of the bloodiest venues of the entire conflict, was the scene of three battles between July and September, each resulting in clear Confederate victories. Meanwhile, the fight for western Virginia saw an encouraging series of Northern successes, at Philippi, and at Rich and Cheat Mountains.

But the first stunning awareness that the war would not end quickly occurred on July 21. A large contingent of Southern forces was threatening Washington, and a swift and decisive Union victory would hopefully shorten the conflict and embolden the people of the North. Brigadier General Irvin McDowell's Union troops met Confederate soldiers under Generals Beauregard and Johnston in Virginia only 25 miles from the nation's capital. Citizens of Washington, secure in their expectation of a successful outcome, arrived in carriages to observe the battle. Many brought picnic baskets. Here, along a little creek called Bull Run, the Confederates first introduced the North to what came to be called the "rebel yell." The Union troops were routed after intense fighting, and retreated in disarray toward Washington, sweeping along with them many terrified picnickers and observers.

The North was in shock. Less than a month later, at the battle of Wilson's Creek, Missouri, the Union army fell to a rebel force twice its size. Following so soon after the humiliating defeat at Bull Run, this was a bitter setback for the North. It was going to be a long war.[8]

On August 6, Congress passed the Confiscation Act, allowing for the seizure of all goods and property used by the Confederacy to further the war effort. This included slaves. General John C. Frémont interpreted this legislation as a license to issue his own Emancipation Proclamation. He instituted martial law in Missouri on August 30, announcing that all the property of Missouri's rebels was confiscated and all their slaves were "declared freemen." On hearing of this, a number of border-state Union soldiers—some of whom owned slaves—threw

down their weapons, refusing to fight a war of liberation. Whether Frémont was seeking an effective way to fight the Missouri guerrillas or
simply grandstanding, he had clearly exceeded his authority. Lincoln
removed Frémont from command in two days.[9]

New York City was clearly feeling the effects of the war. The South had
determined from the outset to break this capital of commerce. The
*Richmond Dispatch* referred to it as "Execrable New York" and likened
it to Sodom, with the distinction that Sodom had one honorable man.
The *Charleston Courier* ranted that "the interests of Christianity, civi-
lization, humanity, and intelligent self-government, require that New
York, the metropolis of shoulder-hitters, prize-fighters, blackguards and
mercantile gamblers should be blotted from the list of cities."[10]

And it looked as though that might happen. Trade with the South,
New York's strongest source of revenue, had virtually ended by July.
As a result, ancillary manufacturing enterprises crumbled. Quiet descended on the shipyards and iron mills; clothing factories and carriage
shops closed their doors. Thirty thousand men found themselves out of
work; it seemed as though the Panic of 1857 had come again.

George Templeton Strong's diary reflects the sobering influence the
war had on the city. In April, he had echoed the patriotic feelings of
most New Yorkers when he wrote,

> Everyone's future has changed in these six months last past. This is to be
> a terrible, ruinous war. . . . I was prosperous and well off last November.
> I believe my assets to be reduced fifty per cent, at least. . . . I clearly see
> that this is a most severe personal calamity to me, but I welcome it cor-
> dially, for it has shown that I belong to a community that is strong and
> generous, and that the City of New York is not sordid and selfish.[11]

Four months later, on August 27, his thoughts had assumed a darker
cast:

> It is almost time for another great disaster. It will occur in Western Vir-
> ginia, probably. Can any disaster and disgrace arouse us fully? Perhaps
> we are destined to defeat and fit for subjugation. Perhaps the oligarchs of
> the South are our born rulers. Northern communities may be too weak,
> corrupt, gelatinous and unwarlike to resist Jefferson Davis and his con-

federates. It is possible that New York and New England and the Free West may be unable to cope with the South. If so, let the fact be ascertained and established as soon as possible, and let us begin to recognize our masters. But I should like a chance to peril my life in battle before that question is decided.[12]

Volunteering in the New York regiments was partly an act of patriotism, and partly a lark; it was also one of the only ways for a workingman to find a regular wage. With the closing of shipyards and factories, there was no work to be found in the spring and summer of 1861, and the offer of a soldier's pay of $13 a month was better than nothing. Or so men thought until they saw battle.[13]

There were, of course, those New Yorkers who still chose to engage in commerce with the South. Some clothing manufacturers surreptitiously made Confederate uniforms, and the National Bank Note Company of New York printed up Confederate bonds and sent them to Alabama. A New York ship, carrying a thousand muskets to Georgia's Southern soldiers, was seized in New York Harbor by the governor's Metropolitan police. Through the influence of Mayor "Fernandy" Wood, the ship was soon released. Wood apologized profusely to the governor of Georgia; he had no control, he said, over the actions of the state-sponsored police force.

As with all wartime economies, however, things improved as manufacturers and businessmen found new ways to meet the needs of the nation. Bumper crops and livestock from the West needed distribution, and with the rivers closed to commerce by the war, railroads became the nation's most natural lifeline. Old lines were improved and extended, and new lines built.[14]

By the time of Nathaniel Gordon's trial, New York's businesses were booming on a number of fronts. Ships were again being built to meet the Union's growing needs. Clothing manufacturers suddenly found themselves responding to the demands of a vast army, as companies filled millions of dollars' worth of contracts, often with substandard goods. Finding themselves at a loss for sufficient material, Brooks Brothers took shredded rags, glued them together, pressed them into a semblance of material, and sewed them into uniforms. These uniforms would literally fall to pieces in the first rain, leaving the unfortunate soldiers nearly naked. Other companies soon learned to cut corners as well. Unscrupulous businessmen manufactured cheap knapsacks, blankets, and hats. In many instances, the soles of the soldiers' shoes were made of wood chips, glued together; they would hold together for perhaps half an hour on the march. A new name was invented to describe this disgracefully substandard clothing and equipment: "shoddy."

Huge profits were also made through the provision of spoiled meat and the sale of old and blind horses. The government was riddled with corruption, and contracts usually went to the supplier who paid the biggest bribe. It was a problem that would plague the Union army throughout the entire war, and would make fortunes for many unscrupulous New York businessmen. There were only a few dozen millionaires in New York City in 1860; by the war's end the number had grown to several hundred. They became known as the "shoddy aristocracy." [15]

New York was busily coping with the war on many levels. Still, a reading of the city newspapers during the summer and fall of 1861 gives the impression that for most New Yorkers, life went on much as before. Knox still advertised fine lightweight summer hats, Laura Keene's Theater featured the comedy *Our American Cousin*, P. T. Barnum promoted the "most extraordinary man in miniature," the Cooper Union offered "Free Lectures on Social and Political Science," and every slave case that found its way into circuit court received coverage in the local press.

New York had always been a bastion of racial hatred, and it was exacerbated by the war. As the city gradually worked its way back from the brink of economic disaster and jobs became more readily available, military enlistment dropped off. But many business owners, in an effort to save money, would hire African American New Yorkers, whom they could pay a lower wage. Should White workers strike for better wages and conditions, the employers would simply hire a "scab" crew, comprised largely of African Americans. Naturally, this infuriated the White working class, many of whom were immigrant Irish and Germans.

New York's African Americans were in an untenable position in other ways as well. Aware that the struggle for national survival was being fought largely over them, many wished to join the fight. But it was consistently made clear to them that this was a White man's fight and that their participation was unwelcome. Still, they continued to try. They drilled on their own, despite police warnings. New York City's Black community offered Governor Morgan three regiments to fight until the war ended; they even volunteered to provide all their own clothes, pay, and weapons. They were refused. So here they were, hated for causing the war, unable to hold their own by fighting in it, and reduced to taking jobs away from Whites when they could find work at all. To make matters worse, there was the growing fear among New Yorkers that once the war was won, hordes of freed slaves would invade the city in search of employment.[16]

Summer passed, and the Gordon case was scheduled to be heard once again in late October. By October 7, Delafield Smith was nearly ready. "I have my additional witnesses," he wrote to George C. Whiting at the Department of the Interior. Smith kept them sequestered so that "nothing but the bribing of Jurors can baffle me." Smith asked Whiting to pass his letter along to Secretary of the Interior Caleb Smith, "and tell him that no labor will be spared to procure a conviction."[17]

Yet Smith was not as ready as he had thought when he wrote to his superior. He had his sailors as witnesses, and he had further researched the issue of Gordon's citizenship. But to his frustration, he did not yet have Lieutenant Todd. He had expected the officer to be released to him in time for the trial, but Todd was still on blockade duty aboard the *Cumberland,* and Smith was understandably reluctant to go to trial without him. The *New York Times,* erroneously referring to him as "Lieutenant Ford," reported that the officer "was a necessary witness . . . and had not arrived yet from the blockading squadron off Charleston. . . ."[18]

On October 18, Smith, wrote directly to the secretary of the interior: "The case of Captain Gordon of the slave ship 'Erie' will, I am confident, with the new evidence . . . result in a capital conviction, to the infinite honor of your department and of humanity." Smith then asked that the case and those like it "be reported stenographically," and the transcripts made available to the press.[19] He realized the significance of the case, and wanted a verbatim record of the trial. Knowing he was about to make history, Smith wanted an accurate record to be kept for posterity. The trial transcript no longer exists, but the parallels in the various city newspapers' coverage indicate that they were working from the same source, and can be relied upon for an accurate account.

The trial had been set for October 23, but was postponed until November 6 to allow for Lieutenant Todd's long-delayed presence. After

Gilbert Dean joined Gordon's defense team, Smith briefly considered reinforcing his own. He decided against it, fearing that adding more lawyers to the government's side would prejudice the jury, making them feel that Gordon was being persecuted.[20]

Smith was concerned about the jury for another reason as well: "Mr. Joachimsen, one of the prisoner's counsel, [has] personal friends of his own German Jewish faith on the jury. . . ."[21] Smith was afraid that the Jews would vote to acquit from a sense of clannishness, rather than any belief in Gordon's innocence.

For his part, defense attorney Dean seems to have been especially selective in his choice of jurors. "Some difficulty," wrote Smith, "was experienced in procuring a jury, the prisoner's counsel challenging each as they were called." Dean sharply questioned each potential juror as to whether he read the daily newspapers, specifically the *Tribune;* its editor, Horace Greeley, was especially vocal in his denunciation of the slave trade, and of the government's failures in prosecuting it. Dean, in referring a juror to a recent Greeley editorial, made his own feelings known, saying "it was the most atrocious article he ever read, calling for the conviction of every man to be tried before this Court."

When it was Smith's turn to question the potential jurors, he left no doubt as to the outcome he sought: when "one juror said he was conscientiously opposed to 'drawing a man up' he was excused." If a man was unwilling to see the defendant hanged, he didn't belong in the jury box.[22] By now, both sides realized that this would not be just another slaving trial.

One would think that the courtroom would be filled with spectators breathlessly hanging on the words of the witnesses and attorneys. But this was not the case. During the course of this trial, as in the first, the courtroom was quiet. The *Post* reporter wrote, "The case attracts but little interest, there being few spectators in court."[23] There really was no reason for the public to take an interest at this point. Articles and editorials on slave-trade issues and cases were now appearing almost daily in the press, and thus far, nothing distinguished the Gordon case from the others being brought before the bar in New York. That was about to change.

The trial commenced with Prosecutor Smith's address to the jury. His first move was to convince them that he had no abolitionist motives for wanting to see Gordon convicted. His opening remarks detailed for the twelve jurors his personal philosophy, beginning with the Fugitive

Slave Act: "A man may believe, above all . . . that the Fugitive Slave law . . . ought to be fairly and faithfully executed. And such, gentlemen, is my own belief."

Apparently, Gilbert Dean had stated or implied to the jury that Smith was an antislavery man: "[My opponent] imputed to me views on the subject of slavery which I do not entertain, and which I never have entertained. I have no ultra views on the subject [of slavery], and never have had. I have no views which any conservative citizen might not entertain on the subject. I do not agree with the peculiar views of those expressed on the subject by the New York *Tribune* and by persons of my own political party. . . ." Smith was letting the "conservative citizens" on the jury know that he was one of them. He disagreed with his own Republican Party, and even shared the average New Yorker's Southern sympathies: "The dearest friends I have on earth . . . are this day in the State of South Carolina, in the Sumter district, and this war has put an end to the visiting and correspondence on any point with endearing friends in that section of the country. I come before you, therefore, without any prejudice in favor of any particular views whatever . . . but simply with the purpose of performing the duty which I owe as an officer of the government, to see that the laws of the United States are enforced."

Smith then drew for the jury that hoary distinction between the slave trade and slavery itself. He had tried this approach during the first trial, but this time he pulled out all the stops: "A citizen may have any opinion that he deems right on the question of slavery . . . and still adhere to the proper administration of the law against the African slave trade, which trade the nations have pronounced a curse, and which all Christendom declares to be against humanity, unjust and impolitic."[24] Clearly, he was working the jury, letting those impaneled New Yorkers know that together, they could do their duty without compromising their personal feelings regarding race and slavery. As he later wrote to Caleb Smith, "I labored to separate the case from all questions as to slavery or slavery extensions in this country."[25]

After explaining the charges to the jury, Smith addressed the question of Gordon's citizenship and once again called on Captain Richard Crockett, the old Portland seaman who had known Gordon and his family since the defendant was a small boy. But this time, Smith called other witnesses to testify to Gordon's American birth. First was Lieutenant Henry Davis Todd. Smith questioned the young officer at length, and Todd's account was consistent with that of the first trial.[26] At day's end, court was adjourned.

But at this point, the prosecution digressed from normal procedure. Justice Nelson, who was sharing the bench with Shipman, responded to a special request from Smith: he "would not permit the jury to separate, but ordered them to be kept together, and not allowed to communicate with any person or with each other on the subject of the trial. Provision is made for their accommodation at the Astor House, and three officers are detailed to keep them in charge."[27] It was Marshal Murray who assumed responsibility for keeping the jurors sequestered. He didn't allow them out of his or his deputies' sight, "even to get a lunch, the Marshal providing them with lodgings . . . and with their means."[28] It was the intention of Smith and Murray that no one be allowed to come into contact with the jurors. Jury tampering might have occurred in the first trial; there would be none of it in the second.

Next day, Smith played his trump card, and called all four of the *Erie*'s seamen who had been brought to New York by the marshal. He began with his star witness, William Martin. Both the *Times* and the *Post* gave detailed summaries of his damning testimony. Martin testified that he had signed aboard in Havana, for what he thought was a legal voyage to the Congo River. He told of the subsequent suspicions of the crew over the cargo and the presence of four Spaniards who did no work on board, of the confrontation with Gordon over the nature of the expedition when the *Erie* was a month out of port, and of Gordon's response that it was a legal voyage and "they had no right to ask such a question." When they sailed into the Congo and anchored 45 miles upriver, Gordon was "on and off the vessel all the time," doing business with the slave trader.

Martin testified that he suffered an eight- to ten-day bout of "Congo fever," and was ordered ashore by Gordon to make sails while he recovered. When he came back aboard, he noticed that all 250 bundles of hoops and shooks had been made into barrels, filled with river water, and stowed. With Gordon still in command, the *Erie* sailed downriver to Sharks Point, where, on August 7, they boarded a cargo of Africans. Martin recalled that Spanish slavers had brought them from shore in launches. "It took about three-quarters of an hour to bring them all aboard; Gordon cut the rags off some of the negroes with his knife; he was looking after the loading of them; Gordon sent the men to one part of the vessel and the women to the other." When they sailed, said Martin, some eight or ten more Spaniards or Portuguese had joined the crew.

Then Martin made the statement that Smith was looking for: "There was no change in the authority of the vessel after the negroes were taken on board."[29] Martin testified that he was at the wheel that night, and that "Captain Gordon . . . and no one else . . . gave him directions as to the course to steer."[30]

When Smith asked when Gordon had made his intentions known to the crew, Martin stated that he, along with the other crew members, were summoned to the afterdeck the night before they boarded the slaves. Waiting for them were Gordon, First Mate Warren, and the Spaniards: "Gordon said they were going to take on a cargo of niggers, and the sailors would receive $1 per head for every negro he landed alive on the coast of Cuba; one of the men asked if they could not get more, and Gordon said no."

Martin concluded his testimony with an account of their pursuit and capture by the *Mohican* between seven and eight o'clock on the morning they sailed out of the river mouth. "Captain Gordon was on the forecastle looking at the Mohican through his glasses. . . . Witness did not know of any Spanish or Portuguese captain or officer being on board."[31]

Smith asked Martin if he had told all he knew. "He replied yes, adding that if they were not satisfied, plenty of men could be got on shore [to support his story]."[32] Martin's testimony was extraordinary. He had given an account of the *Erie*'s entire slaving voyage under the unbroken command of Nathaniel Gordon. It was now up to the defense to try to discredit him.

Joachimsen asked if Martin had ever been on a slaving voyage before signing aboard the *Erie;* Martin acknowledged that he had "previously made one passage in the coolie trade, but had never been to the Congo before."[33] This was not a character endorsement. The coolie trade of the 1850s was similar in most respects to the African slave trade. Poor Chinese were either recruited or kidnapped by coolie agents, kept under guard in barracoons, loaded aboard ships, and delivered mainly to Cuba as cheap labor. They were made to sign contracts of indenture for an eight-year period, since actual slavery was illegal. This was a legal nicety, since the conditions were the same. The

Cubans spoke of "buying," not "hiring" the workers. When they bought a coolie's contract at auction, they were actually buying the person. Between 1847 and 1874, nearly 125,000 Chinese were shipped to Cuba. Most of the coolies were put to work in the sugar and tobacco fields; upwards of 60 percent did not survive their eight-year period of indenture.[34]

If Martin's experience in the coolie trade gave the jury pause, it was quickly dispelled when his three shipmates corroborated his testimony. Their credibility was strong, especially considering they had nothing to gain from giving evidence. No charges had been brought against them, nor were they offered any rewards. They firmly placed Gordon in command of the *Erie,* sailing both into and out of the Congo River. They clearly portrayed him as the guiding force of every aspect of the expedition, down to physically directing the captives to the various parts of the ship.

Smith seems to have changed his mind about using testimony from members of the *Erie*'s disreputable Spanish shadow crew; for his final witness, he called Francisco Sallegosa. Through an interpreter, Sallegosa testified that he was a passenger aboard the *Erie,* having purchased his berth for $100. The Spaniard stated that Gordon, Warren, and Hall were the only officers aboard, and ordered all the work regarding the slaves.[35]

Under Joachimsen's cross-examination, Sallegosa admitted that he was currently under indictment for serving aboard the slaver brig *Bonita;* at the time of his court appearance, he was being held in the Mulberry Street House of Detention. He testified that he, along with two comrades, had shipped aboard the *Bonita* as passengers. (Sallegosa seems to have had a knack for picking the wrong vessels on which to "book passage.") Although he stated that "[I] have not been promised that I should not be prosecuted under that indictment if I would testify in this case," he seems an odd choice for a prosecution witness. Sallegosa's testimony was clearly flawed, and Smith himself would later acknowledge that the Spaniard hurt rather than helped the case.[36]

Still, Smith had delivered on his promise to present a solid case for the prosecution. Todd had spoken again of the condition of the slaves aboard the *Erie;* and the four sailors gave Smith the one thing Todd could not—hard testimony that Gordon had, in fact, been in command of the *Erie* before, during, and after the boarding of the slaves. Smith had also presented new evidence of Gordon's citizenship, making the question of the *Erie*'s country of ownership irrelevant. He had shown that Gordon was an American citizen not only serving on but commanding a proven slaver. Smith concluded his case, and waited to see what rabbits Dean and Joachimsen would pull from their hats.

Joachimsen opened for the defense. His first witness was Ralph Post, who testified that he had formerly owned a three-quarter share in the *Erie*, along with Freeman B. Lewis and G. A. Knudson (our captain in Havana), but "to the best of his knowledge," the ship had been sold in March 1860, prior to sailing from Cuba. As he recalled, the sale price was $13,000, which he divided with his partners after paying some bills.

Delafield Smith, on cross-examination, got Post to admit that he had no idea who the buyer was; the money was paid through Messrs. Hamel & Co. in Havana. Post was very insistent, however, that he had had no connection with Gordon while he and his partners owned the ship.[37] With no specific buyer, no receipt of payment, nor any proof of sale, convincing a jury that the *Erie* had been sold to a foreigner in Cuba would be difficult. The owners had been sloppy in not providing Gordon with a set of false papers prior to his voyage; it would prove a fatal error.

As in the first trial, the defense called a witness to testify regarding the tides at the mouth of the Congo River. This time, it was a Portuguese gentleman, one Jose Morales Faiao, who stated that he "had been several times at the Congo, and knew the location of Sharks Point, where these negroes were taken on board; that there was no tide above Sharks Point, except when it rains, and then it overflows."[38] This was the same point the defense attempted to make in the first trial: if the entire river above the mouth was owned by Portugal; and if the slaves were boarded on the river, in Portuguese territory; then Gordon, his crew, and his ship were outside American jurisdiction. Exactly why Faiao had made several voyages to the slaving ground was not determined.

Once again, the defense called upon First Mate William Warren, who repeated his tale of the Spanish captain, but in greater detail. Warren testified that he had helped unload the *Erie*'s cargo, at which point he was relieved as mate; Gordon then transferred command to a Spaniard named Captain Hill, who "had full charge while we lay in the river." Gordon and Warren, according to the witness, were officially unemployed, and Hill announced that he was now in command. A new Spanish crew came aboard, with a complement of four officers, including one named Manuel. But tragedy struck, said Warren, when Captain Hill died suddenly. Manuel took command, and it was at this point that the slaves were loaded. Neither Warren nor Gordon participated in the process. Warren did not deny the "one dollar a head" story, he merely gave it an innovative twist, stating that Captain Gordon made the offer to the crew through a letter left by the late Captain Hill.[39]

Second Mate Hall was called; he told the same story. Their testimony was no different in substance from those that had been given by captains and mates in countless other slave-trade trials: the captain had turned over command to a foreign officer, the mates resigned their posts upon reaching their destination and discharging their cargo, and the former captain, mates, and crew were merely on board as passengers.

In retrospect, the defense's strategy seems to have changed little if at all from the first trial. Joachimsen made the same points about jurisdiction, ownership of the *Erie,* and the Spanish captain and crew. Apparently, there was nothing more of substance to present. After all, their client had been caught commanding a laden slaver, and aside from sending up a smoke screen to confuse the jury, there was not much more to say. The defense's testimony is transparent; the only wonder is that for nearly 42 years juries had heard virtually the same tale from other accused slavers and then let them go.

The question arises: why bring in Gilbert Dean, if the defense's case remained virtually unchanged, and if the job of calling and rebutting witnesses still fell to Joachimsen? Two reasons: Dean was the perfect man to present and sum up their case. He was an eloquent and effective speaker, and if a decision hung in the balance, Dean's well-chosen words might swing it in their favor. However, if the jury found against Gordon, Dean was also highly experienced in the process and intricacies of appeal, and was acquainted with powerful people in the government.

At ten o'clock next morning, November 8, the jury was escorted back to the box to hear summations. In an age when long speeches were the norm, the two lawyers outdid themselves. True to form, Dean spoke for more than four hours "in an able and argumentative address."[40] Even Greeley's *Tribune* complimented him on his "able plea on behalf of his client," but then went on to say that "Mr. U.S. District Attorney SMITH responded, demolishing his arguments."[41] The *Post* called Smith's address a "convincing and masterly effort,"[42] while the *Herald* praised his "eloquent speech on the evidence and on the enormities of the slave traffic, on which he spoke for more than four hours."[43] Smith had demonstrated that he could play the game as well as Dean. It is unfortunate that neither summation has been preserved. (Smith was sufficiently satisfied with his own presentation to later publish a treatise entitled "Addresses to Juries in Slave Trade Trials.") It wasn't until after six in the evening that Justice Samuel Nelson addressed the jury. Despite his less-than-stellar record in the past adjudication of slave-trade cases, and possibly due to the influence of Judge Shipman, Justice Nelson delivered an "able and direct" charge, which was reproduced verbatim in the city newspapers.

He began by admonishing the jury to confine their deliberations to the "real issues" of the case, and put aside the "wide range of discussion you have heard from the learned counsel on either side." He made the charge very clear: if Nathaniel Gordon is found guilty of enslaving a negro or mulatto, he is a pirate, and he must die. But to find the defendant guilty, he must either be an American citizen who served on a foreign slave ship, or a foreigner who served on an American slave ship.

Nelson effectively dismissed the claim of the defendant's supposed birth under a foreign flag: if Gordon was born to American citizens, it made no difference where the birth occurred; he was, by law, an American citizen. As for the prosecution's claim that he was born in Portland, Nelson put the burden on the defense to show that he wasn't.

Regarding ownership of the *Erie,* Nelson took Ralph Post's testimony apart, pointing out that no documentation existed to prove that the ship had been sold; therefore, the defense's claim of a foreign transfer in Havana didn't hold up.

Having made short work of both the citizenship and ownership issues, Nelson focused the jury on the central issue, or, as he called it, the "merits of the case": did Gordon enslave Africans on the Congo River? He reminded the jury that the four sailors had given identical testimony to the effect that the defendant had done just that, without ever surrendering command or control. After reviewing the high points of their statements, he concentrated on the concept of forcible detainment. The

Africans, he stated, were confined in barracoons and loaded aboard the
*Erie* in bondage and "under moral restraint and fear—their wills controlled by [a] superior power exercised over their minds and bodies. . . .
Any person participating in that forcible detention" is guilty. "As to the
intent of making them slaves: This, undoubtedly, is a question of fact
for the jury."[44]

Nelson's synopsis to the jury was balanced, fair, and comprehensive.
After his charge, the jury retired to consider the evidence. They returned in less than half an hour with their verdict: *Guilty.*


Two factors distinguished this trial from the first. One was the testimony of the four sailors Delafield Smith and Marshal Murray had found
and presented to the jury. Compared to their testimony, the statements
of Warren and Hall came across as exactly what they were—lying attempts to keep Gordon's neck, and ultimately their own, out of the
hangman's noose. But none of this would have made any difference if
a single juror had been bribed. By keeping the jurors sequestered, the
prosecution ensured an honest deliberation.

Delafield Smith lost no time in sending a telegram to Secretary of the
Interior Caleb B. Smith: "I have convicted the Slave Capt. Gordon."[45]

Suddenly, the city awoke to the significance of the Gordon verdict.
The *Herald* editorialized:

> The difficulties which have surrounded cases of this kind, especially in
> the matter of procuring evidence, have heretofore rendered convictions
> almost impossible; but in the case of Captain Gordon the links of testi-
> mony were so unbroken as to afford the jury no opportunity for doubt or
> hesitancy. . . . The charge against the prisoner was piracy, and the
> penalty is death. Whether the extreme rigor of the law be carried out or
> not, the conviction of Captain Gordon will have a wholesome effect in
> checking the unnatural system of slave traffic.[46]

While assigning much of the credit to Delafield Smith's skillful handling of the case, the *Tribune* took a somewhat more pragmatic approach: "Probably the success of the prosecution is due in a great
measure to the fact that the jury was kept together by the Marshal, and
guarded against improper influences."[47]

Henry Raymond's *New York Times* took the reader from the 1820 passage of the Piracy Act through to the Gordon verdict, ending on a triumphant note:

> The Slave-trade has experienced a blow from which, it may be hoped, it cannot recover. Judges Nelson and Shipman, as well as the District-Attorney and the jury, have rendered a public service quite out of the usual routine, and which will entitle them to the thanks of our law-abiding citizens.[48]

Delafield Smith later sent a much longer communication to Caleb Smith. After minutely detailing his efforts and strategy from the time he took over the Gordon case, the prosecutor describes the public response to the verdict:

> The effect in this community has never been paralleled by any criminal conviction in either the state or U.S. courts. Persons crowded into my office, the following morning, and asked if it was really so. As Gordon is an old offender, having been previously on two or three slave voyages, I trust the law may take its course. No fitter example could be made. The cruelty exhibited by the evidence in these cases surpasses the common belief in respect to the atrocities of this trade. . . . I am sorry for the guilty man. But he should think of the agonies of the dying in his ship's hold, where sores and death appeared within a few hours after the living cargo was taken on board.

Smith concludes his letter with a request:

> As I have never sought, in words, to express to the President, my gratitude for the Commission I hold from him, I should be glad, if he would not deem it intrusive, that this letter should be read to him as some evidence that I have not been insensible to the obligation which that Commission has imposed. . . . To be useful, in any degree, to such a Government and such an Administration is the high measure of ambition.[49]

Smith was very pleased with himself, and understandably so. He had accomplished what no prosecutor, law enforcement officer, judge, or juror had achieved in 42 years, and he had done so through skill, dedication, and an innovative approach to the task. Clearly, he wanted not only his boss but also President Lincoln to know of it. Yet his job was far from over; the skillful Dean had immediately applied to the judges to file a motion for an arrest of judgment and a new trial. There was still a long way to go before Nathaniel Gordon's fate was decided.

*(above)* U.S. ATTORNEY E. DELAFIELD SMITH. BY NO MEANS AN ABOLI-
TIONIST, THE NEW REPUBLICAN PROSECUTOR WAS NONETHELESS DETER-
MINED TO ERADICATE THE SLAVE TRADE IN NEW YORK CITY. CAPTAIN
GORDON WAS HIS FIRST TARGET.

*(right)* SMITH'S TELEGRAM TO HIS SUPERIORS ANNOUNCING HIS CONVIC-
TION OF GORDON.

# CHAPTER VII

# SENTENCING

Justice Samuel Nelson scheduled defense counsel Gilbert Dean's request to present a motion for arrest of judgment and a new trial for the following Saturday, November 16. Suddenly, the Gordon case was news, and the motion was published in its entirety in the local newspapers. Dean's main points were these:

- The judge was in error when he told the jury to assume that the *Erie* had been sold to Americans—if it had been sold at all—unless the defense could prove otherwise. It was the *government's* responsibility, said Dean, not the defense's, to prove that the ship was still American-owned.

- The alleged sale of the *Erie* had taken place in Cuba—a foreign country—which should create the presumption that she was sold to foreigners, not to Americans.

- If, in fact, the *Erie* was a foreign vessel, the United States had no jurisdiction to try Gordon, since the offense occurred on the Congo River, and therefore, presumably, in Portuguese territory.

- The court erred in declaring that Gordon was an American citizen, even though born abroad of American parents.

- The indictment was flawed, inasmuch as it did not define the captives "as slaves by the law of any of the United States."

- There was no charge that the offense was committed "forcibly," an "essential requisite of the offence of 'piracy.' " The captives, Dean asserted, might simply have wished to leave the country.[1]

Dean's motion was comprehensive. If he had merely presented it based on the question of Gordon's citizenship, the vessel's nationality alone would have been enough to hang him. Conversely, had Dean addressed only the issue of the *Erie*'s ownership, Gordon could hang as an American citizen. Dean filed his motion based not only on these two issues, but on the use of force as well. Technically, he claimed, if force could not be proven, then a piracy charge could not be supported.

E. Delafield Smith immediately responded, opposing the motion point by point. As to the court's charge regarding Gordon's citizenship, Smith maintained that it was "strictly correct." The burden of proof lay with the defendant to show that he was born abroad, since the evidence established, prima facie, that he was born in Portland, Maine. The same argument applied to ownership of the vessel. Regarding jurisdiction, Smith asserted that it made no difference where the crime had been initiated, inasmuch as the capture itself had occurred on the open ocean, "a place unquestionably within the admiralty and maritime jurisdiction of the United States. . . . The crime was committed at every point" from where the Africans were boarded to the arrest in open waters.

Finally, said Smith, "as to the meaning of the word 'forcibly,' it would be a monstrous perversion to say that a man who commits a crime against the person by a moral sway over his victim, is not guilty because he has proved physical force unnecessary to the complete perpetration of the outrage." Whether the Africans were taken aboard the vessel through the use of physical or psychological violence—"moral sway"—it must be considered forcible. And this was enough to define the captives as slaves. "A new trial should be denied," Smith concluded, "and judgment be pronounced." [2]

The court took Dean's motion under consideration; the judges would give their opinion on November 30. Meanwhile, other slave-trade cases—the fruits of the last-gasp efforts of the African Squadron—were finding their way into the courts, with less dramatic results.

Just four days after the verdict was rendered in the Gordon case, another young man stood before Justice Samuel Nelson and Judge William Davis Shipman. Minthorne Westervelt—25 years old, a member of a venerable Staten Island Dutch family, and grandson of a former vice president of the United States—was facing the same charges as Nathaniel Gordon. Westervelt had served as third mate aboard the *Nightingale,* which had been captured by the USS *Saratoga* the previous April off the coast of Africa with 961 slaves aboard. Westervelt, along with first and second mates Samuel Haines and Bradly Winslow, was brought back to New York to stand trial for piracy. [3]

Westervelt was represented by Charles O'Conor and John McKeon, both former U.S. district attorneys, now earning their livings defending the types of men they had once attempted to imprison or hang. They applied for, and received, the right to a separate trial for their client. O'Conor and McKeon pleaded "ignorance and compulsion" as their defense. Westervelt, they claimed, knew nothing of the nature of the voyage when he signed on; upon discovering its objective, he had no choice but to follow orders. Therefore, they argued, he had had no control over the buying and boarding of the slaves, and was not liable under the Piracy Act. [4]

They went on to "show the good character of the accused," describing him as "the son of a wealthy gentleman of Staten Island, and the grandson of a former Vice-President."[5] Prosecutor Delafield Smith "said he would admit the respectability of the prisoner's family," but that he could present proof that Minthorne's father had told his son "if he went up the Congo River he need never enter his doors again."[6] This would seem to indicate that not only was young Westervelt well aware of the *Nightingale*'s objective long before he stepped aboard her but he signed on despite his father's objections.

Smith argued his case most eloquently, pointing out to the jury that Westervelt's crime was worse than the same offense committed by a common sailor. One couldn't blame a poor seaman for signing on a slaving voyage, when dilettantes such as Westervelt set the example. He didn't need the money, and had gone slaving on a lark, as a "gentle-man mate." Perhaps, said Smith, the defendant was dissatisfied with the ancestral home, and wished to build a mansion for himself "with the gains of adventures which involve the transportation of human beings from their homes in Africa to the strange coast of Cuba, in stifling pens, beneath tropic suns, with the calculation . . . that if two thirds die and one third land, the venture is a fair success!"[7]

In his charge to the jury, Justice Nelson stated that, while "anyone who confined negroes was guilty, circumstances" could compel a man to break the law. He instructed the jury that their decision would hinge upon whether they would hang young Westervelt for not jumping ship when the true nature of the voyage was made clear. He went on to reit-erate the defense's portrayal of the defendant as an intelligent, sensitive scion of a fine old family.

Nelson's charge made it amply clear to the jury that the judge did not want the young man hanged; they returned from their deliberations hopelessly deadlocked, with ten voting to convict and two for acquittal. Next came the discussion of bail pending retrial. Bail should have been out of the question, since this was a capital case. This, however, did not prevent Justice Nelson from bending the law in favor of the "home boy" son of an influential New Yorker:

The prisoner is a young man—I think little over twenty years of age at the time that he was charged with this offence—and . . . down to the time of the commission of the crime he had borne a respectable character. . . . He is now in the Tombs, or in Eldridge Street Jail, among felons and associates undoubtedly tending to corrupt a young mind and young heart. Under all the circumstances we are inclined to admit the prisoner to bail.[8]

Considering Westervelt had voluntarily helped to enslave nearly 1,000 human beings for profit, one wonders what his cellmates could have done to further corrupt his "young mind and young heart."

McKeon requested that bail be set at $10,000; Justice Nelson said that half that amount would suffice (though "the crime was a heinous one," and "the administration of justice should be stern") because "the young man being confined among felons, the Court is disposed to give him an opportunity of enjoying better associations and of avoiding crime."[9]

Despite Justice Nelson's depiction of the prisoner as an impressionable youth of good breeding, Westervelt was clearly as guilty of piracy as Gordon. Even if he were a young socialite on an adventure, he had acted as an officer aboard a laden slaver. This alone should have been enough to put him on the gallows. Smith, sensing the futility of a second capital trial, contented himself with allowing Westervelt to join the army in lieu of facing jail time if he helped the court obtain information proving the American birth of the first mate. Samuel Haines had been unusually brutal in dealing with the captive Africans, and Smith saw a better chance of convicting Haines than he had had with young Westervelt, or with foreign-born second mate Winslow. Ultimately, however, all three of the *Nightingale*'s mates were granted bail, and the charges dropped.[10]

At the same time he was dealing with the *Nightingale,* Smith had to make a decision regarding the prosecution of the sailors from the laden slaver *Bonita* that had been captured at sea the previous October. At least six of her crew lived in the Tombs, awaiting the court's pleasure. But they were all foreign-born, including Blaus of France and Sallegosa of Spain, and Smith thought a conviction unlikely. Therefore, he declined to prosecute, and released all the crewmen.[11]

The same page in the November 26, 1861, issue of the *New York Post* that reports the assignment of bail to Minthorne Westervelt refers to two other slave-trade cases—those of the *Cora* and the *Augusta*. Originally, the *Cora* had been seized in New York Harbor in May 1860 while attempting to embark on a slaving voyage; she was bonded, released, then caught at sea four months later with 705 Africans confined on her middle deck. Owner and captain John Latham and his three mates were taken to New York to face charges under the Piracy Act. Latham "made his escape through the connivance of one of Marshal Rynders's officers," and the first mate crawled, "it was said, through a port-hole while the vessel lay in New York" and swam away. Smith allowed the others to plead to the lesser charge of serving aboard a slaver. Since they had already been languishing in Sing Sing for 14 months, Judge Shipman sentenced them to another 10 months and fined them each $500.[12]

The *Augusta* was yet another example of a vessel that had been previously seized, libeled, bonded, and released to pursue a slaving voyage. The difference was that this time the slaver had never left the New York area. The *Augusta* sailed from the city docks, ostensibly on a whaling voyage, and made for Greenport, near the eastern tip of Long Island. Because Captain Appleton Oaksmith had a history of financing and commanding slave ships, officials found the ship's movements suspicious, and a government agent was sent to Greenport to monitor Oaksmith's actions. The agent determined that the *Augusta* was fitted out more for a slaving expedition than a whaling voyage, and he recommended that she be seized after putting out to sea.

A week later, Oaksmith, his brother, and a crew of around 16 men boarded a sloop at Fire Island to convey them to the *Augusta*. After having toasted the enterprise with a keg of rum, Oaksmith and the crew ran the sloop aground in a storm. Marshal Murray and his deputies, acting upon Delafield Smith's orders, then boarded the sloop and arrested the captain and his entire crew.[13]

A new libel was filed against the *Augusta,* and Judge Shipman, finding "her whaling apparatus . . . inadequate" and "her stores . . . not such as were adapted to a whaling voyage" condemned her.[14] "Meanwhile," crowed the *Post,* "those engaged in this renewed attempt will undoubtedly be personally punished if proved guilty of fitting out their bark for the purpose of dealing in the slave trade."[15]

Once again, this was not to be so. Despite the fact that one of the crew volunteered information that resulted in the arrest of the *Augusta*'s owner, a wealthy New York City merchant, Smith discharged the lot of them. Technically, the crew had not been arrested aboard the *Augusta,* and Smith felt that he had insufficient evidence to procure a conviction.

Oaksmith was next heard of in Boston federal court, where he was convicted of fitting out another of his whaler/slave ships.[16] U.S. Marshal Robert Murray traveled to Boston to attend the trial, and later wrote to

Assistant Secretary of the Interior George Whiting, "I have been absent from town the whole of last week attending the trial of Appleton Oaksmith which was very interesting. I consider his conviction of greater triumph in the cause of the suppression of the Slave Trade than the execution of Gordon the slaver captain."[17] Oaksmith was sentenced to a short term in prison. Three months later, he broke out of jail, leaving a long letter in his cell indignantly protesting his innocence. Nothing further was heard of him.[18]

Though all four of these vessels—the *Nightingale,* the *Bonita,* the *Cora,* and the *Augusta*—were condemned in court for their involvement in the slave trade, nearly every officer and seaman arrested for the same crime was set free. Aside from the conviction of Nathaniel Gordon for piracy, nothing, it seemed, had changed. Gordon was the exception not the rule.

On November 30, Judge Shipman delivered his opinion on Attorney Dean's motion for arrest of judgment and for a new trial in the Gordon matter. Regarding the count of "confining and detaining negroes," Attorney Dean had been hoping to show that the Africans were slaves before Nathaniel Gordon even became involved, thereby proving him innocent of the charge. Shipman responded that the terms of the count were simply "more comprehensive than necessary," and served "to cover the offence." There was, he determined, no fault in the statute.

As far as the nationality of the *Erie,* Shipman stated that the ship had been shown to have been built and owned by American citizens. It lay with the defense to show proof that her status had changed prior to the slaving expedition; this had not been done, beyond verbal testimony that a sale had taken place in Havana. As for Dean's statement that a sale in a foreign country should presuppose the buyer to be a foreigner, Shipman responded that there was "no foundation in law or reason" to support such a presumption.

Shipman next addressed the question of Gordon's citizenship. He stated that the government had proven the charge satisfactorily, and "[w]e are clearly of the opinion that there was no error in this charge." Gordon was, in the eyes of the court, an American citizen, just as the *Erie* was an American ship. Either fact would be sufficient to hang the prisoner.

The final objection that Judge Shipman addressed was the question of jurisdiction. Dean had claimed that the waters of the Congo River where the transfer of slaves occurred were under Portuguese jurisdiction; were the *Erie* shown to be a foreign ship, the court had no legal right to arrest or prosecute Gordon. Shipman gave two answers to the exception. First, as he had already stated, the proof was "clear and uncontradicted that she was an American vessel." Second, the crime had occurred at the mouth of the river, "where its broad expanse is lost in the Atlantic." But this is not even relevant, Shipman continues, since "the proof is clear and uncontradicted that the offence of confining and detaining the negroes on board was continuous and uninterrupted until her capture in the Atlantic Ocean."

All of Dean's objections that Shipman considered germane had now been addressed, and he stated in conclusion, "Upon all these points we are clearly of the opinion that there is no error in the indictment, and that none intervened on the trial."

In a case in which the two judges disagree, the defense is entitled to a "certificate of division," which allows him to appeal to the U.S. Supreme Court. Dean had applied for such a certificate as well, but Shipman denied it, stating that his views "are fully concurred in by Mr. Justice Nelson." Dean had come up empty.

Smith immediately moved that Judge Shipman pronounce sentence upon Gordon; Dean objected to sentence being passed by only one of the two sitting judges. He stated that he had not had time to contact "a single person connected with the case," nor to "consult with any of the jurors" on his client's behalf. Dean claimed that initially, 11 of the 12 jurors were prepared to recommend mercy, and now all 12 were of such a mind. He therefore requested "that passing of judgment might be suspended."

Judge Shipman responded that "one Judge constitute[s] the court," and judgment could be passed accordingly. Besides, he had consulted with Justice Nelson regarding the sentence, and both men were in accord. Therefore, he "deemed it best to pass judgment at the present time."

Gordon was asked to stand. "He did so, the expression of his countenance rapidly changing."[19] He was then asked if he had anything to say as to why sentence should not be pronounced on him. He attempted to smile and responded, "I have nothing to say whatever."[20]

Judge Shipman's sentence upon Captain Gordon is a finely worded speech, which masterfully addresses not only the legal but also the moral aspects of the case. It is deeply moving; the judge himself, by all accounts, was visibly affected as he delivered it.

Nathaniel Gordon, it appears from the evidence in your case, that in the summer of 1860 you sailed in the ship *Erie* from Havana, in the island of Cuba, bound to the coast of Africa. You were master of the vessel, and had on board a competent crew, and a large amount of provisions of a kind and quantity appropriate for food for a large number of persons, and such as is usually carried out in vessels intended for the slave trade.

The ship also had on board a large number of water-casks as well as a quantity of liquor, which latter was to be left in Africa—probably exchanged for the freight which you intended to bring back to Cuba. In command of this Ship, thus manned and provided, you proceeded to the Congo River, on the West Coast of Africa, and then, after landing your cargo and subsequently reshipping all or nearly all but the liquor, and filling your water casks with fresh water, you dropped your vessel down the river to a point a few miles from its mouth, and in a few hours of the afternoon of the seventh of August, you took on board eight hundred and ninety seven of the inhabitants of that country, thrust them densely packed and crowded, between the decks of the ship, and immediately set sail for Cuba.

On the morning of the eighth, in the Atlantic Ocean, about fifty miles from the coast, you were captured by the United States war vessel "Mohican," your ship taken to Monrovia, where all the unfortunate victims of your crime, then living, were put on shore, and you were brought in your ship to this port. Upon these facts you have been accused, brought to trial before a jury of your countrymen, and found guilty of a crime for which the laws of your country adjudge you a pirate and inflict upon you the punishment of death. In the verdict of the jury it is my duty to say that the court fully concurred. The evidence of your guilt was so full and complete as to exclude from the minds of your triers all doubt.

You are soon to be confronted with the terrible consequences of your crime, and it is proper that I should call to your mind the duty of preparing for that event which will soon terminate your mortal existence and usher you into the presence of the Supreme Judge.

Let me implore you to seek religious guidance of the ministers of religion; and let your repentance be as humble and thorough as your crime was great. Do not attempt to hide its enormity from yourself; think of the cruelty and wickedness of seizing nearly a thousand fellow-beings, who never did you harm, and thrusting them beneath the decks of a small ship, beneath a burning tropical sun, to die of disease or suffocation, or be transported to distant lands, and be consigned, they and their posterity, to a fate far more cruel than death.

Think of the sufferings of the unhappy beings whom you crowded on the *Erie;* of their helpless agony and terror as you took them from their native land; and especially think of those who perished under the weight of their miseries on the passage from the place of your capture to Monrovia! Remember that you showed mercy to none, carrying off as you did not only those of your own sex, but women and helpless children.

Do not flatter yourself that because they belonged to a different race from yourself, your guilt is therefore lessened—rather fear that it is increased. In the just and generous heart, the humble and the weak inspire compassion, and call for pity and forbearance. As you are soon to pass into the presence of that God of the black man as well as the white man, who is no respecter of persons, do not indulge for a moment the thought that He hears with indifference the cry of the humblest of His children. Do not imagine that because others shared in the guilt of this enterprise, yours is thereby diminished; but remember the awful admonition of your Bible—"Though hand join in hand, the wicked shall not go unpunished." Turn your thoughts toward Him who alone can pardon, and who is not deaf to the supplications of those who seek His mercy.

It remains only to pronounce the sentence which the law affixes to your crime, which is, that you be taken back to the City Prison, whence you were brought, and remain there until Friday, the seventh day of February next, and then and there, the place of execution, between the hours of twelve o'clock at noon and three o'clock in the afternoon on that day, you be hanged by the neck until you are dead, and may the Lord have mercy upon your soul.

At this point, Delafield Smith handed the death warrant to the judge, who signed it and gave it to Marshal Murray.[21]

The newspapers reported that "as the Judge proceeded . . . [Gordon] grew apparently stronger, and his eye firmer. Towards its close he exhibited less feeling than the spectators in court—much less than the judge."[22]

"Only once," wrote Murray, "did that stoical expression which Gordon's face had assumed forsake him, and that was but momentary, when Judge Shipman uttered the words 'hanged by the neck until you are dead.' When, however, the order was given for his remand, he stepped quickly forward and proceeded with firmness to the Tombs."[23] Elizabeth was awaiting him there, and "an affecting interview took place . . . Mrs. Gordon was overwhelmed with grief."[24]

# CHAPTER VIII

# REACTIONS

Nathaniel Gordon's conviction made it apparent to New Yorkers—as well as to the country at large—that this was no everyday slave-trade case. After 42 years of near total inactivity on the part of the military, the government, and the courts, a man finally stood convicted of willfully trafficking in slaves, and his life hung in the balance. As soon as the judgment of the court became known, editorials began to appear, and they were predictably intense.

The *New York Times,* in a piece published the day after Gordon was sentenced, clamored for his execution: "Capt. Gordon is as responsible for the death of those on the *Erie,* as if he had taken the life of each by his own hand. For once, when no doubt exists as to guilt, a terrible example should be made. It will do more to stop the slave trade than a dozen war vessels on the African Coast."[1]

Gordon's conviction was especially important now that the need for ships to fight the war had compelled the government to withdraw all but one ship from Africa, literally leaving the coast clear for slavers:

> Immunity extended to Capt. Gordon would undoubtedly lead to the fitting out, in our own harbor, of a large number of vessels for the trade. . . . Nothing will deter people from engaging in this infamous but profitable traffic, but the fact that detection and conviction is certain to cost the life of the offenders. To pardon Capt. Gordon would be a most inhuman and mischievous step, and we trust that in this case the law will have its course without mitigation or delay.[2]

The *Herald* took a similar line, stating that Gordon's conviction would have a "wholesome effect" in stopping the "unnatural system of slave traffic."[3] And the *New York Post* proclaimed that what was needed to end the slave trade was to "establish a precedent for administering faithfully the punishment provided by act of Congress for the crime." The *Post's* editor in chief, William Cullen Bryant, added, "We hope the President's good nature will not overcome his duty as guardian of the laws."[4]

The timing of the Gordon case could not have better served the administration. One year after the presidential election, and just in time for Lincoln's first Annual Message to Congress, E. Delafield Smith's success in prosecuting the slaver gave his superiors their most dramatic evidence of the government's new hard line on the trade. And now, both President Lincoln and Secretary of the Interior Caleb B. Smith would go on public record endorsing Gordon's conviction.

In his December 3 report to Congress, Lincoln praised the Department of the Interior's recent efforts in combating the "inhuman traffic," listing five vessels seized and condemned, three men fined and imprisoned, and one captain "convicted of the highest grade of offence under our laws, the punishment of which is death."[5]

Because the responsibility for enforcing the slave acts had been given to his department, the secretary of the interior's Annual Report dealt in much greater detail with the recent arrests and seizures, and addressed the secretary's efforts to educate and encourage its officers toward a more determined pursuit of their duties:

> I caused the marshals of the loyal Atlantic States to assemble at New York for consultation, in order to insure greater concert of action. They were thereby afforded an opportunity of inspecting vessels fully equipped for the African slave trade, and of seeing the arts and devices employed to disguise and conceal the real objects of their voyage, thus enabling them to detect and prevent the clearance of vessels designed for this trade.[6]

This meeting of the marshals, hosted by New York's Robert Murray, amounted to a show-and-tell session; the recently captured and libeled slave vessels acted as floating classrooms for the officers. In its coverage of the event, the *New York Times*, in an editorial entitled "Dying Struggles of the Slave Trade," praised Lincoln and Secretary of State William Seward for giving the traffic their

> first attention, and they have followed it up with vigor and success. The meeting of the United States Marshals . . . did a great deal to infuse vigor and harmony into their actions, and the conviction last week of the captain of the *Gordon* [sic] will satisfy the parties who have hitherto grown

rich on the profits of this nefarious trade, that the law is no longer to be a dead letter. . . . One or two vessels have recently left this port for Portuguese ports with legitimate cargoes, but with the well-understood purpose of refitting *there* and going to the coast of Africa. Through the vigilance of **Marshal Murray,** however, our Government has made full representations to our counsels at the ports in question, and the vessels will be sharply watched. . . . [7]

Secretary Smith's report concluded: "Much credit is due to the United States attorneys and marshals at New York and Boston for the vigilance and zeal evinced by them, and I avail myself of the first occasion to make them this public acknowledgment."[8] The two men most prominently—and deservedly—in line for Caleb Smith's "public acknowledgment" were U.S. Attorney E. Delafield Smith and U.S. Marshal Robert Murray.

Another major event was occurring in the city during the week of Gordon's sentencing: the mayoral election. Although the result would be counted as a political victory for the president, it emphasized the deep divisions among New Yorkers. The irrepressible Fernando Wood was making a bid for reelection, and once again—with the support of his brother Ben's virulent *New York Daily News*—he was using racism and fear as the planks of his platform. The Irish and German workingmen, he proclaimed, would be used to fill the ranks of an army determined to free the Blacks and send them North by the thousands to take the very jobs of their liberators.[9] (The *New York Daily News* was so vitriolic a critic of the war that the federal government temporarily suspended its postal rights, effectively stopping publication for nearly a year.)[10]

Wood had previously split with Tammany Hall and formed his own branch of the Democratic Party. He was confident of victory, but this time he faced a daunting challenge. Tammany was running C. Godfrey Gunther, a city businessman and former fireman, hoping to draw the German and Irish votes since Tammany's appeal was largely to the poor workingman.

The Republican Unionists supported George Opdyke, a highly successful merchant. He drew his support from other city businessmen, including the government contractors. Opdyke's party played down any hint of abolitionist sentiment, and presented their candidate, a Lincoln man, on a platform of Unionist patriotism. All three parties enjoyed a share of popular support; New York was indeed a divided city.[11]

The Republican newspapers were soon attacking Wood on two fronts—his on-again, off-again loyalty to the Union, and the blatant corruption that had marked his administration. The *Times* and William Cullen Bryant's *Evening Post* fired daily salvoes, calling Wood a "secessionist mayor" and a "vile and calculating traitor."[12] Bryant accused him and his brother of leading a "Secessionist Association in New York" consisting of "the most virulent and notorious sympathizers with the South."[13]

A bipartisan rally was held for George Opdyke at the Cooper Institute, touted as the "largest political demonstration that has occurred in this city since the Presidential election," where members of both parties set aside their political differences in support of the war effort to save the Union. The hall was completely filled—"seats, aisles, stage and corners"—as ex–Supreme Court justice Edward Cowles presided.[14] Among the luminaries who spoke were E. Delafield Smith, Henry Raymond of the *New York Times,* and former U.S. attorney (and counsel to slavers) John McKeon.[15] In his speech in praise of the candidate, prominent New York attorney John H. White listed Opdyke's qualifications, among which were: "He has been . . . a faithful public servant, a sincere philanthropist and an honest man" and "he has no brother Ben to counsel with."[16]

The morning after Election Day, a poem presumably written by William Cullen Bryant himself appeared on page one of the *Post,* entitled "Fernando's Soliloquy."

Oh, now, forever,
Farewell the City Hall! Farewell dear Ben!
Farewell all Hackley contracts, and big jobs
That bloated my ambition! Oh, farewell!
Farewell the *nay*-ing power, by which I fooled
The people as I pleased—the Japanese,
And Royal Prince, that helped so much to feed
The pomp and circumstance of Gotham's Mayor!
And oh, ye lager, whiskey-drinking throats,
That clamored oft so loudly for "Fernandy,"
Farewell! Fernando's occupation's gone![17]

Yes, Fernando Wood had lost the election—as had Tammany's man Gunther. "We have chosen for our mayor," crowed the *Post,* "a man known for his probity, his honor, for all the qualities which our merchants most highly value."[18]

Given New York's strong Democratic history and its opposition to Lincoln, the government in Washington had been understandably concerned with the outcome of the mayoral contest. Word of Opdyke's victory, Bryant wrote, "fills Washington with rejoicing. . . . Democrats are as much rejoiced as Republicans—I mean, of course, the better class of democrats."[19]

The results of the election were not quite the Republican triumph the newspapers proclaimed it to be. Opdyke won only a third of the 74,300 votes, indicating that the victory was less an endorsement of the Republican platform than the result of the rift in the Democratic ranks: the Republicans had not won the election so much as the Democrats had lost it.[20] Nor was Opdyke, for his part, the white knight portrayed by the press. A longtime clothing manufacturer, he had made a good deal of his money producing cheap clothes to be used by Southern slaves. Just a few months before the election, it was George Opdyke, in his capacity as clothing inspector, who had approved the shoddy uniforms produced by Brooks Brothers. Before the war ended, a noted statesman said of Opdyke that he "had made more money out of the war by secret partnerships and contracts for army clothing, than any fifty sharpers in New York."[21] As mayor, however, he would prove himself a strong supporter of both the administration in Washington and the war effort.

One fact was apparent from the mayoral election of 1861: New York was a city engaged in a tug-of-war with itself. On the one hand, here was the Gotham that early on had marshaled a large, dedicated force to resist the troops of the South. Its soldiers even helped guard Washington from Confederate attack. New York's shipyards were rapidly turning out vessels of war, while her manufacturers supplied the Union with uniforms, weapons, horses, and equipment. During one week alone in November 1861, New York generated nearly $3 million in revenues from military contracts. Through the efforts of the city's Sanitary Commission in caring for the North's sick and wounded soldiers and improving conditions in the army camps, New York rightfully earned respect throughout the North.[22] Three of the major city newspapers— Horace Greeley's *Tribune,* Henry Raymond's *Times,* and William

Cullen Bryant's *Evening Post*—were constantly hammering home the Union anthem, and backing the Lincoln administration and the war effort.[23] Here, then, was a metropolis moving toward growth and enlightenment.

Even so, there was the New York that drank from the same political cup as the errant South. Arguably the "most southern of northern cities," Gotham soon became a bastion of Confederate sympathy and opposition to the war. A large portion of New York's population was rabidly racist. They violently opposed abolition, and bought into the poisonous rhetoric of such hate-mongers as Isaiah Rynders and the Wood brothers.

The election of Opdyke, however, gave some satisfaction to an administration in Washington with far greater issues to address. Emboldened though he was by New York's mayoral results, Lincoln was busy at the same time trying to avoid a war with Britain. Confederate President Jefferson Davis, in his continuing attempt to gain support and recognition from the nations of Europe, had selected two statesmen—James Murray Mason of Virginia and John Slidell of Louisiana—to act as commissioners and to woo the governments of England and France. They sailed from Havana in November, bound for London on board a British mail packet, the *Trent*. Shortly after leaving port, she was intercepted at sea by the USS *San Jacinto,* under the command of Captain Charles Wilkes. In direct violation of maritime law, Wilkes sent an armed party aboard the *Trent,* and when the British crew resisted, "a force became necessary to search." The Americans arrested the Southern emissaries and their secretaries, and steamed north with their prisoners. When the *San Jacinto* reached Highland Light off Cape Cod, she picked up Marshal Murray, whose orders were to take Mason and Slidell into custody and deliver them to the military prison at Fort Warren, in Boston Harbor.[24] One week later, Murray escorted his prisoners ashore, turned them over to the Fort's commander, and returned to New York on November 25—in time to hear sentence pronounced on Gordon.[25]

Wilkes was feted throughout the North and lauded as a hero in the press. Secretary of the Navy Gideon Welles publicly approved his actions, and he was officially thanked by the U.S. House of Representatives. However, in the words of one modern historian, "No international incident better illustrates the stupid thoughtlessness of popular clamor."[26] Wilkes's actions violated the rules of neutrality on the open ocean. He had boarded a foreign vessel under arms, searched it illegally, and forcibly removed and confined its passengers. He had, in fact, done exactly what the United States had been accusing England of doing ever since the Revolution.

England was not about to tolerate this affront. When informed of the incident, the prime minister, Lord Palmerston, shouted at his cabinet, "You may stand for this but damned if I will!" He sent 8,000 troops to Canada and placed a fleet of steam-powered warships on standby. Lincoln's newly appointed minister to England, Charles Francis Adams, wrote to his brother from London, "This nation means to make war," while his son Henry referred to those who had praised Wilkes's actions as a "bloody set of fools." [27]

As most clear-thinking Americans would have agreed, a war with England at this time was the last thing the Union needed. The armed forces of the North were already hard pressed to hold their own in the existing struggle. Fortunately, for all its talk of war, England behaved with admirable restraint. For America's part, calmer heads prevailed as well, mainly those of Lincoln, Seward, and Adams. On December 21, the *Post* reported that "the town is quiet today. . . . The intimations given out this morning by the State Department convince the timid that the war cloud, which . . . shadowed the nation, has passed away . . . simply because the two nations are disposed to avoid a war, especially at this time." [28] Seward wrote a note to Lord Lyons acknowledging that Wilkes had acted without authorization and that the two Confederate diplomats would be "cheerfully released." However, Seward couldn't resist a bit of British-bashing, reminding the gentleman of England's long record of maritime misbehavior, and ending his letter with, "If the safety of this Union required the detention of the captured persons[,] it would be the right and duty of this government to detain them." [29] In other words, we're letting them go, but we don't have to if we don't want to!

Meanwhile, as New York's political conflict, a real war at home, and a potential war with Britain played out through December 1861, Nathaniel Gordon languished in his dank cell at the onset of a cold New York winter, while his lawyers tried every avenue that might spare his life. Since his transfer to the Tombs several months earlier, Gordon had been denied all visitors, with the exception of his attorneys and his wife. The toll on both Gordon and Elizabeth was terrific. Although Gordon managed to maintain his stoic carriage after his conviction, his physical condition continued to deteriorate. He rapidly went from a man who had once been "thick-set and muscular, and evidently possessed [of] great physical strength" to a wraith of near skeletal proportions. And he would grow ever more gaunt as the day of his execution approached.[30]

The strain upon Elizabeth can only be imagined. The young woman had been transported from her home in Portland, Maine, to a nightmare of a city whose very government sought her husband's death. She had no money, and "her pecuniary means [were] derived exclusively from benevolent persons," presumably friends and supporters of Gordon.[31] And still, every day, month after month, Elizabeth made her way to the unimaginably depressing City Prison to visit her doomed husband.

Elizabeth's circumstances gave her little to look forward to if Gordon was executed. Short of remarrying, there were few opportunities for a penniless widowed mother, and none of them was attractive. Married at 15, Elizabeth probably had little education and few, if any, marketable skills. If she were handy with a needle and thread, she might earn pennies a day doing piecework at home or sitting at a sewing machine in a dusty factory. There were, however, many more seamstresses than there were jobs, and she would be competing with thousands of soldiers' wives and widows. She couldn't become a nurse for the Union, because she was too young and attractive. The Department of Female Nurses, under the rigid leadership of Dorothea Dix, required women to be at least 30 years old and "plain in appearance."[32]

Perhaps she could have found a position as a housemaid or "maid of all work." Daily, she would carry water and coal to every room, make and light the fires, empty and clean chamber pots, set and clear the table for each meal, and clean the entire house. As with most jobs open to women, the pay was pitiful and the hours impossibly long.[33] Women were the "lowliest . . . workers, subject to the worst wages and most brutal labor practices."[34] Still, there was one profession that was, and ever had been, women's domain: prostitution.

Whatever fate awaited her husband had been well earned. The press was right; every African whose death had come as a result of Gordon's chosen career, every family destroyed by his voyages, gave ample justification for his sentence. But tragically, Elizabeth Annie Gordon and her young son were caught in the swell.

• • •

A marked change had occurred in the general perception of Gordon's case. As Marshal Murray would later write,

> During the summer of 1861 [after the first trial], the subject of the further prosecution was treated by Gordon and his friends with ridicule on the ground that a conviction for the capital crime . . . was impossible. But after sentence public opinion changed; only the slavers pooh-poohed the idea of his execution. They still tried to persuade him that the punishment would be commuted to a term of imprisonment, or that he would be forcibly rescued. This was done partly to keep his mouth shut, it being feared that in his last extremity he would inform against the different merchants for whom he sailed, or whom he knew to be interested in the traffic.[35]

Nathaniel Gordon was not without his supporters, chief among whom was his lawyer. The indefatigable Gilbert Dean, with the aid of his partners, Beebe and Donahoe, would continue to explore every possible recourse on his client's behalf. Having failed to win a retrial, Dean's best hope now lay with the one man who was in a position to spare his client's life—President Abraham Lincoln.

# CHAPTER IX

# THE AWFUL CHANGE

President Abraham Lincoln had earned a reputation for the liberal use of the power to pardon. He was, to some, a man of compassion and mercy; to others, a sentimental meddler who was continually undermining military discipline and the sanctity of the courts.

Two men who felt that Lincoln had to be protected from his own kinder instincts were members of his own cabinet—Secretary of the Navy Gideon Welles and Attorney General Edward Bates. The president, Welles confided to his diary, "is always disposed to mitigate punishment, and to grant favors. Sometimes this is a weakness."[1] Edmund Stedman, Lincoln's pardon clerk, wrote, "My chief, Attorney General Bates, soon discovered that my most important duty was to keep all but the most deserving cases from coming before the kind Mr. Lincoln at all; since there was nothing harder for him to do than to put aside a prisoner's application and he could not resist it when it was urged by a pleading wife and a weeping child."[2]

Edward Bates himself defined Lincoln as an ideal man, with but one weakness: "I have sometimes told him . . . that he was unfit to be entrusted with the pardoning power because he was almost certain to be affected by a touching story."[3] Lincoln's correspondence secretary, William O. Stoddard, said that Lincoln was "downright sure to pardon any case" in which he saw "a fair excuse for pardoning. . . . Some people think he carries his mercy too far."[4] According to one historian, "Lincoln himself seemed to be aware of his susceptibility to yield to a woman's entreaty."[5]

It is hard to imagine the constant assault upon Lincoln's sensibilities by the petitions of desperate people. Take, for example, the letter of young Sally Petty:

"Mr President Lincoln

Dear Sir I take my pen with a broken heart to try to write you a few lines. I am all alone I cannot write for weeping I am a poor little helpless girl of 13 years O Mr Lincoln if I could only see you and tell you all about O Mr Lincoln they have sentenced my papa Mr F. Petty to be shot. O Mr Lincoln wont you pardon him. O Mr Lincoln my papa is not gilty [sic] of what they charge him that very night he stayed at home with me and mother. O how can I live and no papa to protect me, O Mr Lincoln read the life of Mr Napoleon and see where he pardoned a man for his little girl and O can you be harder hearted than he was.

O Mr Lincoln have you got no little girls and suppose you was in papa place and your little girl was to beg a man for mercy and he was to grant it. O would you not love him; O how papa would love you. O how can I stand it. O pardon, O pardon my papa Mr Lincoln, O if I could see you, I would kiss your feet

O Mr Lincoln have mercy—have mercy—O pardon my papa. O how can I live, O how can you refuse, O hear the petition of a poor distracted child pleading for the life of her papa.

O if I knowed how to ask you in the humblest way I would [be] a Servant for you for the pardon of my papa, O how can I live, O Mr Lincoln show this to your little girls and ask them, to plead with you for my papa O God how can I live. O Mr Lincoln I do not know what to say I have said all that I can say—if you let my papa be killed it will kill me and mother too.[6]

The touching letter goes on for several similar paragraphs. No record has survived as to the nature of Mr. F. Petty's offense, nor, sadly, of Lincoln's disposition of the matter.

There were three areas in which Lincoln's pardoning power pertained. The first of these related to cases in the civil courts—murder, treason, assault, mutiny, embezzlement, rape, violation of the Fugitive Slave Act, and the slave trade. According to the records of the State and Justice Departments, Lincoln reviewed approximately 456 civil cases, 375 of which received pardons. Four of these were slave-trade cases. Of the roughly 81 instances in which clemency was not shown, three related to the slave trade.[7]

The second category in which Lincoln had pardoning power was in military cases. It was here that Lincoln received the most criticism for what was perceived—not without some justification—as his interference in the flow of military justice and discipline. Lincoln did, in fact, have a tendency to pardon boys who had fallen asleep on guard duty or who had deserted. He usually sent them back to the ranks, either to serve out their terms or to fight until the war ended. His inclination toward mercy was certainly not lost on his generals. William T. Sherman made his frustration known in an 1864 letter to the judge advocate general, writing that he planned to "execute a good many spies and guerillas—without bothering the President. Too many spies and villains escape us . . . and we all know that it is very hard for the President to hang spies, even after conviction, when a troop of friends follow the sentence with earnest . . . appeals."[8]

General Joseph Hooker once sent an envelope to the president containing the cases of 55 convicted and doomed deserters; Lincoln merely wrote "Pardoned" on the envelope and returned it to Hooker.[9] One historian has written, "Lincoln probably did commute sentences and pardon offenders too freely for military discipline. . . . Sometimes . . . his contemporaries believed, with good cause, that less clemency would have been a policy of mercy in the long run." General Sherman commented that "forty or fifty executions now would in the next twelve months save a thousand lives."[10]

But Lincoln's approach to clemency for those in the ranks was neither whimsical nor haphazard. He was pragmatic—or, as one Lincoln scholar puts it, "discriminating."[11] He believed that the most serious offenders should be punished, and they often were; there were 267 men executed by the military during the war.[12] But he would not countenance taking life if no good would be served. He made it clear to General George Meade that he was "unwilling for any boy under eighteen to be shot."[13] As a rule, he disallowed shooting men for desertion: "Must I shoot a simple minded soldier boy who deserts, while I must not touch a hair of the wily agitator, who induces him to desert? I think that in such a case to silence the agitator, and save the boy, is not only constitutional but withal a great mercy."[14]

The third class of cases calling for Lincoln's mercy had to do with those in rebellion against the government. This being the Civil War, more than half the country fell in this category—including Southern soldiers and officers, Confederate government officials, and civilians. It also pertained to those Northerners, including the copperheads, who had foresworn their support of the war in order to pursue their own ideas of reconciliation with the South. Some of these cases proved downright embarrassing to the president.

While in command of the Union Army's Department of Ohio, General Ambrose Burnside took it upon himself in April 1863 to issue "General Order No. 38," stating that anyone "declaring sympathies for the enemy" would be liable to punishment by military court. It so happened that one of the most vocal opponents of the Lincoln administration, Ohio Democratic congressman Clement L. Vallandigham, chose that time to make a speech accusing the government of deliberately and needlessly prolonging the carnage. Burnside promptly arrested him, tried him by military tribunal, and sentenced him to prison.

Lincoln was mortified. He knew that by punishing Vallandigham, he would be creating a martyr, and encouraging further outbursts by thousands like him. Conversely, releasing the congressman would be perceived as a sign of weakness. Lincoln took a middle road, and an unusual one at that: he commuted Vallandigham's sentence from imprisonment to banishment, and deported him to the Confederacy! According to his brother's biography, Vallandigham sneaked back North in disguise the following year and immediately took up where he had left off, pillorying Lincoln and the war in speeches across Ohio. Despite the fact that the terms of Vallandigham's banishment stipulated a prison term should he return, Lincoln wisely chose to ignore him.[15]

Lincoln's attitude toward the South reflected the greatest expression of his mercy. He wanted nothing more than a return of the seceded states to their former place in the Union. Although he had given his approval, early in the war, to the laws passed by Congress for the stringent punishment of those convicted of treason, Lincoln was "ready at any time to grant a general amnesty with a remission of all penalties except the loss of property in slaves, if the measure would hasten the return of peace and the end of the Confederacy." Although this offer of amnesty and pardon did not extend to the South's leaders, he allowed that they might also petition for pardon, which he would grant "if it seemed prudent to do so." He did so on a number of occasions. And most significantly, he made his intended plan for reconstruction known long before the war ended, as an indication to all in rebellion that they could, in fact, go home again.[16]

None of this is to imply that Lincoln was always a soft touch. An old friend wrote that the president "would strain a point to be kind, but he never strained it to breaking. He would be just as kind and generous as his judgment would let him be—no more."[17] One historian provides a description of Lincoln which is both succinct and accurate. Lincoln's writings "do not give the impression of a folksy and jocular countryman swapping yarns at the village store or making his way to the White House by uncertain and awkward steps or presiding like a father, a tear in his eye, over the tragedy of the Civil War. . . . This is a Lincoln intent, self-controlled, strong in intellect, tenacious of purpose."[18]

Lincoln brought to each case his fine sense of justice, and he knew when to let the law take its course. He offered no pardon to bounty jumpers or recruiters for the Confederacy. He refused to show favoritism to officers over enlisted men and turned a deaf ear to the pleas of repeat deserters and of soldiers whose offenses smacked of meanness or brutality.[19] And he always looked to the consequences of his actions.

Not all of Lincoln's pardons were expressions of kindness and compassion. Being an astute politician, sometimes Lincoln granted clemency for the sake of expedience. In 1864, in order to help secure New York State in the upcoming presidential election, he pardoned a condemned contractor at the request of three prominent New York statesmen. In another instance, Lincoln, at the request of influential Massachusetts senator Charles Sumner, dismissed the proceedings against an obviously guilty group of Boston contractors who had defrauded the government in filling naval contracts.[20]

But one of the most dramatic cases in which Lincoln refused to intercede with the course of law was that of Confederate officer John Yates Beall. Beall was the embodiment of the Victorian concept of chivalry and courage, a Southern beau ideal—young, handsome, and selflessly dedicated to the Cause. Born to an old and distinguished Virginia family, Beall studied law at the University of Virginia. When his father died, he returned home to run the family farm, Walnut Grove. When war broke out, the twenty-six-year-old Beall enlisted in the famed Stonewall Brigade of the Second Virginia Regiment. He was one of Virginia's first volunteers.

Shortly thereafter, he was shot while leading a charge at the Battle of Falling Waters. During his convalescence in Richmond, he designed a scheme to release the more than 3,000 Confederate prisoners of war (all officers) from the dismal Union prison on Johnson's Island, Lake Erie. He took his plan to President Jefferson Davis and Secretary of the

Confederate Navy S. R. Mallory. Because an attack on Johnson's Island would have to be launched from Canada, Davis and Mallory were hesitant to approve the plan for fear of offending Great Britain. They did, however, encourage Beall to form a company of rangers, for the purpose of harassing Union shipping along the Chesapeake.

Beall organized his band of partisans and staged several raids along the Lower Potomac. Finally, Davis approved the Johnson's Island plan, and Beall crossed into Canada, joining a band of Southern raiders. On September 19, 1864, they seized two Lake Erie passenger steamers, from which they intended to board and capture the USS *Michigan,* a 14-gun warship that guarded the island. They would then turn the *Michigan*'s guns on the fort and liberate the prisoners. The plan went awry, however, and Beall escaped into Canada.

Less than three months later, Beall made his way to upstate New York, where he was captured in an attempt to derail a train carrying Confederate prisoners. He was taken to Fort Lafayette in New York Harbor, where he was tried by court-martial on charges of being a spy and "guerillero" (guerrilla). Five witnesses appeared for the prosecution, none for the defense. His attorney argued that Beall was not a spy, but an officer in the Southern navy; he presented a letter to that effect from Confederate President Jefferson Davis. The court refused to admit the letter and in short order found Beall guilty and sentenced him to be hanged on February 18. Through a friend, Beall sent the trial record to President Lincoln, with the attachment, "Some of the evidence is true, some false. I am not a spy or guerillero. The execution of the sentence will be murder."

Protests poured into Washington from both North and South. Patriotic Unionists, including numerous congressmen, begged Lincoln to grant clemency to Beall. General (and future president) James A. Garfield wrote the president, recommending "a temporary reprieve, at least." Beall's supporters retained Orville Browning, an old friend of Lincoln's, to act on the prisoner's behalf. Browning brought Lincoln a petition signed by six senators and 81 members of the House of Representatives seeking mercy for young Beall. They submitted, not unreasonably, that "Beall is a Captain regularly commissioned in the Rebel services, and that Jefferson Davis . . . publicly asserted that the several acts specified in the charges against said Beall were done under his authority and direction." Beall, they asserted, was merely following his president's orders as a loyal officer.

The list of supplicants who visited Lincoln included the librarian of Congress, the president of the Baltimore & Ohio Railroad, the governor of Massachusetts, former postmaster general Montgomery Blair, and Beall's sister. Confederate brigadier general Roger Pryor, freshly released from Fort Lafayette military prison, visited Lincoln to plead for Beall's life. After listening respectfully to all that Pryor said, Lincoln showed him a telegram from Union general John Dix, who had overseen Beall's trial and imprisonment, stating that the prisoner's execution was vital for the "security of the community." There had been a recent unsuccessful attempt by Confederate saboteurs to burn New York City, and Dix was convinced that Beall was involved, though there was no evidence to support this suspicion, nor was this the crime for which Beall stood accused and convicted.

On the morning of Beall's scheduled execution on Governors Island off New York City, the young prisoner received his mother and various friends and clergymen. He asked to have his picture taken; the photograph shows a handsome, serene-appearing young man with strong features and a neatly trimmed goatee, dressed more for a dance than an execution. Marshal Murray then entered Beall's cell in company with the executioner. Beall stood, saying that he was at their service, and commented, "It is only a question of muscular power; I think I can bear it." He was bound and escorted to the gallows. Looking at the sky, Beall said, "The sun shines brightly; I now see it for the last time." Marshal Murray asked Beall if he had anything to say, to which he replied, "I protest against the execution of this sentence. It is absolute murder— brutal murder. I die in the defense and service of my country."

Just before the cap was drawn over the young man's face, Murray again asked if he had any final words. Beall answered, "No. I beg you to make haste." The signal was given, and Captain Beall was hanged. "His fortitude and courageous bearing were commended even by his enemies."[21] Shortly after Beall's execution, the outraged editor of the *Richmond Enquirer* wrote, "True to their cowardly instincts, the Yankees carried out their mad purpose of hanging Captain Beall on last Friday. The Yankees, it will be recollected, trumped up the charge against him of being a 'spy and guerilla,' but the truth is, he was merely a prisoner of war."

The president was deeply affected by Beall's execution. The day the young officer was hanged, Lincoln sank into a depression, and his sadness lingered for some time. A full month after the event, when his friend Illinois lawyer and Republican congressman Henry Bromwell visited the White House, Lincoln complained of the constant pressure to pardon or reprieve men. He spoke of the unending line of petitioners:

> It seems to me they will wear the very life out of me; but then all these other matters are nothing to these cases of life and death—and there are so many of them, and they all fall on me. I reckon there never was a man raised in the country, on a farm, where they are always butchering cattle and hogs and think nothing of it, that ever grew up with such an aversion to bloodshed as I have and yet I've had more questions of life and death to settle in four years than all the men who ever sat in this chair put together. But, I've managed to get along and do my duty, as I believe, and still save most of them, and there's no man knows the distress of my mind. But there must have been some of them I couldn't save—there are some cases where the law must be executed . . . there was this case of Beall on the lakes. That was a case where there must be an example. They tried me every way. They wouldn't give up; but I had to stand firm on that, and I even had to turn away his poor sister when she came and begged for his life, and let him be executed, and he was executed, and I can't get the distress out of my mind yet.[22]

The Lincoln that is seen here is a man who is empathetic and kind, but also "self-controlled" and "tenacious of purpose." He is the leader of a powerful war-torn nation, keenly aware that his decisions—great and small—inevitably have to reflect that nation's greater good. And so it would in the case of Nathaniel Gordon.

In late January 1862, Gordon's attorney became one of Lincoln's petitioners; he traveled to the nation's capital to appeal to the only man who could spare his client. The *New York Times* tells of Dean's first visit to the White House:

> Gordon's able and pertinacious counsel, Judge Gilbert Dean, went immediately to Washington, and urged the President to pardon him, or change his punishment to that of imprisonment for life. The Judge laid before Mr. Lincoln all the evidence in favor of his client, as the District-Attorney had previously done all that was against him; and the President, according to the statements of both of these learned gentlemen, gave the subject his earnest and careful attention. At length he decided that he

could not find it to be his duty to interfere. He admitted that it was hard for a man to lose his life for violating the law, which had been a dead letter for forty years, but did not see that that fact would warrant him in overruling the courts, or setting aside a law in Congress.[23]

Meanwhile, petitions containing thousands of names found their way to Lincoln's desk, pleading for clemency. Two arrived from Portland, Maine, Gordon's home city, listing a combined total of 18,000 names: "While we condemn the crimes for which he stands convicted," one of the petitions begins, "as we do all other crimes of a heinous character, we cannot forbear craving from you Executive clemency. We do not presume to ask for an unconditional pardon, but we do humbly pray that Captain Gordon's sentence may be commuted to imprisonment, even though your Excellency should make it during his life— and we do this in behalf of a young and devoted Wife and infant Son, for a most excellent and highly respectable Mother, for fond Sisters, and an extensive circle of the most respectable connections."

The second group of Portland petitioners, also acknowledging the "justice of the proceedings," accounted themselves "deeply moved by a painful sympathy for the aged and venerated mother of the convict, for his wife and only child, and for his other near relatives . . ." Writing several years after the execution, Marshal Murray was correct in stating, "Many who considered that Gordon fully deserved his impending fate could not help but sympathize with his unfortunate wife and child."[24]

At one point, Lincoln received a letter from the famed and respected pastor of Portland's High Street Congregational Church, the Reverend John W. Chickering, who had known Gordon all his life and had been his parents' pastor. Nathaniel, he wrote, "was once a boy in my Sunday School, I cannot do less than present his broken hearted mother before you as one among the many aspects of this dreadful case. He is the only son of his mother & she a widow, respectable & estimable. Her distress can be (partly) imagined." He urges Lincoln to let the mother's plight "have its due weight in deciding the question between justice and mercy."[25] Presumably, had Nathaniel Gordon been an orphan and a bachelor, he would have elicited little sympathy indeed.

As the *Times* article indicates, E. Delafield Smith had arrived in Washington ahead of Gilbert Dean. Fearing that public pressure might tempt the president to spare Gordon's life, Smith had hurried to the

White House four days ahead of Dean to implore Lincoln to refrain from interfering. Ethan Allen, one of Smith's assistant U.S. attorneys, described the prosecutor's meeting with the president:

> When he met Mr. Lincoln, as he afterward reported to me on his return, Mr. Lincoln took out from his desk the reprieve already prepared and laid it before him. He picked up a pen, which he held in his hand while he listened to the argument of Mr. Smith on the imperative necessity of making an example of this man Gordon, in order forever to terrorize those who were engaged in this business.
>
> Mr. Lincoln listened to him very patiently and with a sort of wail of despair (as it was afterward described), flourishing the pen over the reprieve he said: "Mr. Smith, you do not know how hard it is to have a human being die when you know that a stroke of your pen may save him." He threw down the pen, however, and Gordon was executed in New York.[26]

Smith need not have worried about Lincoln's resolve. Ethan Allen's little tale of Smith showing the proper course to a wailing and wavering Lincoln makes for a good story. After all, what better light in which to show oneself than as the man who kept the president from weakening in so crucial a case? But it has more than a touch of the apocryphal about it, and it fails to address one vital fact: Lincoln, from the beginning, had no intention of sparing Nathaniel Gordon's life.

Despite the president's assurance that the sentence would stand, Delafield Smith was still concerned that Lincoln would waver. He took it upon himself to write a letter to a "prominent official" in Washington, most probably his boss, Secretary of the Interior Caleb B. Smith, urging his support. The letter appeared, certainly not by accident, in the *New York Times*. The prosecutor clearly fears the possibility that his hard-won victory would slip away; the tone of his letter has a hint of desperation.

> Sir—I felt it my duty to say to you that public opinion here is manifest, earnest and almost unanimous against any commutation of the sentence of the court in the flagrant case of Gordon. It is widely felt that his execution will strike a blow at the Slave-trade, such as it has never received. It would stamp it, in the minds of sea-faring men, as infamous and degrading. Imprisonment, though for life, bears no such stigma in their minds.

Smith was concerned that anything short of execution would be seen as a victory for New York's slave traders, who "have hung their heads under the imminence of our proceedings in this case." Mere imprisonment would not only prove them right in the prediction that no man would ever hang for slaving, it would give them reason to expect "that a pardon will come in future."

> Cruel, unscrupulous and sordid, Gordon is now convicted for the fourth offence. The sentence pronounced upon him by Judge Shipman, with the commentaries in your report and in the President's message, ought not to be read by mankind in the light of a subsequent commutation of a just, wise and necessary punishment. I bear Gordon no ill-will; but I trust that this revolting, sickening traffic may not grow bold again under a relaxing attitude of the Government.

Smith warns the president against listening to men who, though seeking executive clemency, were "paid to intercede for interference, or are professionally employed for that purpose." He refutes Dean's claim that nearly all the jury would speak for mercy: "Eight of the Jury yesterday declared to me that Gordon should be executed, and they say that but one of the Jury would now sign any petition." (In fact, two days after sentence was passed on Gordon, the *Tribune* published an article stating that "eleven of the jurors had desired to add to the verdict a recommendation of mercy and an appeal to Executive clemency."[27] A later edition of the *Post* refuted this claim: "It has been asserted that all the jurors on the trial of Captain Gordon united in the petition to commute his sentence. This is a mistake; at least eight of the jurors refuse positively to join in any effort to commute the sentence."[28])

Smith continued,

> It is said that the Government has heretofore not performed its duty.
>
> There are two answers to this. First, the crime is intrinsically so cruel and atrocious, that none but a heartless and depraved man could commit it after once (much less three times) witnessing and participating in its horrors. The poor savages begin to die before all are on board the ship. Terror, suffocation, sores and anguish unutterable plead in vain. The slave captain knows nothing of pity. But, secondly, how can we execute in other cases if we do not in this? I believe I shall procure the conviction

of Haines, mate of the slaver *Nightingale,* whose brutality and cruelty are dreadful to contemplate.

I know that the President and his advisors are wiser than I am, and perhaps I ought to do no more than inform him of the means taken here to obtain applications for clemency.

I write unofficially, but leave my letter to any use (if any) to which you may think proper to put it.[29]

Smith had clearly exceeded his authority; it was presumptuous of him to admonish Lincoln in his duties, especially in a public letter. One unanticipated result was a verbal duel with another attorney. John McKeon, former U.S. attorney, staunch Democrat, and current legal counsel for Samuel Haines, first mate of the slaver *Nightingale,* was furious. The *Times* gave him equal play, and he responded with a missive dripping with sarcasm and condescension:

During several years of service as Public Prosecutor of the State of New York, and of the United States, for this District, I have no recollection of ever interfering with applications for pardon or commutation of punishment in cases involving severe punishment, much less the life of a convict, except when requested by the Executive to whom, by the Constitution of the State or of the United States, the power of pardoning was intrusted [sic]. I considered my duty closed when the trial . . . was concluded. The duty of the District Attorney in executing the severe exaction of the law having been discharged, it was not, in my opinion, proper for him to intrude his judgment upon the officer who had the exclusive authority to temper justice with mercy, unless the opinion of the District Attorney was required by such authority.

It appears your course of proceeding differs from mine. In your *unofficial* letter (which is stated in the *Times* of this morning to have been addressed to a prominent *official* at the National capital) you have given your opinion in the exigency of the execution of Gordon, convicted of having been engaged in the Slave-trade. The letter appears not to have been in answer to any request of the Executive of the United States, but the unsolicited expression of your earnest desire, unofficially given, that Gordon should be hung in obedience not only to the sentence of the law, but also the requirements of public opinion. Against this declaration, as an individual, I have no right to complain. I am not counsel for Gordon, but I am for Haines, who is under indictment for being engaged

in the Slave-trade, and of which charge he declares his innocence. I have
a right to complain that you have unnecessarily dragged into your letter
in the paragraph in which, after speaking of the absolute necessity of executing Gordon, you state: "But, secondly, how can we execute on other
cases if we do not in this? I believe I shall procure the conviction of
Haines, mate of the slaver *Nightingale,* whose brutality and cruelty are
dreadful to contemplate."

This unfortunate man, Haines, is to be tried for his life. Is it just, is it
fair that you should prejudice *his* case in the opinion of the community,
from which the jurors to try him must be selected? What *evidence* has
been presented in Court in his case as yet, on which you have reason to
believe that his "brutality and cruelty are dreadful to contemplate"? This
man's life is as much in your hands as mine, and you, as public prosecutor, have no right to poison the public mind against him. . . .

The jury who will hear the evidence on both sides must determine
this question, not the District-Attorney. . . . You must not blame me for
protesting against publications which are not only, in my judgment, not
called for by official position, but are . . . well calculated to endanger the
life of my client. You cannot blame me for interposing my shield and
protecting my client from such assaults.[30]


As a veteran prosecutor, John McKeon was far more familiar with the
workings and parameters of the office of the U.S. attorney than was
Delafield Smith, a relative neophyte with less than a year's experience.
Strictly speaking, McKeon was correct on a number of points. First,
popular opinion was not the selling point upon which Smith should
have based an appeal to Lincoln. Further, it was neither professional
nor ethical of the U.S. attorney, once a verdict had been delivered and
sentence passed, to lobby against clemency. Smith was clearly not responding to a request from Lincoln for his opinion; he was attempting,
unsolicited, to influence the president, both in print and in person.
McKeon was also within his rights to object to Smith's comments about
Haines; it was inappropriate for the prosecutor to publicly taint the case
of a man who had not yet had his day in court.[31]

McKeon, on the other hand, had never won a death sentence against
any of the slavers whom he tried as U.S. attorney (though of all of
Smith's predecessors, he had come closest. Back in 1854, it was Mc-
Keon who had prosecuted Captain James Smith, only to have his conviction thrown out by Justice Nelson). Newcomer Delafield Smith had

won a capital conviction, and it was a landmark case of stunning proportions. Smith was justifiably concerned for its outcome.[32]

The pressure to spare the slaver increased as the time set for his execution drew nearer. James Gordon Bennett's *New York Herald* pled for clemency: "It must be admitted that the punishment of death is too severe a penalty to attach to what is, in this point of view, the mere violation of a commercial law; and it is very doubtful whether a more mitigated penalty . . . would not be more efficacious in putting a stop to the trade."[33]

By January, the *Times* reported, "a strong and well-concerted effort is making to procure from President Lincoln a pardon for Gordon, the convicted slave-trader. The movement is headed by the Hon. George Evans, at one time a United States Senator from Maine. . . . We are . . . to believe that the appeal is exclusively to mercy, founded doubtless upon the youth of the condemned, the grief of his family and friends, the gravity of his punishment. To such appeals the President cannot be insensible."[34]

Lincoln was constantly receiving communications from men of high regard, seeking mercy for Gordon. On January 27, 1862, Edward P. Cowles, a former justice of the U.S. Supreme Court, wrote Lincoln a typical letter.

Sir:

It is not without misgivings, nor until after much reflection, that I join with the Hon. George Evans and others in asking for a commutation of the sentence of Captain Gordon, lately convicted in this district of engaging in the African slave trade. It is unnecessary to say that I abhor the crime for which he is convicted. I feel, with all correct thinking men, that this traffic should be annihilated by the strong arm of the government. It is not to be overlooked, however, that for some years past the efforts of the government to break up this traffic and punish those engaged in it have not been characterized by much apparent earnestness or rigor. It is scarcely two years since it was stated here by the public press that the then prosecuting officer of the government [Roosevelt] had openly avowed in court his reluctance to press prosecutions against those charged with this crime, saying that the changed public sentiment of the world rendered convictions almost impossible. Unfortunately, there was at that time much apparent truth in the alleged observation. Government then seemed to be regarding this crime with diminished abhorrence. So at last those engaged in the traffic evidently thought, and such too was the painful belief of many good men. . . . Now, however, there exists a more concentrated sentiment upon the subject of this traffic.

Government and its officers and the courts are acting with stern vigor in the enforcement of existing penal laws on this subject. Probably we shall soon have even more stringent ones to aid them in their efforts.

Had this man's crime been committed after he had been warned by this renewed and vigorous action of the government and its officers of this newly awakened determination to break up this trade and punish with the full rigor of the law those engaged in it, I would not now join in asking for an interposition of Executive clemency in his behalf. But in view of all the foregoing observations—If a commutation can in this case be granted, yet with a full understanding that it will not be drawn in precedent, but that henceforward this crime shall be met with the full measure of punishment denounced against it by law—I am of opinion that it would be both merciful and wise to commute the sentence of Captain Gordon.[35]

On February 3, 1862—just four days prior to Gordon's scheduled execution—Secretary of State William Seward sent Lincoln a note, asking him to see "Lieut. Colonel Joachimssen [sic] . . . a good and loyal citizen of New York who desires an opportunity of speaking with you in regard to the case of Nathaniel Gordon."[36] The officer was none other than Philip J. Joachimsen, Gordon's former counsel, who now commanded the 59th New York Regiment of Volunteers and would soon be brevetted a brigadier general. Presumably, he was hoping that his new status as a military officer would carry some weight with the president. He was mistaken.

Equal pressure was put upon Lincoln by those who supported Smith's opinion and advocated hanging Gordon. Senator Charles Sumner of Massachusetts visited the White House on February 1, and later wrote his friend, the famed Catholic scholar and essayist Orestes A. Brownson, "Yesterday I told the Prest. that though I am against capital punishment, I am yet for hanging that slave-trader condemned in New York. It must be done (1) to deter slave-traders, (2) to give notice to the world of a change of policy & (3) to shew that the Govt. can hang a man."[37]

Ralph Waldo Emerson, at that time America's preeminent literary scholar, traveled to Washington in late January for the express purpose of encouraging Lincoln to stand firm. He reported that Lincoln "was not quite satisfied yet and meant to refresh his memory by looking again at the evidence."[38]

On January 31, Emerson attended an exclusive meeting with Secretary of State William Seward, Senator Charles Sumner, Governor John A. Andrew of Massachusetts, and wealthy Boston philanthropist, abolitionist, and counsel to the president, John Murray Forbes. Emerson wrote in his journal that, as they sat in Seward's "dingy State Department," breathing the fumes of the secretary's half-smoked cigar, Forbes commented that "he saw there was an effort making to get Gordon the slave-trader pardoned. He hoped the Government would show to foreign nations that there was a change and a new spirit in it, which would not deal with this crime heretofore. Seward looked very cross and ugly at this; twisted his cigar about, and I thought, twisted his nose also, and said coarsely, 'Well, perhaps you would be willing to stand in his place,' or something like that, and rather surprised and disconcerted Mr. Forbes."[39]

Forbes wrote a letter to Lincoln, which he had published in the *New York Post,* urging Gordon's execution in the strongest possible words: "Is he, like the rattlesnake in camp . . . to be released? The great want of the hour is to see one spy . . . hanged. . . . But if this one wish of the nation can not be gratified, can we not at least hang one of the pirates who have sacrificed such hecatombs of Africa?"[40]

The considerable space that the Gordon case occupied in the newspapers grew as the scheduled day of his hanging drew near. One of the most comprehensive articles was published in the *New York Times* on January 28. It detailed the various efforts afoot to reprieve Gordon, and dramatically addressed the reasons why his death was necessary:

> The Government of the United States, in common with certain European Governments, has, for forty years, spent uncounted millions for the suppression of the African slave-trade. It has maintained a squadron for a long period upon the African coast for no other purpose. To this object it has sacrificed the lives of numberless valued officers and men, who have either died on the station from the malarious influences of the climate, or have brought away the seeds of disease to shorten their lives at home.

All this costly vigilance, attended with some success in capturing and condemning as prizes vessels caught in the fact, has had no effect in curtailing the traffic. It has rather flourished more rankly. And this for the reason that while slave-trading is declared to be piracy, the slave-trader has never been regarded as a pirate. If he has been tried as such, his own craft, or that of counsel, or the leniency of a jury in refusing to inflict punishment for a crime in connection with which none of their number had a direct personal concern or apprehension; or the interposition of ill-judged clemency on the part of the Executive, having saved the culprit from the penalty of his offense. The kidnapper has found captains, mates and seamen to navigate his vessel, though at heavy price, because captains, mates and seamen have been sure, that while their wages would be double, their risk would be no greater than upon a round voyage to Liverpool and back.

The time has long gone when this idea of impunity should have been corrected. What it has cost in dollars to this Government; what it has cost in suffering to the hapless African, we cannot calculate. But now, when we are engaged in a life and death struggle with an enemy whose design is to revive the Slave-trade with all its horrors, as soon as his independence shall have been securely achieved, it is more than high time to assure mankind, that we do in all honesty regard man-stealing as a crime of the utmost atrocity, and to demonstrate our purpose to vindicate it as such upon all who are proved guilty. The victim in the present circumstance is young, and more is the pity; but also more is the necessity of his punishment. It is to the young, the daring, the unreflecting, the temptation of the slave-trading capitalist is offered  Without the help of that class, their commerce would cease. It is the young and the unthinking who need a warning, a warning so tragic and memorable that not all the thirst for gold which may prompt them to embark in this inhuman business can overcome the horror of the example. Gordon has deliberately placed himself where he may legally be presented as such an example. Every consideration of justice, of true clemency (which has regard to the innocent many rather than to the guilty individual) and of public policy, demand the execution of the sentence of the law upon this most unhappy criminal; and we doubt not the President will so answer the prayer of these petitioners.[41]

The article exaggerates both the government's expenditures for the eradication of the slave trade and the primary goals and success of the

African Squadron. Still, it is an eloquent, brilliantly stated endorsement of Gordon's sentence.

The *Post* took a more diplomatic approach in advising against commutation: "What is needed to put an end to the slave-trade is to establish a precedent for administering faithfully the punishment provided by act of Congress for the crime. We hope the President's good nature will not overcome his duty as guardian of the laws." (It is interesting to note that Lincoln's reputation for clemency was so widespread, yet he had only been in office less than one year.)

A newspaper editorial from Gordon's home state of Maine took a similar tone:

> It is said that this unhappy wretch has hosts of friends who are . . . turning heaven and earth, to effect his pardon. Whether the President will bow before the blast which is being raised in his behalf, time will tell. Upon his determination . . . hang vast results. Our own opinion is, that if capital punishment is justifiable in any case, it is in the case of the slave trader, and if Gordon expiates his . . . offense against heaven and humanity upon the gallows, no one save his guilty companions and sympathizers will complain.[42]

Lincoln had viewed the evidence, considered the prospect of allowing Gordon his life, and rejected it. As he would tell Illinois congressman Henry Bromwell in late March 1865, "There was that man [Gordon] who was sentenced for piracy and slave-trading on the high seas. That was a case where there must be an example and you don't know how they followed and pressed to get him pardoned, or his sentence commuted; but there was no use of talking. It had to be done; I couldn't help him."[43]

On February 4, 1862, Lincoln wrote, "I think I would personally prefer to let this man live in confinement and let him meditate on his deeds, yet in the name of justice and the majesty of law, there ought to be one case, at least one specific instance, of a professional slave-trader, a Northern white man, given the exact penalty of death because of the incalculable number of deaths he and his kind inflicted upon black men amid the horror of the sea-voyage from Africa."[44]

Lincoln had always considered the North as culpable as the South for the growth of slavery in America: "When southern people tell us they are no more responsible for the origin of slavery, than we; I acknowledge the fact."[45]

To truly understand Lincoln's public policies and personal beliefs, we must, at least temporarily, take our lead from the thinking of the time, and distinguish between the slave trade and slavery as an institution. Admittedly, it is at best an artificial distinction, but one that will help in understanding the man's actions.

When he was first elected, Lincoln walked a careful line regarding the issue of slavery. He clearly disapproved of it, and his opposition to its expansion into the Territories had not only been part of his campaign platform in 1860, but his personal and political philosophy for many years before. In Peoria on October 16, 1854, he debated Illinois senator Stephen A. Douglas, seasoned Democratic campaigner and renowned orator. This was by no means his first face-off against Douglas, but it was the debate that showcased his views on both slavery and the slave trade. The argument that Lincoln used would remain the same all the way to the White House.

The speech was masterful. Douglas had earlier sponsored a bill espousing a program of "popular sovereignty," advocating free choice on the issue of slavery in the Territories of Kansas and Nebraska. The bill passed, and as the Kansas-Nebraska Act, it was signed into law by President Franklin Pierce. As one historian put it, now "the expansion of slavery was not simply an issue; it was a fact."[46] As Lincoln saw it, Douglas—and Congress at large—had broken faith with the Founding Fathers and the Constitution regarding the spread of slavery. Douglas had asserted that it was the "sacred right" of the citizenry to decide whether to bring slaves into the Territory of Nebraska.

Lincoln responded with finely honed sarcasm:

If it is a sacred right for the people of Nebraska to take and hold slaves there, it is equally their sacred right to buy them where they can buy them cheapest; and that undoubtedly will be on the coast of Africa; provided you will consent not to hang them for going there to buy them. . . . I am aware you say that taking slaves from the States to Nebraska, does not make slaves of freemen; but the African slave-trader can say just as much. He does not catch free negroes and bring them here. He finds them already in the hands of their black captors, and he honestly buys them at the rate of about a red cotton handkerchief a head. This is very cheap, and it is a great abridgement of the sacred right of self-government to hang men for engaging in this profitable trade![47]

Lincoln carefully laid out for his audience the intentions of the framers of the Constitution, and their subsequent actions for the eradication of the slave trade.

At the framing and adoption of the constitution they forbore to so much as mention the word "slave" or "slavery" in the whole instrument. . . . In that prohibiting the abolition of the African slave trade for twenty years . . . the thing is hid away, in the constitution, just as an afflicted man hides away a wen or a cancer, which he dares not cut out at once, lest he bleed to death; with the promise, nevertheless, that the cutting may begin at the end of a given time. Less than this our fathers COULD not do; and more they WOULD not do. . . . But this is not all. The earliest Congress, under the constitution, took the same view of slavery. They hedged and hemmed it in to the narrowest limits of necessity.

In 1794, they prohibited an outgoing slave-trade—that is, the taking of slaves from the United States to sell.

In 1798, they prohibited the bringing of slaves from Africa, into the Mississippi territory. . . .

In 1800, they prohibited AMERICAN CITIZENS from trading in slaves between foreign countries—as, for instance, from Africa to Brazil.

In 1803, they passed a law in aid of one or two State laws, in restraint of the internal slave trade.

In 1807, in apparent hot haste, they passed the law . . . —the very first day the constitution would permit—prohibiting the African slave trade by heavy pecuniary and corporal penalties.

In 1820, finding these provisions ineffectual, they declared the trade piracy, and annexed to it, the extreme penalty of death. While all this was passing in the general government, five or six of the original slave States had adopted systems of gradual emancipation; and by which the institution was rapidly becoming extinct within these limits.

Thus we see, the plain unmistakable spirit of that age, towards slavery, was hostility to the PRINCIPLE, and toleration only by NECESSITY.

But now it is to be transformed by "sacred right." . . . Near eighty years ago we began by declaring that all men are equal; but now from that beginning we have run down to the other declaration, that for SOME men to enslave OTHERS is a "sacred right of self-government." These principles cannot stand together. They are as opposite as God and mammon; and whoever holds to the one, must despise the other.[48]

Over and over, in speech after speech, Lincoln hammered home his message that the Founding Fathers had it as their high objective to end the institution of slavery through the eradication of the slave trade: "Why did those old men . . . decree that slavery should not go into the new Territory? Why declare that within twenty years the African Slave Trade . . . might be cut off by Congress? . . . What were [all these acts] but a clear indication that the framers of the Constitution intended and expected the ultimate extinction of that institution."[49]

Lincoln was convinced, and he voiced it repeatedly, that Douglas's plan for the expansion of slavery into the Territories would not only foil the plans of the country's founders, it would cause a resurgence of the slave trade. "I now put this proposition that Judge Douglas' popular sovereignty applied will re-open the African slave trade, and I will demonstrate it by any variety of ways in which you can turn the subject or look at it."[50]

Lincoln was clear on his personal feelings toward slavery: "I have always hated slavery, I think as much as any Abolitionist."[51] But he made no secret of his position on the legality of slavery where it already existed, the Fugitive Slave Act, and African Americans as a race. He stated in July 1858, "I have said it a hundred times, and I have now no inclination to take it back, that I believe there is no right, and ought to be no inclination in the people of the free States to enter into the slave States, and interfere with the question of slavery at all. I have said that always. . . . When it is said that I am in favor of interfering with slavery where it exists, I know it is unwarranted by anything I have ever *intended* and, as I believe, by anything I have ever *said.*"[52]

Regarding emancipation, Lincoln stated, "Shall we free them and make them politically and socially our equals? MY OWN FEELINGS WILL NOT ADMIT OF THIS, and if they would[,] the feelings of the great mass of white people would not. . . . A universal feeling, whether well or ill-founded, cannot safely be disregarded. We cannot make them our equals."[53] And these views extended to the placement of African Americans in government: "Senator Douglas remarked, in substance, that he had always considered this government, was made for the white people and not for the negroes. Why, in mere point of fact, I think so too."[54]

For Lincoln, however, this did not justify their enslavement. Continually, Lincoln put forth the question, in one form or another, "whether the negro is *not* or *is* a man: If the negro is *not* a man, why in that case, he who *is* a man may, as a matter of self-government, do just as he pleases with him. . . . If the negro is a *man,* why then my ancient faith teaches me that 'all men are created equal'; and that there can be no moral right in connection with one man's making a slave of another. . . . Nothing stamped with the Divine image and likeness was sent into the world to be trodden on, and degraded, and imbruted by his fellows." [55,56]

Douglas published a list of questions in the Chicago *Times* in an attempt to embarrass his opponent—but Lincoln forthrightly answered each one at the 1858 Freeport debate:

On the repeal of the Fugitive Slave Act: "I do not now, nor ever did, stand in favor of the unconditional repeal of the fugitive slave law."

On the admission of more slave states to the Union: "I do not now, nor ever did, stand pledged against the admission of any more slave States into the Union."

On the abolition of slavery in the District of Columbia: "I do not stand to-day pledged to the abolition of slavery in the District of Columbia."

On the prohibition of the slave trade between states: "I do not stand pledged to the prohibition of the slave trade between the different States."

Lincoln elaborates, saying that he has always felt the South to be "entitled to a Congressional Fugitive Slave Law," and that he "would not be the man to introduce it as a new subject of agitation upon the general question of slavery." He goes on to explain that although he is not formally *pledged* to these various issues, he nonetheless has specific feelings about them. He "should be exceedingly glad to know that there would never be another slave State admitted into the Union." He would also be "exceedingly glad to see slavery abolished in the District of Columbia." As to the question of the "abolition of the Slave trade between the different States," Lincoln equivocates, saying that "it is a subject to which I have not given mature consideration." [57] This is hard to believe.

Shortly after his election to the presidency, Lincoln wrote a "private and confidential" letter to his new secretary of state, William Seward. In it, he states,

As I have all the while said, on the territorial question—that is, the question of extending slavery under the national auspices—I am inflexible. I am for no compromise which *assists* or *permits* the institution [of slavery] on soil owned by the nation. And any trick by which the nation is to acquire territory, and then allow some local authority to spread slavery over it, is as obnoxious as any other. . . . I am against it.

But then he goes on to say,

As to fugitive slaves, [slavery in the] District of Columbia, slave trade among the slave states, and whatever springs of necessity from the fact that the institution is amongst us, I care but little, so that what is done be comely, and not altogether outrageous.[58]

How, then, do we reconcile the apparent dichotomy between the Lincoln who considers slavery a consummate evil, and fights unceasingly to keep it out of the Territories, with the man who voices, time and again, his support for the Fugitive Slave Act, his unwillingness to consider wholesale emancipation as a viable option, and his refusal to interfere either with slavery as it exists in the South or the slave trade between the Southern states? Lincoln himself provides the answer:

We must not disturb slavery in the states where it exists, because the constitution, and the peace of the country, both forbid us. We must not withhold an efficient fugitive slave law, because the constitution demands it.

We want, and must have, a national policy, as to slavery, which deals with it as being wrong. . . . [W]e must, by a national policy, prevent the spread of slavery into new territories, or free states, because the constitution does not forbid us, and the general welfare does demand such prevention. We must prevent the revival of the African slave trade, because the constitution does not forbid us, and the general welfare does require the prevention. . . . The people—the people—are the rightful masters of both congresses, and courts—not to overthrow the constitution, but to overthrow the *men* who pervert it.[59]

Herein lies the key. As far as Lincoln was concerned, nothing outside the Constitution had a claim to national or governmental legitimacy. It was his rock and his foundation, and he was fully prepared to put aside

his personal feelings on specific issues—strong though they might be—
in deference to it. Lincoln would have all change for the "general welfare" made in accordance with the Constitution. What in him might
have appeared to be ambivalence, or wavering, or weakness, what in
his views might have seemed contradictory, were in reality reflections
of a lifelong commitment to the strength and workings of this extraordinary document.

If slavery was to end, it must be through the force of law. Lincoln
was the foremost member of the new Republican Party, and "Republicans . . . think slavery is wrong; and . . . like every other wrong which
some men will commit if left alone, it ought to be prohibited by law.
They consider it not only morally wrong, but a 'deadly poison' in a government like ours, professedly based on the equality of men."[60]

When he became president, national and political considerations
kept him from immediately considering "a national policy . . . which
deals with [slavery] as being wrong." For one thing, he knew that the
goodwill and loyalty of the border states men, many of whom were
slave-owners, were crucial to winning the war. When General Frémont
issued his ill-conceived proclamation of emancipation, numerous soldiers in the border companies threw down their rifles in clear refusal to
fight for the Black man. And this Lincoln could not afford. There were
many loyal men in the North as well—strong Unionists—who had no
interest in supporting a war to free slaves.

But Lincoln knew that eventually the issue of emancipation had to
be addressed. He was fond of saying in his speeches, "A house divided
against itself cannot stand. I believe this government cannot endure
permanently half Slave and half Free."[61] (On one occasion, Stephen
Douglas "made great complaint" about the remark, at which point Lincoln acknowledged that he had not coined the phrase, but merely bor-
rowed it from Roger Pryor—a Southerner, a Confederate general, and
the editor of the *Richmond Enquirer!*)[62]

Emancipation would come; Lincoln recognized its inevitability. But
groundwork would have to be painstakingly laid, and steps gradually,
slowly, and diplomatically taken.

Lincoln had no such ambivalence regarding the slave trade; he hated
it. And more to the point, the law forbade it. In his Peoria speech, he
suggested that Southerners, in kinship with the North, saw slavery as a
great wrong, and the slave trader as an arch villain:

The great majority, south as well as north, have human sympathies, of which they can no more divest themselves than they can of their sensibility to physical pain. These sympathies in the bosoms of the southern people, manifest in many ways, their sense of the wrong of slavery, and their consciousness that, after all, there is humanity in the negro. If they deny this, let me address them a few plain questions. In 1820 you joined the north, almost unanimously, in declaring the African slave trade piracy, and in annexing to it the punishment of death. Why did you do this? If you did not feel that it was wrong, why did you join in providing that men should be hung for it? The practice was no more than bringing wild negroes from Africa, to sell to such as would buy them. But you never thought of hanging men for catching and selling wild horses, wild buffaloes or wild boars.

. . .

You have amongst you, a sneaking individual, of the class of native tyrants, known as the "SLAVE-DEALER." He watches your necessities, and crawls up to buy your slave, at a speculating price. If you cannot help it, you sell to him; but if you can help it, you drive him from your door. You despise him utterly. You do not recognize him as a friend, or even as an honest man. Your children must not play with his; they may rollick freely with the little negroes, but not with the "slave-dealers" children. If you are obliged to deal with him, you try to get through the job without so much as touching him. It is common with you to join hands with the men you meet; but with the slave dealer you avoid the ceremony—instinctively shrinking from the snaky contact. If he grows rich and retires from business, you still remember him, and still keep up the ban of non-intercourse upon him and his family. Now why is this? You do not so treat a man who deals in corn, cattle or tobacco.

And yet again; there are in the United States and territories, including the District of Columbia, 433,643 free blacks. At $500 per head they are worth over two hundred millions of dollars. How comes this vast amount of property to be running about without owners? We do not see free horses or free cattle running at large. How is this? All these free blacks are descendants of slaves, or have been slaves themselves, and they would be slaves now, but for SOMETHING which has operated on their white owners, inducing them, at vast pecuniary sacrifices, to liberate them. What is that SOMETHING? Is there any mistaking it? In all these cases it is your sense of justice, and human sympathy, continually telling you, that the poor negro has some natural right to himself—that those who deny it, and make mere merchandise of him, deserve kickings, contempt and death.[63]

Kickings, contempt, and death for the slave trader. . . . Whatever his feelings on equality, or the Fugitive Slave Act, or abolition, there was no mistaking how he perceived the slaver. If slavery was, in Lincoln's words, a "moral, social and political evil," then the slave trader was the soulless tool of its existence.[64]

On one of the numerous occasions when Lincoln was asked to consider mercy for Nathaniel Gordon, his response reflected this view:

I believe I am kindly enough in nature and can be moved to pity and to pardon the perpetrator of almost the worst crime that the mind of man can conceive or the arm of man can execute; but any man, who, for paltry gain and stimulated only by avarice, can rob Africa of her children to sell them into interminable bondage, I never will pardon.[65]

The law was unwavering in its language on the eradication of the slave trade, and it was absolutely essential that the new administration make its position clear. Lincoln was very specific in that regard: "The slave trade will never be put down till all our laws are executed, and the penalty of death has once been enforced upon the offenders."[66] All that was required was the right set of circumstances for an example. Nathaniel Gordon provided it.

Putting an end to the slave trade wasn't Lincoln's only reason for denying Gordon clemency. Gordon would die because at bottom, the sentence was just and appropriate. His was not the case of a sixteen-year-old boy falling asleep on picket duty, or a frightened soldier running from the terrors of battle. There was nothing in Gordon's offense or personal history, with the exception of his family, to call forth the compassion for which Lincoln was known. Sparing Gordon would do nothing to further the Union cause; on the contrary, while there were thousands upon thousands of young men dying in the field, it would be highly inappropriate to grant clemency to a man whose crimes had contributed, in a small but undeniable way, to the war that was claiming so many lives.

Still, many who advocated death for Gordon feared that ultimately

Lincoln would give in to his compassionate nature. They need not have been concerned. He soon gave the country his answer: a two-week reprieve, followed by the execution. Lincoln was aware that many influences—Gordon's lawyer, the shadow slavers, news of the petitions, and history itself—had led Gordon to expect clemency. The president felt that a strongly worded proclamation would let the prisoner know that there was no hope of commutation or pardon, while giving him time to make his peace with God. On February 3, 1862, Lincoln discussed his resolution of the Gordon affair with the cabinet. They all concurred with his proposal; the following day, he wrote a letter to Attorney General Bates, asking if, as chief executive, he could legally grant the brief reprieve to Gordon. Bates responded immediately:

> I have no doubt that you can. The Constitution . . . plainly gives you power to grant reprieves as well as pardons, & that without any exception, but cases of impeachment. A reprieve does not annul the sentence, as a pardon does. It only prolongs the time, & fixes a day for execution, different from & more distant than the day fixed by the Court.
>
> . . .
>
> My answer is confined to the single question of your lawful power to do the thing, which is clear & plain. I say nothing about the justice or expediency of using the power, because upon that branch of the subject, no question is propounded to me.[67]

In his diary entry of the following day, however, Bates makes it clear that he *verbally* advised the president *against* issuing a respite to Gordon:

> The Prest. is in trouble about granting a *reprieve* for Gordon—the pirate—the first conviction under the law making the African slave trade piracy—I, being confined at home, sick, he wrote a note for my *legal opinion* whether he could grant a reprieve without entirely remitting the death penalty! Of course I answered that there was no doubt about the *power.*
>
> I told the Prest.—verbally, that I did not see any good reason for interfering at all unless he meant to pardon or commute—that there were men watching opportunities against him, and that by interfering at all he might give them a handle.

He sd. he had no intention to *pardon* Gordon but was willing to give him a short respite, and that yesterday at C.[abinet] C.[ouncil] all the members present, (tho' not asked as a *cabinet*) agreed to it—And said he'd consider it a little more.[68]

It is not difficult to see Bates's point; Gordon was a multiple offender caught in a brutal capital offense. Even the protests and appeals made on Gordon's behalf freely acknowledged the abhorrent nature of his crime, as well as the need to put a stop to it.

Lincoln wrote the following proclamation on February 4:

Whereas, it appears that at a Term of the Circuit Court of the United States of America for the Southern District of New York, held in the month of November, A. D. 1861, Nathaniel Gordon was indicted and convicted for being engaged in the Slave Trade, and was by the said Court, sentenced to be put to death by hanging by the neck, on Friday the 7th day of February, A. D. 1862;

And whereas, a large number of respectable citizens have earnestly besought me to commute the said sentence of the said Nathaniel Gordon, to a term of imprisonment for life, which application I have felt it to be my duty to refuse;

And whereas, it has seemed to me probable that the unsuccessful application made for the commutation of his sentence, may have prevented the said Nathaniel Gordon from making the necessary preparations for the awful change which awaits him;

Now therefore, be it known, that I, Abraham Lincoln, President of the United States of America, have granted, and do hereby grant unto him, the said Nathaniel Gordon, a respite of the above recited sentence, until Friday the twenty-first day of February, A. D. 1862, between the hours of twelve o'clock at noon and three o'clock in the afternoon of the said day, when the said sentence will be executed.

In granting this respite, it becomes my painful duty to admonish the prisoner that, relinquishing all expectation of pardon by Human Authority, he refer himself alone to the mercy of the Common God and Father of all men.[69]

With the execution of Gordon, the president could at least achieve one clear-cut, dramatic victory at a time when military triumphs were rare. Lincoln was far from pleased with the war's progress. The Union defeats at Bull Run and Ball's Bluff had stunned the nation. Major General George B. McClellan, the gifted organizer who had replaced the ancient Winfield Scott as general-in-chief of the Union army, was already showing the arrogance and unwillingness to fight that would so infuriate the president over the next several months. And the Confederacy was expanding—the loyalties of Missouri and Kentucky were split, and while both remained officially in the Union, rebel factions in both states were sufficiently strong that the Confederate Congress, in November, had admitted Missouri as its twelfth state, with Kentucky soon to follow.[70] But one of Lincoln's biggest headaches came from the formation of the Joint Committee on the Conduct of the War.

Alarmed at the recent defeats, Congress created the Joint Committee—known as the "War Committee"—to delve into the workings of the armed forces. It functioned under the leadership of Senator Benjamin Wade of Ohio, a prominent Radical Republican, and Republican senator Zachariah Chandler of Michigan. There was no aspect of the military that they didn't scrutinize. On the positive side, the heavily partisan committee found flagrant examples of fraud, bungling, and general corruption in the areas of contracting and purchasing. Their research into the maltreatment of Union prisoners in the Southern camps led directly to reform measures and brought more public support for the war effort.

Unfortunately, this group of politicians, who were "nearly bereft of critical military knowledge and experience," also took it upon themselves to study the reasons behind the North's defeats. Their solution to what they perceived as command deficiencies was to support the placement of antislavery Republican generals in positions of high command. Overall, the committee's continuous attempts to run the war proved a constant frustration to the commander in chief. Lincoln prevailed on some occasions; on others, he gave in to political expediency and let the committee have its way.[71]

Now, in the case of Nathaniel Gordon, Lincoln could show Congress, the military, the nation at large, and the nations of the world, that the new government had the commitment and the fortitude to take an old, dusty, but potentially powerful law and allow it to work in the manner intended by its authors so many years before.

There was another major reason for the president's refusal to grant mercy to Gordon, one that would not become evident for another two months. It involved reaching an accord with Great Britain. Relations between the United States and Britain had been strained since the beginning of the conflict. Largely for economic reasons, the British government was sympathetic to the South. As late as October 1862, Chancellor of the Exchequer William Gladstone would state, "There is no doubt that Jefferson Davis and other leaders of the South have made an army; they are making, it appears, a navy; and they have made what is more than either—they have made a nation. . . . We may anticipate with certainty the success of the Southern States so far as regards their separation from the North."[72] And Queen Victoria, by declaring both the North and the South to be "belligerents," implicitly placed them on equal footing and gave tacit recognition to the Confederacy. The *Trent* affair, involving the illegal boarding of a British vessel, brought the United States and Britain to the edge of conflict. Relations would remain tenuous throughout the war, with the South receiving Britain's unofficial encouragement all the while.

And every now and again, Her Majesty's navy still managed to ruffle American feathers. On February 21, 1862—the very day of Gordon's scheduled execution—an article entitled "Outrage of an American Seaman" appeared in the *Springfield Daily Republican:*

> A British commander attempted to take a seaman from an American vessel by force, but the Federal gunboat Iroquois protected the man. The governor of St. Thomas notified the Britisher that the guns of the fort would aid the Iroquois. The British Admiral arrived subsequently, who reprimanded the commander and duly apologized to [U.S.] consul Edgar.[73]

Any British attempt to stop a suspected slave ship flying the American flag was still viewed as an act of outright aggression. But the U.S. Navy was devoting most of its energies to the war, rather than the search for slavers, and with the recall of nearly all the African Squadron, U.S. maritime efforts to end the slave trade practically ground to a stop. It was essential that the president take steps to ensure that this would not happen. Lincoln sent a message to the Senate on April 10, 1862: "I transmit to the Senate, for its consideration, with a view to ratification, a treaty between the United States and Her Britannic Majesty, for the suppression of the slave trade."[74]

Through Secretary of State Seward, the president had very quietly negotiated a treaty with Lord Lyons, giving Britain full approval to board and search suspected American slavers. Additionally, there would be provision made for shared courts for the adjudication of the resultant cases. This treaty would be implemented by a congressional act in July. London, it can be assumed, was following the Gordon case with some interest; the new administration's level of commitment to the enforcement of America's slave laws would let Britain know just how serious Lincoln was about eradicating the traffic.

In their biography of Lincoln, John Nicolay and John Hay, the president's former secretaries, wrote:

> No less to fulfill the dictates of propriety and justice than for its salutary influence on the opinion of foreign nations . . . [the president] secured the passage of "An act to carry into effect the treaty between the United States and Her Britannic Majesty for the suppression of the African slave-trade," approved July 11, 1862. That this action betokened more than mere hollow profession and sentiment is evinced by the fact that under the prosecution of the Government, the slave-trader Nathaniel P. [sic] Gordon was convicted and hanged in New York on the 21st of February, 1862, this being the first execution for such crime under the laws of the United States, after their enforcement had been neglected and their extreme penalty denied for forty years.[75]

The *New York Times* put it succinctly: "Henceforth the Government of the United States washes its hands completely of all complicity in the Slave-trade."[76]

With the execution of Captain Gordon, the stage was set for the passage of a succession of slavery-related acts.[77]

Lincoln sent a special message to Congress on March 6—scarcely two weeks after the hanging—recommending the adoption of a joint resolution that any state willing to adopt a program of gradual emancipation would receive cooperation—and compensation—from the federal government. The following week, a law was passed that prohibited the military from returning slaves who had escaped to their ranks. A month later, on April 16, Lincoln signed into law an act that freed all slaves within the District of Columbia, and granted compensation to their former owners. On June 19, all slaves within the territories were declared free, with no provision for compensation to their masters. In July, the second confiscation act was passed, taking the law regarding slaves and the military even further: it provided that all slaves fleeing to the Union lines were automatically declared free. It also stipulated that the slaves of all who were guilty of treason, including those who supported the Confederacy, were "forever free of their servitude, and not again held as slaves." Finally, on January 1, 1863, Lincoln issued the Emancipation Proclamation, which was, in many respects, less impactful for its actual provisions than for the title itself. In fact, the acts of the previous several months had gone as far as—and to some degree, farther than—the proclamation. But at least the concept of total emancipation was now before the nation and the world as a major item on the administration's agenda, as well as a vital component to the pursuit of military victory.[78]

Any single one of the above reasons would have justified Lincoln's determination to let stand the sentence of the court. Combined, they formed a powerful argument indeed. This may well be what Lincoln meant when he said it was his "duty to refuse" clemency to the slaver. Nathaniel Gordon would hang.

## CHAPTER X

## LAST ATTEMPTS

When Secretary of State William H. Seward received President Abraham Lincoln's proclamation granting Gordon a two-week respite, he immediately sent the documents to Marshal Robert Murray, who received them early on the morning of February 6. Murray hurried with them to the Tombs. In the company of Moses Grinnell and Simeon Draper, two members of the New York City Commission of Public Charities and Corrections, Murray walked into Gordon's cell, where the prisoner was conversing with Reverend Amzi Camp, a Methodist minister. The *Herald* reported the exchange between the marshal and Gordon:

> The Marshal said, "Good morning, Captain Gordon."
>
> "Good morning, Marshal, sit down."
>
> The Marshal [said,] "I have a commutation from the President which I propose to read to you."
>
> Gordon said he expected it. The Marshal produced the paper and read it to the unhappy man, and then told him not to have the slightest hope of ultimate pardon or further commutation; that the President had acted very humanely in giving him [Gordon] time to meet his Maker and prepare himself for another world.
>
> The prisoner received the intelligence, for which he had been somewhat prepared, with a calm despondency. The Marshal told him that if he had anything to say, he would come to him at any time. Gordon said he would prefer to speak to him now.

At that point, Grinnell and Draper left the cell, and Gordon "spoke feelingly of his wife and child, and felt deeply for their condition." Murray then did an unusual thing. He promised Gordon that he would personally raise enough money "in this city to place them beyond the immediate want of pecuniary means, and begged of him not to let their necessities press upon him now."

Gordon and Murray spoke for some time, and at the end of the conversation, Gordon requested a change of diet, which Murray "gratified out of his private purse."[1] Murray's actions, unprecedented though they were, were far from altruistic, although he certainly must have felt compassion for Gordon's family. He reveals his motives in a February 18 letter to George Whiting at the Department of the Interior. It would appear that Murray, Whiting, and presumably both Caleb Smith and Delafield Smith, were hopeful that Gordon would reveal the names of his backers:

Dear Sir,

I have received your note of the 17th . . . asking whether Gordon has made any disclosures?

I would state, in reply, that about two weeks ago, I really thought Gordon intended to make a confession, but his manner has altered since then, and he is particularly reticent. No doubt this change was produced by the false hopes of pardon, held out to him by his council [sic] and friends; for I have done all in my power to gain his confidence, and have given him a liberal diet, at my own expense, in lieu of the prison fare, besides promising to raise a sufficient sum, after his execution, to place his wife and child above immediate want. It is my opinion, that he will die without revealing anything of importance; if he should, however, make any disclosures, I shall communicate promptly with the Department.[2]

Gordon was "somewhat prepared" for the news because he had first heard it from his wife the previous day. When she arrived, he was in the middle of an interview with the *New York Times*. The resulting article appeared in the next morning's edition.

The case has been pressed before the President by ex-Judge Dean, and by other professional and friendly counsel, to such an extent that up to yesterday afternoon, Gordon entertained hopes of pardon. So long a time, however, had elapsed without an interference, that he began to have fears for his life. We had a brief conversation with him yesterday [February 5], during which Gordon expressed the feeling that it was very hard to enforce suddenly and with extreme rigor a law which, for 40 years, had been but a dead-letter. He said that in his opinion the best thing that could be done was to pardon him, and then issue a proclamation that thereafter any and all parties convicted of the crime should be dealt with as the law demands.

Various incidental remarks concerning his past life, showed plainly that he considers himself a very fair-minded and kind-hearted man. He was, he states, always kind to his men and his passengers; and all who had once sailed with him, would do so a second time. In reply to a question as to the absolute necessity of death on the part of many of the slaves in the hold, he stated that the deaths occurred mainly after the ship had become a prize; that half a dozen or so men were put on the slavers to sail them, who were unacquainted with the captives or their language; and that, in consequence, the negroes, unable to make their complaints or desires known, would suffer.

During the interview, Mrs. Gordon, a very pretty, bright and intelligent woman, of not more than 22 years of age, hurried into the corridor, and with trembling hand, gave her husband tidings of the boon for which they both so long had waited.

It was a respite for two weeks.

Gordon received it very coolly, but was evidently very grateful for the little, which may be but the seed of a greater personal benefit. He said he had nothing to say to the public, his views on the subject of so hasty an enforcement of the law were known, and the rest must be left with the President. His family—a wife and a boy four years old—live in Williamsburg, and everything that loving heart or willing hand can do to ameliorate his condition, is cheerfully performed.[3]

The strong language of Lincoln's brief reprieve, clear though it was, did nothing to discourage further attempts to change the president's mind. It gave them, if anything, a greater, more desperate intensity. Marshal Murray himself exceeded the responsibilities of his office and traveled to Washington to meet with the president and present him with "proof" of Gordon's guilt in order to prevent a commutation of his sentence.

Gordon, on one his previous slaving voyages, had allegedly stolen the brig *Camargo* from Levi Fenner and converted it to a slave ship for a voyage from the Congo to Brazil. "By a singular coincidence the widow of the owner of the Camargo arrived in New York from San Francisco a few days before [Gordon's] execution, and brought with her indisputable testimony," Murray later recorded.[4] He interviewed the widow and "delivered to President Lincoln certain papers furnished me by Mrs. [Arvilla] Fenner, disclosing the fact, that Gordon had stolen the Brig 'Camargo,' belonging to her husband, and proceeded with her to the coast of Africa, and after taking on board a cargo of negroes, thence proceeded to the coast of Brazil."

It had long been rumored that Gordon had eluded capture by disguising himself as a woman. Mrs. Fenner's information confirmed this: "After discharging the negroes and selling them, he burned the vessel, and made his escape in women's clothes."

Murray made no secret of why he went to the trouble of carrying this information to the capital: "These papers were delivered to the President by me, about a week previous to Gordon's Execution, in order to prevent a commutation of his sentence."[5]

Murray does not indicate what Mrs. Fenner was doing in New York, aside from "coincidence." Her knowledge of the *Camargo*'s voyage, and the part played by Gordon, no doubt had come from her late husband, and so could not be considered firsthand information nor proof in a court of law; nonetheless, it served to provide further support for what had already been strongly suspected. And it had an interesting effect on Gordon. Until now, he had denied any involvement in prior slaving expeditions. But according to Murray, "After his recognition by this person he ceased to make a mystery of his voyages, although still extremely cautious in his choice of confidants."[6] It was probably Murray who told Gordon about the Fenner interview, possibly hoping that Gordon would open up about his backers.

No sooner had word of Lincoln's proclamation of reprieve become known than the members of the press assigned their own spin to it. The *New York Evening Post,* unwilling to take the president's statement at face value, viewed the respite as a big mistake:

It is a false clemency which has granted a respite of the sentence passed upon Gordon. . . . If there are to be no more examples of capital punishment, if the gallows is to be dispensed of in all cases, if the sentence of every felon who has committed a capital crime is to be commuted to some milder form of punishment, the public would, of course, be informed of it. We should be given to understand that the humanity of the President would not allow of his consenting to the violent death of even the vilest criminal. . . .

. . .

If an ordinary murderer, who has taken a single life for the sake of a single purse, deserves to die a single death, the slave-trader deserves to die a thousand. . . . There is no murder more deliberately plotted than those he commits—there is no cruelty practiced in modern times so horrible as his. . . . This Gordon is a veteran slave-trader, a man-stealer and man-slayer by profession, hardened in cruelty. . . . The retribution he has so richly earned and so long escaped should be certain and swift.

. . .

The skulking villains, some of them men of capital, concerned in the slave-trade, in this city . . . feel that the existence of their horrible traffic depends on this man's escape. If he is hanged, the slave-trade receives its death-blow. . . . To avoid this they would make large sacrifices and pay enormous sums of money. They have procured a respite from the gallows . . . for the wretch whom they used as their instrument, and hope undoubtedly to make this respite the first step in his progress to immunity from punishment. [If Gordon is not hanged,] it will be said that we administer justice on the slave-trader in the same hesitating, procrastinating spirit that we are making war on the rebels.[7]

In this one article, the editor has managed to misinterpret Lincoln's proclamation, imply that he is under the influence of the slavers, and impugn the war effort. It is correct, however, in its perception that people on both sides of the issue were keenly aware that considerably more was at stake here than the life of one offender.

The *Times,* understanding the reprieve for what it was, saw the broader picture, stating that it was indeed necessary to "fire a ball cartridge at the Slave-trade in New-York, after which blank cartridges may be tried. . . . It is necessary to show European Powers . . . that there has been a change in the Administration, and that a slave-trader may be hung, even in New-York City."[8] It didn't really matter how subsequent cases were adjudicated, so long as the law, in this one specific instance, was satisfied.

One person who apparently did believe the words of the proclamation was Nathaniel Gordon himself. The *Post* reported on February 11 that Marshal Murray had visited the prisoner in the Tombs; Murray found that Gordon was "extremely depressed in spirits, and signified to the officer that he had given up all hope of a further respite or commutation of sentence."[9]

Gordon's attorney was far from through. Having had no success in his initial meeting with Lincoln, Gilbert Dean appealed to the U.S. Supreme Court on February 15. The chief justice at this time was Roger B. Taney, notorious for his decision in the Dred Scott fugitive slave case. Dean first applied for an arrest of judgment, for what he claimed were "irregularities and errors in the proceedings." He was basing this on the small technicality that no record of the conviction appears to have been kept. This application was denied. He then requested that his case be certified to the Supreme Court based on a "division of opinion." He charged that since only one of the two presiding judges on the case actually delivered the sentence, there might have been a difference of opinion between them, which would clear the way for an appeal to the Supreme Court. Two months earlier, Judge Shipman had specifically told Dean this was not the case, but by this time, Dean was turning over every card he had. Taney denied this application as well, reiterating that the circuit court had been unanimous in its decision.

Dean then applied for a writ of prohibition, charging an irregularity in the proceeding, and also a writ of certiorari, which would mandate Judge William Davis Shipman and Justice Samuel Nelson to send all "papers . . . and proceedings" to the Supreme Court. This would presumably give the Court access to the actual court records and documents, upon which Dean could base his appeal. It would also stop the wheels on the execution.

Taney received Dean's application on a Friday; he delivered his decision on Monday, February 17. His response to Dean was brief and definitive: "This motion cannot be sustained." Taney pointed out that the Supreme Court had no jurisdiction over a case that had been adjudicated in the lower court, since there had been no division of opinion between the two judges. Once the verdict of the circuit court was delivered, barring some irregularity, there was no possibility of appeal. And Taney confirmed to Dean that there had been nothing amiss in the proceedings of Gordon's trial. Therefore, the Supreme Court had no legal right to examine the records of the lower court, nor to impose itself on the decision, nor yet to prohibit the marshal from "performing a duty which the Circuit Court had a lawful right to command"—i.e., directing the execution of Captain Gordon.[10] The slaver had four days to live.

Meanwhile, there was an air of fear and anxiety in the White House that had nothing to do with Gordon, the war, or the nation. Two of the president's sons, eight-year-old Tad and eleven-year-old Willie, were seriously ill, probably from typhoid. Tad improved, but Willie's condition worsened. Of Lincoln's children, Willie was the closest to him in manner and nature—a "near-clone of his father," as one historian has written. Lincoln doted on the boy. According to a neighbor in Springfield, Willie was "the true picture of Mr. Lincoln, in every way, even to carrying his head inclined toward his left shoulder." The child was "bright, sensible, sweet-tempered and gentle mannered."[11]

On February 18, Attorney General Edward Bates wrote in his diary, "The Prest.'s 2d. son, Willie, has lingered on for a week or 10 day[s], and is now thought to be *in extremis*[.] The Prest. is nearly worn out, with grief and watching."[12]

The same day Chief Justice Taney was delivering his decision to Gilbert Dean, President Lincoln received a letter from Rhoda E. White, the wife of a New York judge. She had come to Washington with Captain Gordon's wife and mother to plead for clemency. Her letter caught Lincoln at his most vulnerable.

> I would not intrude upon the sanctity of your sick room and upon your hours of grief but for the sake of Mercy, and for the sake of an afflicted Mother and wife who are bowed down with sorrow and look to God and to you to lift the heavy burden they are suffering under.
>
> The case I plead for, is that of Nathaniel Gordon now under sentence of death—He must be executed on next Friday, unless the Almighty through you, interposes.
>
> His wife, an interesting woman of twenty two and his aged Mother are here, and through me *implore* you to commute the punishment to *imprisonment* for Life. They do not, nor will they *ever* ask you for pardon.
>
> They present to you a Petition from over eleven thousand of our citizens of New York who are warm and earnest upholders of the Government. The sympathy of the State of New York is in favor of a commutation of the punishment and as that State is in favor of abolishing Capital punishment such a favor from you will be in conformity with the sentiments of the people[.] Please consider the following reasons why we ask and you dear Sir may grant our request.
>
> 1st—Mr Gordon was engaged in the Slave trade at the time when many *then* in power upheld it, and engaged in it—*not since the War began*.

2d—The Government wishes to make an example of Mr Gordon—To pardon him might offend Justice—But have the hearts of our Rulers and people become so hardened that *imprisonment for life* will not answer the ends of Justice—"Forgive us our trespasses as we forgive others"—Is not imprisonment for life equal to death?—You will not, without reflection, I feel sure, Mr Lincoln[,] deny the Petition of so many, when it is not an unreasonable one. Our most prominent men are not opposed to it. I fear that selfish motives have influenced those who desire the contrary.

The poor man has only a few days to live please let his poor wife know the decision as speedily as possible, and let her return to her unfortunate husband. The Attorney General will be kind enough to let me know your decision—

May Our Lord direct your decision and we will be resigned.[13]

Lincoln refused to see them. Mrs. White and the Gordon ladies were granted an audience with Mary Lincoln. Mary, unstable at the best of times, had no doubt come from the bedside of her two sons in order to meet with the desperate women. During the interview, Elizabeth Gordon even presented the First Lady with a poem of her own composition:

To Mrs. President Lincoln.
Madam,

Within your power it lies to save
My husband from an early grave;
And rescue from a life of shame,
The wife and child who bear his name

He may have erred—but can *I* touch
The faults of one I still love much
With pen of censure—and destroy
The father of my little boy?

For that boy's sake, oh, lady dear,
For the poor father interfere!
Obtain his life—if nothing more.
Mercy—is all that we implore.

His wife and mother, well I know,
You will your sympathy bestow,

Will grant the favor we invoke,
And save him from the fatal stroke.

Yes; you will kindly intercede
For *Gordon's life,*—for which we plead;
Nor will you let us *vainly* sue
Our hopes depend alone on—*you.*

If blessings buy a grateful heart
Besought of God, can bliss impart,—
Or human happiness improve,—
Sorrow and sickness far remove?;—

That lot is yours! For not one day
Will I allow to pass away,—
But what I'll raise my fervent pray'r
That He your life will bless and spare.

That ev'ry kindness you dispense
May meet on earth rich recompense;
And the boon my husband given
May find a sure reward in Heaven.[14]

Obviously touched by Elizabeth Gordon's plight, Mary Lincoln attempted to discuss the subject of Gordon's commutation with her husband. In the words of Robert Murray, "The President . . . would not
allow his wife to broach the subject, and poor Mrs. Gordon returned to
New York heartbroken and disconsolate."[15]

Lincoln sent the petition that Mrs. White carried to Washington—the
second he'd received from New Yorkers regarding Gordon—to Attorney General Bates for review, along with the letters from Rhoda White
and Elizabeth Gordon. Bates responded immediately.

½ past 2 p.m. Feb. 18 1862

The papers sent over to me half an hour ago, being two letters & several rolls, numerously signed, all relate to Capt. Nathaniel Gordon, under
sentence of death on a conviction of piracy, in the African Slave trade.

The papers, all of them, ask that Gordon's sentence be commuted to
imprisonment for life. No reasons are given to shew a doubt of the guilt
of [Gordon.] The papers contain no suggestion of any impropriety in the

legal proceedings. And these are the only papers in the case which I have seen.

I see nothing in the papers, as presented to me, to make it proper for you to interfere, to stop the course of law.[16]

Bates was feeling fairly smug when he later entered an "I-told-you-so" in his diary:

Two weeks ago, I warned the Prest. against granting a respit[e] to Nath[aniel] Gordon, under sentence of death, for Piracy (slave trade). . . . I was convinced (and told the Prest. so) that the reprieve wd. be taken as an implied promise of pardon or commutation, however strongly he might asseverate to the contrary[.]

And now, my prediction is verified. Mrs. White (wife of Judge White of N.Y.) with the mother and wife of Gordon, are urging both the Prest. and me to commute the sentence to imprisonment for life.[17]

That same day, Lincoln received yet another appeal from Gilbert Dean. Undaunted by his rejection by the Supreme Court, he had assembled a new list of issues—some more germane than others—with which to change the president's mind. Dean based his "right to address you on behalf of my client" on the *Times*'s publication of Delafield Smith's open letter to the secretary of the interior.[18]

Dean begins by disputing Smith's claim that New York stood in favor of Gordon's execution. Just refer to the petitions signed by "Lawyers and Laymen, Clergymen and Citizens—the Senators and members of Assembly of New York City."

He points out that a recent New York State statute stipulates that only the crimes of treason and murder are to be punishable by death in the state of New York, and that a full year must pass between sentencing and execution. Further, no execution could take place until the court record has been certified by the clerk of the court, and approved by the governor. Dean "was astonished" to find that there was no record of Gordon's conviction. "I have applied to the Supreme Court of the United States . . . the motion is denied." In a statement rich with unintended irony, he claims that the rights of property in the courts receive more favorable treatment than those of men: "Human life is of less consequence than Bales of Cotton—or Boxes of Dry Goods." The hundreds of Africans who died at Gordon's hands apparently did not factor into either Dean's argument or his thinking.

Dean then presents the argument that Gordon had not actually enslaved the Africans himself; he was merely taking them, already in chains, from one port to another. In the words of one historian, Dean was claiming that his client was merely in the *"transportation* business."[19]

He continues with the "dead letter" argument so popular among Gordon's supporters: Gordon is the first man sentenced under a law that had lain dormant for more than 40 years; show him mercy, and hang the *next* man to violate it. The law, Dean claims, "has been a dead letter, because the moral sense of the community revolted at the penalty of death imposed on an act when done between Africa and Cuba, which the law sanctioned between Maryland and Carolina. . . . It was, nay it is, lawful to carry a child born in Virginia to Louisiana and there to sell him to perpetual slavery—is it an offence then deserving death to bring a barbarian from Africa to the same place?" It was a viable question, and went directly to the heart of the contrived and twisted distinction between the slave trade and the institution of slavery in the United States. The question was also academic; the law had been passed decades earlier for the express purpose of eradicating the slave trade, and it had remained on the books all the while his client was breaking it.

Others deserving of the death penalty, argues Dean, have been convicted and allowed their lives: "While the prison doors are opening to Convicted Pirates and acknowledged Traitors, the Gallows is being erected for Gordon, and why? Is the moral crime of which he is guilty greater than those you are releasing?"

Dean's remaining arguments hold no legal weight whatsoever. He points out that the United States is alone among nations in demanding the death penalty for acts of piracy. Finally he begs Lincoln not to allow the "exultation of the people over National Victories" or the "eve of the preparation for solemnizing the Anniversary of the 22nd Febry to be marred by the creaking of the gallows—or saddened by the report of the dying groans and struggles of a human being sacrificed to appease the spasmodic virtue of men, who are loudest in their demand for the abolition of the death penalty, as more barbarous than the slave trade and more vindictive than murder."[20] In short, Dean didn't think it appropriate to hang a man so close to Washington's Birthday!

Instead of responding to this appeal himself, Lincoln instructed Dean to deliver it directly to Attorney General Bates. Apparently, Lincoln enclosed a memorandum, now lost, directing Bates to study the appeal as quickly as possible. The attorney general received the letter—and the lawyer—near midnight, and responded immediately:

> I have without a moment's delay examined the package of papers which you sent to me yesterday, as I perceive by a memorandum endorsed by you, dated "Feb. 18, 1862." The package was handed me within the last half hour (¼ to 12 M.) by Mr. Dean of New York, and I have had time barely to read the papers.
>
> As you require my immediate attention to the matter, you will not expect me to furnish any detailed answer to Mr. Dean's argument, in his letter to you, dated yesterday. Indeed there is a good deal in that letter which I should not answer, if I had abundant time. Whatever is there said about public opinion in New York—the New York Statute, and Mr[.] Delafield Smith's letter to some one not named—and the impolicy of allowing Gordon to be hanged upon the eve of a national festival, and especially when other pirates, and numerous traitors are allowed to escape. These, I should decline to answer, because, in my opinion, they do not touch the matter in hand.
>
> Mr[.] Dean insists in his letter, that there is *not any record* of the sentence against Gordon—not that the Court did not pronounce sentence, and that the clerk did not write it down in the record book—for that is not denied—but he insists that there must be a *judgment-roll* (which we know embraces the whole record of the case) made out and filed in the clerk's office—and that roll, he assumes, is the only record of the case, and that without it, there cannot be a lawful execution.
>
> That is not my opinion. I see nothing in the papers or the case, to impeach the legal validity of the sentence pronounced upon Gordon.
>
> If it be true, as Mr[.] Dean supposes, that there is no record of the judgment, then he ought to ask a full *discharge*, and not a *commutation*—for it is plain that commutation assumes the legality of the judgment, and only changes and mitigates the punishment.
>
> It is not pretended that Gordon is not guilty, nor that he had not a fair trial. But it is ins[is]ted that it is hard to punish him, because his is the first conviction under the Statute. I do not perceive the force of that argument—Some one must be the first; nor can I understand why the first convict should be spared, in preference to subsequent convicted offenders.

If the case itself afforded grounds for pardon or commutation, I would lean to the side of lenity; but I do not think that the President is justifiable in interposing his authority to arrest the execution of a statute merely because he thinks the law too hard or too severe. That would be to set himself above Congress, & to assume the *dispensing power,* which even the people of England never patiently submitted to, when exercised by their kings.

Upon the whole, I give my advice that you do decline to interpose any further, to arrest the course of law, in the case of Nathaniel Gordon.[21]

Why did Lincoln send all this material to Bates? Was he, in fact, looking for a way to let Gordon off the hook? Absolutely not, and he had already told Bates as much. It was, however, within the parameters of Bates's job as attorney general to consider the legality of specific issues and documents, as they pertained to national welfare. A part, at least, of Dean's appeal was based on strictly legal questions, so it was appropriate that the president solicit the opinion of the nation's foremost attorney. Also, Lincoln was undergoing an almost incomprehensible strain: while he was entertaining the arguments of Gilbert Dean in the White House, his child lay dying in a nearby room. Perhaps he simply needed to share the burden—to let someone else take a part in saying, "No." In any case, Nathaniel Gordon now had only two days to live.

Back in New York, the tension heightened. On the night of the nineteenth, large handbills were "affixed on the walls . . . and extensively posted through the town and suburbs":

CITIZENS of NEW YORK!—*Come to the Rescue!*

—Shall a JUDICIAL MURDER be committed in your midst, and no PROTESTING VOICES be heard against it?

Captain Nathaniel Gordon is sentenced to be executed for a crime which has been virtually a dead letter for forty years. Shall this young man be quietly allowed to be made the victim of fanaticism? Let the generous and humane who are in favor of commutation of the death penalty in his case assemble at the Merchants' Exchange on Thursday, February 20, at three o'clock, and make themselves heard on Gordon's behalf at the White House.[22]

The *New York Herald* reported on the twenty-first that the meeting was attended by "quite a number of persons, composed principally of shipowners, ship agents, shipmasters and longshoremen . . ." A number of merchants, arriving at the Exchange to transact their usual business, were surprised by the gathering, and almost to a man proclaimed their support for the government's case. When Marshal Murray returned from his visit to Washington the previous day, it was with the news that President Lincoln was resolved to let the sentence stand, and that was good enough for them. By the time the meeting came to order, there were only 150 protesters in attendance. They were addressed extemporaneously by a Thomas Tomlinson, who had "never heard of the meeting until a few minutes since," knew nothing of "both Gordon and the merits of the case," and was moved to speak only through a sense of "humanity and pity for the wife and child." It was resolved that a telegram be sent to the president, and a collection was taken up; the total contribution came to $11.77.[23]

Marshal Murray relates that "the meeting was poorly attended, and without result, those present belonging to the class known as 'political dead beats,' a hybrid between the incendiary and the sharper."[24] All in all, the rally was a fiasco.

Nor was the marshal himself spared the heat of either the pro- or anti-Gordon faction. He received

a variety of communications on the subject of the execution—pamphlets for and against capital punishment—letters approving [my] conduct in the case—and others of a threatening nature, of which latter, the subjoined is the most innocent:

"Sir, If you have any regard for yourself, your family, your reputation, you will not hang that man Gordon, for it will be nothing short of murder, and the stigma of it will stick while you live. Resign sooner, by all means, a thousand times over. Do not commit murder. Cut your right arm off first."[25]

Just who were these citizens of New York who signed petitions, printed and distributed handbills throughout the metropolitan area,

and organized protest meetings? There is no doubt that the slaving interests of the city were well represented, for they had the most to lose
by Gordon's execution. There may be some truth to the allegation that
they had put considerable money behind organizing a movement on
the prisoner's behalf (although this is doubtful, considering they contributed nothing to his defense, daily needs, or his family's well-being).
However, this cannot tell the whole story. When petitions containing
names numbering in the tens of thousands are sent to Washington, we
must assume that a fair number of the signatories are everyday, well-
intentioned citizens who honestly reject the notion that Gordon must
die. Marshal Murray (referring to himself in the third person) confirms
this in his history of the case: "A deputation of influential merchants,
*not* connected with the slave trade, waited also on Mr. Murray and besought him to apply for, or recommend a pardon, but the Marshal
knew his duty better, and painful as it was to refuse, he was obliged to
do so." [26]

The press was not unsympathetic to the efforts of Gordon's counsel:

> Thus all efforts in Gordon's behalf at Washington were baffled, and
> Judge Dean, thoroughly exhausted, left the capital on Wednesday night
> [February 19], reaching his home yesterday morning [the twentieth].
>
> He had hardly breakfasted, when certain features in the case, which
> had . . . developed during his prolonged absence, were brought before
> his notice, and deeming them worthy of at least an argument before the
> Court, he hastened thither. [27]

And so, for the third time, Gilbert Dean appeared in circuit court
opposite Delafield Smith and before Judge Shipman; this time, he submitted an application for a writ of habeas corpus. He presented the argument that the Tombs was a *state* prison "for the confinement of
capital persons," and as such was not automatically available to the federal government for executions, without consent of the state. Dean
cited examples of Massachusetts and other states that had refused the
United States the use of its prisons "for certain purposes." Further,
claimed Dean, by the Act of 1860, the state of New York had refused
the use of its jails—and specifically the city prison—for executions. Finally, Dean objected to a technical flaw: the court seal was missing
from the sentencing document, thereby making it invalid.

Smith dispensed with Dean's objection to the use of the Tombs by introducing a note from Simeon Draper, president of the New York City Department of Public Charities and Corrections. On January 29, Marshal Murray had requested the "necessary permission that the execution shall take place in the yard of the City Prison at the time appointed."[28] As confirmation, Draper gave Smith a copy of his response, dated February 19, assuring Murray that the "Warden of the City Prison will render the usual facilities required on such occasions."[29] So much for the issue of venue.

As to Dean's objection to the absence of the court seal, Smith assured him that it could easily be affixed to the document, although he didn't really see the point. The decision now lay with the judge.

Rather than rule immediately, Judge Shipman called a two-hour recess to allow himself time to consult with Judge Betts. When Shipman returned to the courtroom, "twilight had fallen on the outer world, . . . and the gas was lighted." The judge was visibly nervous. He "had a painful duty to perform, and was well aware that his decision now would be final." The case had recently attracted a great deal of attention among New York's legal community, and there were several prominent attorneys in the courtroom, in addition to Smith and Dean. They sat "in the darker portions of the room, waiting with ill-disguised anxiety" as Judge Shipman prepared himself. He "fumbled with the gas fixtures, turned the fluid on and turned it off," and then softly delivered his decision. He said that it was not necessary to affix the court seal to validate the sentence, and that the decision to hang the prisoner in the yard of the city prison "was not lightly or thoughtlessly given, but that after due care and investigation the Court had decided upon the time not only, but also the place."[30]

There was nowhere left for the defense to go; it was over. Gilbert Dean had done "all that human ingenuity or legal acumen could suggest," and Judge Shipman's decision affected him deeply. Physically and emotionally exhausted, he rallied as the other lawyers in the room gathered around him and praised his efforts.[31] Even the aggressively pro-execution *New York Times* grudgingly gave Dean his due: "We can hardly reproach the counsel of a man under sentence of death, for attempting any expedient, however desperate, and taking any ground, however doubtful, in hope of freeing their client."[32] Later, the *Times* would concede that "[e]very exertion was tried, every argument possible was urged before the Courts to break down the conviction or the sentence."[33]

Earlier that day, Dean's partner, former judge Beebe, played a last, desperate gambit: he rushed to Albany to ask New York's Democratic governor Edwin D. Morgan to intercede with the president on Gordon's behalf. It would prove a futile effort; Lincoln rejected the governor's appeal, as he had all others before. He assured Marshal Murray that "no change in the sentence would be extended by him." Armed with this information, Murray told the superintendent of the government telegraph offices not to allow any messages through regarding Gordon on either the day before or the day of the execution, "unless delivered to him personally by the President or Secretary Seward."[34]

The *Times,* under the banner "THE EXECUTION TOMORROW," stated that "NATHANIEL GORDON, the convicted slave-trader, will tomorrow suffer the penalty of the law. The most earnest efforts have been made to avert his fate. . . . The firmness of PRESIDENT LINCOLN contrasts with the feebleness of MR. BUCHANAN. . . . New-York needs to have this aspersion of encouraging the trade in negroes wiped out. It can only be done by satisfying the world that our abhorrence for the crime prevails over a pardonable tenderness for the criminal."[35]

Meanwhile, at twilight, just as Judge Shipman was delivering his final decision, young Willie Lincoln died. His father, in unimaginable pain, stood by the child's bed and sobbed. When his secretary walked into the boy's room, Lincoln looked up and said, "My poor boy, he was too good for this earth. I know that he is better off in Heaven, but then we loved him so. It was hard—hard—to have him die!"[36] It was a blow from which Lincoln would never recover. On April 14, 1865, more than three years later, he said to Mary, "We must be more cheerful in the future; between the war and the loss of our darling Willie, we have been very miserable." That evening, Lincoln attended a performance of *Our American Cousin* at Ford's Theater; he never came home.[37]

# CHAPTER XI

# THE GALLOWS

At 3 o'clock on the afternoon of February 20, just as Judge Shipman was calling a recess to consider Gilbert Dean's last desperate attempt to save his client's life, Nathaniel Gordon's wife and mother visited his cell. Gordon's mother, still a devout member of Reverend Chickering's Congregational Church of Portland, spoke long and earnestly with her son, in a last effort to "renew to her wayward boy, the lessons which in his earlier years, she had endeavored to instill in his breast."[1] He listened quietly, politely, then assured her that he would die unafraid and with a clear conscience. "Pressing her son to her sorrowing heart, she commended his soul to an all-wise and all-loving Saviour, and then, with one long tender embrace she burst into an agony of grief and left the room." For a few moments, Gordon was "solemn and mute."[2]

It was now time for Gordon to bid farewell to Elizabeth. He "spoke most tenderly of his little son, who was absent," regretting the "stigma that would naturally rest" on the boy.[3] Elizabeth tried to cheer him—and herself—by telling him that the president might yet approve a commutation. At some point, however, word arrived from Gilbert Dean that all hope was gone. Gordon was not surprised at this, but it "struck a . . . tangible death-blow to the deceitful hope with which his poor wife had deluded herself." For the first time, Elizabeth seemed to realize that her husband must die; she fell to the floor in a faint. When she was revived, she sobbed miserably, clinging fiercely to her husband. In the presence of such pain from the woman he loved, Gordon's stoic self-control finally broke, and he "cried like a child."

Here was the culmination of the long months of giving daily support to her husband in the most horrific of circumstances, and it took a terrible toll. This was their last parting, and "worn by . . . hope and fear, and final despair," and after a "convulsive attempt at a rational farewell,"

Elizabeth fainted again, and had to be carried out of the cell. By this time, it was 6 P.M.

Gordon regained his own composure; an hour later, he received Marshal Murray, who kept him company while he ate his dinner and wrote letters to family and friends until 10 o'clock. Warden Charles Sutton then allowed him to walk up and down the corridor. Gordon "lit a cigar, had a glass of whiskey, conversed on indifferent subjects,"[4] and "amused (or shocked) his keepers by singing to them Portuguese songs."[5] At one point, he actually joked about his impending death, saying that the executioner "would not require a heavy weight to raise his body, as he had fallen away in flesh since his imprisonment." Finally, before retiring, he asked Marshal Murray to stage the execution at the latest possible moment allowed by the sentence, promising that he would not try to do away with himself in the meanwhile. The marshal agreed that the hanging would take place at 2:30 P.M., and that Gordon's body, in accordance with his wishes, would be turned over to his friends.[6] Gordon thanked the marshal for all his kindnesses, saying that he bore him no ill will. At around midnight, Murray left the Tombs for the night, leaving two deputies outside the open door to keep watch over the prisoner. A lamp remained lit in the cell, as Gordon, still partially dressed, threw himself on his cot and fell asleep.[7]

All evening, a detachment of Marines marched back and forth in front of the entrances to the prison; there had been rumors of an attempted rescue, and the government was taking no chances. No one suspected that the attempt to foil the execution would come not from outside the prison, but from within. The culprit would be Nathaniel Gordon.

At 3 A.M., Gordon awoke with a start, looked at his watch, muttered something to himself, and lay down facing the wall.[8] Shortly thereafter, the deputies noticed that he appeared to be sleeping very fitfully. When they entered his cell, they saw that he was in convulsions—"his features horribly contorted, his eyes bloodshot, fixed, and almost protruding from their sockets, and his extremities cold and stiff. He was awake, but sensible to nothing but pain."[9] The deputies found a small paper packet under the blanket. Gordon had taken strychnine.

The officers immediately raised the alarm. Three highly competent physicians—Doctors Simmons, Wood, and Hodgman—were called. Two were in private practice, the third associated with New York Hospital. By the time they arrived, the convulsions had become increasingly violent. Soon, Gordon went rigid, his pulse nearly undetectable. The doctors immediately pumped his stomach, catheterized him, and ordered Gordon to be dosed with brandy and whiskey, to counteract the effects of the poison. His jaws had locked shut; the doctors had to pry them open with a medical instrument to pour the alcohol down his throat. For the next four hours, Gordon went in and out of consciousness, suffering horrific cramps in his stomach and limbs. For a time, the doctors felt certain they would lose him, but eventually "his eyes opened and shut; his features, though haggard, resumed a more natural expression; and the numbness and cramps . . . totally subsided." By 10 A.M., on February 21, he was able to look around at the people surrounding his bed, and in the mistaken belief that he was dying, cried "in a triumphant, spiteful tone, 'I've cheated you! I've cheated you!' "[10]

Exhausted by the effects of the strychnine, as well as the desperate ministrations of the attending doctors, Gordon fell back on the bed and slept quietly for half an hour. He awoke lucid, though shaky, and asked for some whiskey. Revived by it, he arose and put on his coat. Deputy Borst asked the nature of the poison and how he had acquired it. Gordon replied, "Strychnine. A good many may accuse my wife of a hand in this affair. I have only to say that in time of peace prepare for war." Gordon said that he'd carried it with him since his first arraignment, and added, "The little bench you sit on, if it was examined and could speak, could possibly tell some tales about it." He told Borst to upend the stool, showing him a narrow crack under the seat, in which he had hidden the small packet. Although Gordon had been moved from another cell the night before, and his clothes and furniture carefully searched to prevent just such an eventuality, the poison had been secreted well enough to escape scrutiny.[11]

Gordon admitted to his keepers that he had intended only to feign sleep and swallow the poison when his guards relaxed their vigil. But, exhausted, he fell into a deep slumber, and slept until 3 A.M. He awoke with a start, retrieved the packet, drew the blanket over his head, and shook all the strychnine powder onto his tongue. Perhaps because the dose was too powerful for his weakened system, he immediately vomited, denying himself the quick, private death he had sought.

Gordon said he had "suffered the agony of a dozen deaths" and begged the doctors to "give him something to put an end . . . to his misery." Superintendent Draper, Warden Sutton, and Marshal Murray told Gordon they viewed his attempted suicide as an act of cowardice; understandably, the prisoner disagreed, firmly stating that had he succeeded, "they would have been spared the necessity of a hanging." He then asked for pen and paper, and in a cramped but legible hand, he wrote two final letters. These provide, through Gordon's own words, a rare window into his mind regarding his image of himself as a man of honor, his view of District Attorney Smith's conduct during the trial, the court's decision, his concern for his wife and child, and, clearly, his unequivocal belief in his own innocence of the charges. The first letter was directed "To the Public."

I have left these few lines to be published after the sentence of the law shall have been carried out. To those that signed the petition for the commutation of sentence, I return them my sincerest thanks for the kindness. I feel that I do not deserve the fate which has befallen me, and I have far less on my conscience to answer for than the District Attorney who could tell a deliberate falsehood for the sake of taking my life, and he dare not deny the charge of getting up in the court and telling the jury that if I were convicted, he would be the first man to sign a petition for my pardon, and then request the Executive not to commute the sentence, seems as though he did not scruple much which way he obtained his ends so long as he succeeded. I did not think that if he did not wish to do me any good, that at least he could have let me be tried for my life without interfering. He has pursued me with the ferocity of a bloodhound, and now that I am no more, I suppose he is satisfied. I think that I die a good deal easier than he can, for I never yet told a lie to take a man's life. I understand he charges me with being sordid and cruel, which I denounce as false. During the time I have had charge of a vessel (which has been since 1846) I have never been brought before a court for cruelty to any man under my charge; nor have I ever had a man or officer refuse to sail with me a second time. But I do not feel any animosity against him—I only make a plain statement of facts.

To Judge Dean who acted as my counsel, I have only to say that he has done all that lay in the power of man to do for me, he has nothing to reproach himself with, nor has it been through mercenary motives, for he has not been paid by slave-traders, to my knowledge, for his services as intimated in Court by the District Attorney, and I have no reason to doubt that his services were actuated by a desire to save my life, more than anything else. For all his efforts in my behalf, I return him my most sincere thanks.

To those who have so warmly interested themselves in me, although strangers, I can only return my thanks. I know that public opinion, if it could have its way, would be strongly against the sentence being carried out, but it is ordained that I must be a victim to those that have been so clamorous for my blood. I can only say that as you mete it out to others, so it shall be meted out to you. I do not feel so much regret at dying as I do in leaving an unprotected wife and child to the mercy of the world— one who for a period of seven years has always been a true and faithful wife in prosperity and adversity. I hope and trust that they will be cared for when I am gone, and I feel that they will.

Had I have committed a murder, I should have said that I deserved no mercy, but my hand is not stained with the blood of any man. *I have no feeling that I have done any wrong action,* and I die perfectly easy, so far as that is concerned. I have not injured any man knowingly through the whole course of my life.

And in conclusion, all that I have to say is that I have been dealt with most cruelly and unjustly but I can say nothing that will avail me anything. I can only leave it in His hands who governs the destiny of the whole universe.

Nathaniel Gordon[12]

The second letter, of a much more personal nature, was addressed "To All My Friends."

This letter will be handed to one of you, whom I shall designate to be read after the sentence of the law has been carried out. May God bless you all for your kindness and generosity, and the interest you have taken to save me from such a bad fate!

You, all of you, know that the stories circulating about in regard to my cruelty are nothing but base fabrications to injure me, and were got up expressly by those bloodhounds who are so clamorous for my blood. May God forgive them as I do!

*I have no trouble of conscience. I never harmed a human being in my life,* to my knowledge, but I tell you I can consider the District Attorney in no other light than that of a murderer. A man that will get up in court and tell a jury if they will convict, he will be the first man to sign a petition for Executive clemency, and then go and request him not to commute the sentence is not a man, but a brute. I leave him to God and his own conscience. He has accomplished his bloodthirsty and cruel work, and his victim has passed away from the busy scenes of life, where you all, my friends, sooner or later will have to be; but I hope and trust that your fate will be a far different one from mine—that you will live to enjoy the pleasures of this world to a good old age, and be prosperous and happy. For your indefatigable efforts in my behalf, I now only say, you have the gratitude of my wife and myself. Words are too feeble to express my thanks for all that you have done for me and the partner of all my joys and sorrows.

I do not feel afraid to die. Death is but a momentary pang—it is soon over, but such a death my very soul abhors. To have perished in a shipwreck, or in the natural way, would have been nothing, and I feel that my fate is an unjust one—that I do not deserve it. I trust that I shall meet with more mercy at the hands of God than I have at the hands of that man who so malignantly and cruelly persecuted me. But mark my words, and watch well his course, and if he does not suffer for all he has done to me, it is because there is not an avenging God. I leave him in His hands to deal with as he sees fit. I say nothing; whatever he has done to me I freely forgive, as I trust for forgiveness hereafter myself. But he has not only taken my life, he has embittered the life of one far dearer to me than life itself—one, who through all my troubles, has been a comforter, and who has never for a moment faltered in her devotion towards me, whose very existence was bound up in mine, and who has shewn herself not only by words but acts, a true woman—one who had a heart, and who was worthy of all the love and affection that could be bestowed upon her.

And now, my friends, when I am gone I know you will not forget her. You all know the situation in which I leave her and her poor fatherless child. Advise with her for her best interests and welfare; comfort and console her under this terrible affliction. She has, as it were, a father and mother in Captain Woodside and his wife, whose kindness words can never express, and I know they will always feel interested for her; but I fear the blow will be one from which she will never recover. We have lived together for seven years, and our lives have been one course of sunshine and happiness, and I know her feelings towards me are those of a true hearted woman. I feel that it would have been a great satisfaction to me to have been spared to watch over her and that child, and protected them, but I have to leave this world at a time when it would have been a source of satisfaction to have lived.

It is a very true saying that at about the time we are ready to live, we die; but the will of God must be done and we must submit to it. A man must fulfill his destiny, no matter what it is. Little did I think that this would be mine, and I sincerely hope that none of you will ever have to suffer the same. I owe mine in part to the state of the times and the misrepresentations that have been made to the President by those whom I never injured in thought, word or deed. Imprisonment for life was not enough to satisfy their vengeance; nothing but my life would answer. I can imagine them when I have passed away, going to their homes exulting in the death of their victim—their only regret being that they could not burn me at the stake like the savages of old; but I have but one life to give them.

And now, my dear friends, I bid you adieu. I feel that had public opinion been listened to my fate would have been far different. But John Brown must be avenged, and unless God in His mercy should interfere, I must die; all that I can say is, that I meet a death that is undeserved.

Yours truly,
Nathaniel Gordon[13]

Gordon's allegations of unethical behavior on the part of District Attorney Smith were completely unfounded, nor had Smith made a statement regarding clemency once Gordon was convicted. Smith himself had requested a "shorthand-writer" to record the transcript of the entire trial, knowing well the significance of the case and his role in it. Although the transcript itself has been lost, Marshal Murray's invaluable account states that Smith's prescience in hiring the stenographer showed Gordon's charge to be totally unfounded.[14] Additionally, Gilbert Dean left virtually no rock unturned in his defense campaign; he would not have hesitated to decry any impropriety directed toward his client. There is no mention of questionable conduct on the part of the prosecution in any of Dean's motions or correspondences.

In his letters, Gordon denies any wrongdoing, by repeatedly claiming to have "never harmed a human being" in his life. It had been determined beyond doubt that he had commanded a slave ship on at least four voyages and seen a heavy loss of life among the captive Africans. At first denying any involvement in the slave trade, Gordon eventually "ceased to make a mystery of his voyages" when confronted with incontrovertible proof. And yet, he fails to see himself as the catalyst of so many innocent and tragic deaths. His reasoning is clear—and infinitely sad: he simply didn't view the Africans as human beings. As far as Nathaniel Gordon was concerned, they were merely chattel—goods to be delivered with as little "spoilage" as possible, for a profit. Loss of life among his "cargo" merely represented the cost of doing business, not the willful destruction of human life.

It would have been understandable had Gordon merely shared the prevalent racial views of his time, holding the White race superior to the Black. But to deny—unto death—the very humanity of the Africans bespeaks the depravity to which District Attorney Smith referred in court, and supports the "stories of . . . cruelty" which Gordon so vigorously denied in his last letters. As captain, he was personally responsible for every death that occurred both on board his ships and as a result of his enterprises. The day after Gordon's death, the *Christian Intelligencer* stated it most eloquently:

> Here was a man who had doomed hundreds of innocent victims to a horrible death for the mere lust of gain now passing into eternity without betraying the least sense of the enormity of his crime! With his dying lips he charged the one chiefly concerned in convicting him with violating pledges never given and with breaking promises never made. Thus he went into eternity, not with penitence and confession, but with a lying and malignant spirit, to make the moral aspects of the scene even more dreadful than those of the physical or material.[15]

His concern and pleas for the welfare of his wife and son were both heart-wrenching and real. Elizabeth was a constant presence throughout his 16 months of imprisonment. Murray states

> Gordon himself in spite of his natural and assumed stoicism reciprocated her attachment. To her he was always gentle and affectionate. . . . His love for her was sincere and unselfish. . . . She well deserved all the de-

votion he could give and all the praise and admiration that strangers
might lavish. For Gordon, individually, there existed very little sympathy,
it was compassion for his poor suffering wife that created as much interest in his case.[16]

Gordon conversed "rationally and coherently" with his keepers after
completing his letters, apparently recovered from his suicide attempt.
By this time, it was mid-morning. At some point, he asked to see
Marshal Murray on a private matter. When the marshal went to
Gordon's cell, the prisoner asked him to cut off a lock of his hair and
to give it, along with his watch and ring, to Elizabeth after his death.
Murray agreed, and, "quite overcome with emotion," left Gordon
alone.[17]

At 11 o'clock, a company of Marines under the command of Captain
Cohen entered the prison, marched to the courtyard, and went into formation at the gallows, their bayonets fixed and their muskets loaded.
They were accompanied by a military band playing somber music.
Armed Marines also guarded the outer doors to the prison, where a
large crowd milled. Threats had been made against officials, and a
rumor had surfaced of a plot to storm the Tombs. Despite the pitiful
turnout at the previous day's support rally for Gordon, the mayor intended to be ready; he assigned a large force of city police to maintain
order in the streets.[18]

At 11:30, Dean desperately played one last card. He came to the
Tombs, found Murray, and told him that Governor Morgan had inter-
ceded by sending a telegram to President Lincoln in a last-minute attempt to save the prisoner's life. Dean begged Murray to delay the
execution in the hope of a reprieve, but the marshal held firm. Gordon
would be hanged as scheduled.[19]

The courtyard in which the scaffold stood occupied the center of the
prison, and measured roughly 45 feet by 75 feet. The walls surrounding
the yard were sufficiently high and thick that nothing within could be
seen or heard from the street or the buildings nearby. The practice of
staging an execution in a cloistered space was a relatively new one.
Until 1836, executions in New York, as elsewhere in the country, were
publicly held events, serving the dual function of morality lesson and
entertainment. Bleachers were often constructed at government expense, and venders sold food and "spirituous liquors." Ballads known

as "broadsides," falsely purporting to be the victim's own lyric account of his misdeeds, were cheaply printed and sold under the gallows, while nearby homeowners sold viewing perches on fences and rooftops. A Massachusetts magazine, the *Escritoir,* printed its disgusted account of a public hanging in 1826, stating "all the public gatherings and drunken bouts put together, could not equal it. . . . Rioting, drunkenness, and every species of disorderly conduct prevail on such an occasion to an extent never witnessed from any other cause."[20] Henry Wadsworth Longfellow observed a hanging in 1854:

> Then within a prison-yard,
>     Faces fixed, and stern, and hard,
>         Laughter and indecent mirth;
>     Ah! It is the gallows tree![21]

New York was one of the first states to legislate against public executions, and to place local officials in charge of attendance. This eliminated the riffraff and ensured that the audience would be relatively well behaved. Attendance was limited by space; prior to each execution, thousands of people pressured the sheriffs and marshals for tickets of admission. When there were more applicants than space permitted, the officers' selection was often politically motivated. As one historian of the subject wrote, "The genteel had taken the whole show for themselves."[22]

This was no guarantee, however, that an execution would not occasionally turn into a circus. One such spectacle occurred in July 1860, at the same time Nathaniel Gordon was trading whiskey for slaves on the Congo River. A convicted murderer named Albert W. Hicks was scheduled to face the New York gallows. Hicks, a notorious street tough and career criminal, had taken an ax to the captain and two mates of the oyster sloop *E. A. Johnson.* Because he also attempted to steal the boat, the charge against him was one of piracy rather than simple homicide, and as such was a federal offense. "The Pirate Hicks," as he came to be known, was originally slated to die in the courtyard of the Tombs, but it was decided to hang him on federal rather than city property. Bedloe's Island, future site of the Statue of Liberty, was selected.

P. T. Barnum, the master showman, was always on the lookout for a curiosity. He made a deal with Warden Sutton of the Tombs to get a death mask of Hicks as well as the felon's clothes for his museum in exchange for $25 for Sutton and two boxes of cigars and a new suit of clothes for Hicks. (Presumably, the deal was made far enough in advance of the hanging to allow Hicks time to smoke his cigars.) When the suit was delivered, Hicks objected to its poor quality, and with ironic humor complained it "wouldn't last." Warden Sutton had a fine suit of clothes custom made, at taxpayers' expense. In recognition of Hicks's offense, it featured embroidered anchors and gilt buttons. Hicks would face oblivion in sartorial splendor.

On the morning of July 13, the infamous U.S. marshal Isaiah Rynders escorted the prisoner to a steamer at the Canal Street dock, where they were joined by 1,500 festive spectators and the hangman, Joseph "Little Joe" Atkinson. Little Joe had successfully dispatched dozens of felons, and was now being relied upon to provide a serviceable exit for Hicks. Once aboard, Rynders suggested a short trip up the Hudson, so the "guests" could take full advantage of the clear and lovely day. The marshal, ever a crowd-pleaser, stood on the bridge and acted as tour guide, his sword of office in one hand and a voice trumpet in the other. When the steamer finally docked at Bedloe's Island, Hicks was duly hanged, as some 10,000 additional people cheered from boats and stands, and hawkers sold food and beer to the crowd.[23] Shortly after Hicks's festive end, there appeared a broadside ballad called "Hicks the Pirate," which was written to commemorate the event, and sung to the tune of the Irish traditional ballad "The Rose Tree":

> Twixt heaven and earth suspended,
>     On Bedloe's Island Hicks was hung,
> Some thousands there attended,
>     To see the horrid murderer swung.[24]

Marshal Robert Murray was of a different stripe than Rynders. He was sickened by the hundreds of applications for guest passes to Gordon's execution, and personally oversaw and controlled the list of invitations, making certain that decorum would be maintained. There would be no repetition of the Hicks debacle; Gordon would die in an atmosphere of solemnity befitting the occasion.

Early in the morning, the ground of the Tombs courtyard had been covered with hemlock boards, possibly due to the uncertainty of the February weather. Roughly one-third of the yard had been fenced off, to accommodate the spectators. This left a 15-foot clear space around the gallows, allowing the marshal and his deputies to move "unrestrained." The prison yard could hold 500 people, but Marshal Murray was strict in his selection, and on this day there would be only 400 in attendance—300 by invitation, the rest in some official capacity— Marines, prison officials, reporters, clergy. Only upon presentation of their tickets at the prison door would the observers be allowed entry.[25]

The scaffold stood in the center of the courtyard, a "bare and horrible sight." The gallows itself was a curious device. The structure consisted of two uprights and a crossbeam connecting them at the top. Adjoining one of the uprights was a "sentry box" large enough to accommodate and conceal the executioner. From the center of the crossbeam hung a rope, the end of which featured an iron ring. The rope ran up and along the crossbeam through a series of pulleys, connecting to a heavy weight. This weight hung down into the sentry box, where a length of cord held it suspended approximately four or five feet above the ground. The condemned man would stand beneath the crossbeam with a five-foot length of rope around his neck. At one end, under his left ear, was a slipknot; at the other, an iron clasp. At the appropriate moment, the executioner would link the clasp to the iron ring of the main rope, place the black hood over the face of the condemned, and disappear into the sentry box. The box had a peephole through which he could watch for the signal. When the marshal raised his sword, the executioner cut the cord holding the weight. The weight would plummet to the ground with an audible "thud" as the body was jerked upward, with a violent enough motion to—hopefully—break the neck and cause instant death.[26]

Marshal Murray, in his account of the Gordon case, includes a detailed comparison of this type of gallows, dubbed the American system, with that used in England at the time. The English gallows, he wrote, dropped the victim through a trapdoor, resulting in strangulation rather than a broken neck. The victim fell only a short distance through the trap—to strangle in full view of the public—with only the lower body below the platform. It was not until the mid-1870s that the British government devoted any effort toward merciful executions.[27]

America, on the other hand, was undergoing a major transformation regarding hanging. Most, by their very nature, were not humane events. In colonial times, the victim was simply walked up a ladder with a rope around his neck, the other end having been tied to a tree or beam. When he reached the appropriate height, he was pushed, or "turned off" the ladder, to strangle until dead.[28] Gradually, formal structures ("scaffolds") were built, with a trapdoor upon which the victim stood. The result was often no better, however. For various reasons—poor calculations of body weight and distance of fall, an inexperienced executioner, a rope with too much stretch—the victim usually suffered prolonged strangulation and a painful death. Until the late 1700s, this was either viewed as an unfortunate but sometimes unavoidable aspect of the execution, or as an outright bonus to the spectators. But Americans of the early to mid-1800s came to believe that, although executions were certainly necessary for the preservation of the common good, the *act* of hanging a person need not—indeed, should not—be a painful experience.[29]

Consequently, attempts were made to design a system that would take the felon's life but at a cost of little or no pain. In an effort to develop a humane system of hanging, every possible aspect of an execution was examined, including the heft and stretch of the rope, the height and weight of the victim, the drop, and the level of experience of the hangman. A new system was tried in 1831 on New York Harbor's Ellis Island, where convicted pirate Charles Gibbs was to be hanged. A complex system holding weights totaling 560 pounds was attached to the hang rope, which in turn was attached to Gibbs; as the weights dropped, he was jerked into the air.[30]

Refined even further, this type of gallows became known, appropriately, as the "Upright Jerker." The idea behind it was that the victim's neck was more susceptible to immediate fracture by the sudden application of large weights than by simply dropping him through a hole in the floor. By 1845, the Upright Jerker had become New York City's official gallows. It was soon adopted by other New York counties, as well as by Pittsburgh, Charleston, and Chicago.[31] As its popularity spread, so, too, did the desire to stage as painless an event as possible.

Unfortunately, the Upright Jerker proved as fallible as the other systems. Two years before Gordon's appointment with the hangman, James Stephens was brought under the Jerker. The deputy was careless in cutting the string holding the weights, and the crowd watched aghast as the rope slowly ran off the cleat, raising Stephens off the ground, inch by inch, to a height of four feet, where he died "after eight minutes of gurgling and contortions."[32] Sometimes, as in the case of the ironically named James Stone of Washington, D.C., the weights were so heavy that the victim's head would be ripped from his body.[33] When operating at maximum efficiency, the system usually still failed to sever the spinal column. As early as 1852, the *New York Times* urged, "Let some less revolting plan than hanging be fixed upon. The bullet, the guillotine, the garrote, are incomparably better in the eye than the gallows."[34] But it was the gallows that awaited Nathaniel Gordon.

At noon, in company with Marshal Murray, four deputies, and various members of the press, Superintendent Simeon Draper entered Gordon's cell and informed him that the time had come. Gordon was momentarily stunned, having prepared himself for the latest possible execution of the sentence, and responded, "I thought it was not to take place until 2 o'clock." Draper explained that by attempting suicide, Gordon had broken his promise to the marshal, and that Murray had consequently ordered the hanging to take place as soon as was legally possible.[35]

After his initial reaction, Gordon quietly accepted Draper's pronouncement, and the preparations began. The Reverend Amzi Camp entered Gordon's cell for the last time to pray for him. Apparently, Reverend Camp was a man with a mission; he had met Gordon after his conviction and had been "unceasing in his professional attentions to [him] from the day of sentence to the final hour." A reporter for the *New York Times,* anxious to satisfy the readership's interest in "Gordon's feelings in view of the future world," interviewed the reverend after the fact:

> I have attended Gordon regularly for sometime past, with a view of bringing his mind to a just realization of his situation. He was always respectful, but his manner led me to infer that, while he would not repulse or rebuff me, he wouldn't feel very bad about it if I should keep away. He was thoroughly stoical. . . . I went into his cell last night about 9 o'clock, and prayed with him, but he didn't seem to care much for it. He seems to have no conscientious regret for what he has done, and his

only care seems to be for the welfare of his wife and child. Finding that my visit could be of no possible use, I urged him to think of his near approach to eternity, commended him to the mercies of our Redeemer, bade him farewell, and left.[36]

While Murray's account also describes Gordon as "unmoved" by the clergyman's prayer, another reporter, this one from the *New York Herald,* wrote that the prisoner "listened attentively . . . and expressed a fervent hope that he might be the recipient of God's mercy and pardon."[37] If he responded in this way to Camp's efforts, it was probably just as a courtesy to the long-suffering and frustrated reverend. There would be no last-minute bid for salvation.

A deputy marshal then bound Gordon's arms and placed the black hood atop his head. A chair was set for him outside his cell. Noticing his watch was no longer hanging over his bed, Gordon said, "Where's my watch? I won't stir out of this cell 'til I know where my watch has gone to!"

Murray reminded Gordon that he held his watch, as Gordon had earlier requested, along with the prisoner's ring and the lock of his hair, to give to Elizabeth. His memory jogged, Gordon calmly walked into the prison corridor and took his seat.[38] At this time, the Portland reporter "had now a chance to observe what manner of man he was. His frame was small but sinewy. The pallor of his countenance, contrasting with the black cap, was almost ghastly, and he was much emaciated from over a year's confinement in prison."[39]

Seated in the midst of the standing officials and reporters, Gordon listened with visible impatience as Murray read—"in a distinct voice, tremulous with emotion"—President Lincoln's earlier two-week reprieve, then the death warrant. These were trying formalities but necessary, in accordance with law. Then Murray asked if he had anything to say. Gordon stood, and with "considerable animation," said,

Yes, sir, I have something to say, but I won't detain you long. I have to thank you, Marshal Murray, your deputies, Mr. Draper, and Mr. Sutton and his Warders for the uniform kindness I have experienced. You have all shewn me every indulgence consistent with duty. I hope God will reward you. I also thank, from my heart, Judge Dean, my counsel, and all who have interested themselves in my behalf. But there is one I do not thank, though I bear him no grudge. He has *not* acted fair. When a man begs a jury only to convict a prisoner and that he will then be the first to intercede for him, but afterwards does all in his power to prevent that prisoner's pardon, he must be a mean fellow. *Nothing is too bad for such a man.* I thank you all again. Pray do not forget my dear wife and poor little child; they are quite destitute. I should die happy if I knew that they were provided for. I have no more to say.[40]

At one point during his speech, Gordon's legs trembled. Some reporters mistook this as a sign of inebriation. When a deputy offered assistance, Gordon indignantly rebuffed him and continued his death speech, which "was delivered ever more distinctly, and in that part alluding to the District Attorney, with more bitter emphasis."[41] Gordon walked outside at 12:20 and, in the heavy silence, was escorted across the prison yard. The procession was led by two deputies, followed by Marshal Murray and then Gordon, flanked by two more deputies. Behind them came another contingent of deputies, along with physicians, the coroner's jury, and the reporters. Marshal Murray wore a brand-new uniform of blue, faced with two rows of brass buttons. On his breast shone a gold shield reading "U.S. Marshal," on his head was a ceremonial cocked hat. He carried a sword at his side.

The silent crowd through which Gordon passed consisted entirely of men; in that time, women would not have been invited. (Even if they were allowed, Elizabeth certainly could not have borne it, nor would Gordon have wanted her there.) Those witness who weren't in uniform were dressed in dark frock coats and tall silk hats, a few in bowlers. The reporters were busily scribbling in their notepads; the others stood with their hands at their sides, or clasped behind their backs, or in their pockets for warmth, since the day was chilly. All conducted themselves with decorum.

When Gordon took his place beneath the rope, he spoke in a soft, friendly tone to Bill Isaacs, the executioner. "Bill, I'm an old salt. This sort of death is hard lines. Make the knot run easy, and fix it on the right side."[42] Isaacs did so, although the prescribed place for the knot was on the left. Gordon's thoughts now were of his wife and son, and after shaking hands all around, he addressed Murray for the last time: "Don't forget your promise." Again to Isaacs: "Make short work of it now, Bill. I'm ready."[43]

The cap was drawn down over Gordon's face, and without hesitation, Murray waved his sword. The cord was cut, and Gordon's body shot four feet into the air; except for some minor convulsive twitching of the hands and a slow scissoring of the legs, his body hung still, "a lump of dishonored clay."[44] The reporter for the *New York Herald* commented, "It has seldom been our lot to witness an execution where the culprit suffered less than Gordon did."[45] As was customary, the marshal let the body hang for 15 minutes before ordering it lowered sufficiently for Doctors Finnell, Kimbark, and Shrady to examine it for heartbeat and pulse. They found none; however, Murray thought it advisable to allow Gordon to hang for another few minutes.

Nathaniel Gordon's body was taken down at 12:45 and carried to an outbuilding, where the coroner held his inquest. When the cap was removed, it was observed that there was no facial discoloration; a "meaningless smile sat on the blanched lip," and a "glassy look stared from the half-closed eyes."[46] The coroner determined that death had been instantaneous, due to fractures of both neck and thyroid cartilage.[47] If Gordon had any luck at all since the moment of his arrest a year and a half earlier, it was in his final moments, when the Upright Jerker functioned as it was supposed to and allowed him a quick and presumably painless death. Nathaniel Gordon was then placed in a coffin and, in accordance with his request, delivered that evening to Elizabeth at the Williamsburg home of Captain and Mrs. Woodside.[48]

Word of Gordon's execution spread rapidly. Brief, straightforward articles appeared in newspapers from Portland, Maine, to Richmond, Virginia, capital of the Confederacy. The *Richmond Examiner* reported the event without editorializing.[49] The *Christian Intelligencer* saw the execution as a means of cleansing New York's reputation. Shocking as the hanging might have been,

[W]e have among us those who will not be deterred by methods less severe. And *New York* has long enough borne the disgrace of being the *greatest depot of the slave trade in the world.* Here scores of ships have been fitted out yearly on the negro stealing business. Men have been convicted but slipped their necks from the noose of the law by the connivance of our authorities. . . . But they can do it no longer. . . . Let those who were associated with [Gordon] beware. Their turn may come next.[50]

As Lincoln had anticipated, London had been following the case with interest. On March 8, the *London Daily News* published an article reflecting British response to the execution. It is exceptional in its concise evaluation of the significance of the event, and of Lincoln's role in it.

Our American telegram yesterday contained the short and simple statement that "Captain Gordon has been hanged." It would not be strange if, in the absence of all explanation, some who read this said to themselves, that that was the Captain's affair. Yet Captain Gordon's execution was by no means an event of merely personal interest. On the contrary, throughout America it is understood to be full of significance. It is an index of the quality of Mr. Lincoln's government, of its strength of principle, and the consistency of its policy, and *it marks the end of a system*. Gordon was tried and convicted as the Captain of a slaver and was sentenced to death. Under Pierce, Buchanan and Presidents of their stamp, his condemnation would not have caused his friends any serious alarm. It was well understood on all sides that there were legal forms, decent, proper in a Christian and civilized nation; and solemn sentences passed on persons proved to have participated in the African slave trade were not at all objected to as long as they were not carried out. The prospect changed, however, when Mr. Lincoln was made President. . . . Still when a slave captain was actually convicted and sentenced to death, it was very generally doubted whether the government would hold firm. Presidents who [were] quite prepared to condemn the African slave trade . . . recoiled from the thought of strangling a white man who had removed some black men from a state of barbarism to a Christian country. Mr. Lincoln, they said, although a free soiler, was not a fanatical abolitionist and would think twice before he sacrificed the life of a man of Anglo-Saxon blood to a sentiment in favor of the negro. These people, however, forget the difference between principle and sentiment. . . .

There is not a kinder man in the world than Mr. Lincoln; but neither is there a man who better understands how cruel may be this indulgence of fond sentiment at the expense of duty. Captain Gordon would have had a better chance had his life depended on the decision of some impulsive negro-phile, instead of being at the disposal of the severe, deliberative, but inflexible tenant of the White House, a man who, amidst the severest trials has never swerved a hair's breadth from the policy which he professed when he was a candidate for office. Those who knew President Lincoln well said that he would not lose the precious opportunity to strike a blow at a system which costs hundreds of lives yearly. . . . They said Gordon would certainly be hanged. They were right, and from the Bight of Benin to the Coast of Cuba the man-stealer will tremble.[51]

This was the response that Lincoln had sought, and it paved the way for the Seward-Lyons agreement, known officially as the Treaty Between the United States and Great Britain for the Suppression of the Slave Trade.

New York's Republican press exulted at the execution. The day after Gordon's death, the *New York Times* printed a typical editorial, praising President Lincoln for standing firm in the face of tremendous pressure and supporting the "mighty power of justice which this unfortunate man [Gordon] had put in motion against himself." More than the federal government, New York City itself had stood in desperate need of vindication. The article delivers a scathing indictment of the city, sparing no branch of New York society: "[T]he majesty of the law has been vindicated, and the stamp of the gallows . . . set upon the crime of slave-trading. . . . And it was time." The merchants of New York, their consciences deadened by their "cursed greed for gain," were responsible for Gordon's actions, while the clergy, in refusing to speak out, had caused the entire community to lose "their sense of the wickedness of the trade." This explains why Gordon "should . . . four times have gone into a traffic to which the law had affixed the penalty of death[.]" New York's guilt, the article continues, is massive:

> This City has exerted a terrible influence in that direction. She might well send petitions signed by twenty-five thousand names in Gordon's favor, for his blood lies partly on her skirts. New-York has been most deeply engaged in the traffic. Her merchants have largely profited by its blood-stained gains.

With so many involved in the commerce, and so many more looking the other way, no one expected the law to be carried out. "The oft repeated refrain," says the writer, "was, 'They dare not hang him.' Was it a surprising thing that he should have transgressed the law . . . ? "

It is appropriate, according to the article, that many in New York worked to save the man; after all, they were the ones who put him in this situation. The reader shouldn't think of Gordon as blameless, however:

> He must have known when he did what he did that, if he was convicted of the act, the penalty was death. He doubtless had no expectation of being caught. . . . He did not expect to be convicted if he was caught. He relied upon legal quibbles and difficulties of proof. But when a man yields to temptation upon such a reliance, he cannot complain if it fails him.

And again, there was sympathy for Elizabeth:

> We are sorry for his family and friends, but we cannot but rejoice that the Slave-trade has received so heavy a blow. Our City has been disgraced long enough. Our whole country has shared that disgrace. We rejoice in the belief . . . that the sternness with which the law had been carried out in this instance will be effectual for the destruction of so enormous a crime within the borders not only of this City, but of the whole land.[52]

The *Post* and the *Tribune* printed editorials of like tone and substance. Washington's Birthday, the national holiday that Gilbert Dean was so anxious not to stain with his client's blood, was observed at New York's Cooper Union with speeches by several political luminaries. Far from dampening the spirit of the occasion, Gordon's execution was noted as a cause for celebration. Keynote speaker George Bancroft, noted historian and former secretary of the navy, referred to Gordon in his oration:

> If the opinions of Washington on slavery and the slave trade had been steadily respected, the country would have escaped all the calamity of the present civil war. . . . Yesterday the sentiment of Jefferson, that the slave trade is a piratical warfare upon mankind, was reaffirmed by carrying into effect the sentence of a high tribunal of justice; and to save the lives and protect the happiness of thousands a slave trader was executed as a pirate and an enemy of the human race.[53]

(The irony that the wealth and status of both Washington and Jefferson depended entirely on slave labor, their "opinions" notwithstanding, seems to have escaped Bancroft.)

The newspaper reporters and editors of 1862, as now, recognized that sensationalism enhanced sales. As they would with any newsworthy event, the members of the press—those who witnessed the execution as well as many who received their information secondhand—all gave the events of the day their own twists on the truth. The Springfield, Massachusetts, *Daily Republican* of February 22 wrote, "Gordon, the slaver captain, was executed at New York, at noon, on Friday. He made no speech. He attempted suicide Thursday night by smoking cigars saturated in strychnine."[54] Ignorant of Gordon's explanation of the presence of the poison in his cell, most reporters merely assumed he had smoked cigars—"segars," as some papers put it—soaked in poison. This became the generally accepted version.

A more damaging assertion that played repeatedly in the press, casting aspersions directly on the conduct of Marshal Murray himself, was the claim that Gordon was drunk and went to his death an insensible and pathetic figure. The reporter for the *Portland Advertiser* wrote that "the physicians had poured down such quantities of stimulants— whiskey and brandy—that he may be said to have died drunk."[55] The writer for the *New York Herald* put it forth that Gordon "tottered to the scaffold like a man half dead with fear or stupefied with liquor, it is hard to say which."[56]

Even the *New York Times* observed that "he had just sense enough left to endeavor to follow out the suggestion of the well-meaning deputy, who told him to die like a man, and to walk to the rope, so that no one could accuse him of fear. . . . The noose-knot was adjusted under his ear, and he stood, an unthinking, careless, besotted wretch waiting for he knew not what, when with a jerk he went high in air, and fell to the length of the rope, still senseless, still unfeeling, still regardless of pain or pleasure."[57]

Two days later, the *Times* printed an editorial protesting the "barbarity of his execution." The article claimed that he was "lifted into his place, held up while the fatal cord was placed around his neck, and the last lingering relics of his life were thus extinguished." It went on to suggest that Gordon was already a dying man at noon, and that Murray should have delayed the hanging until 2:30, either to allow the prisoner to die in peace or, in the unlikely event that he rallied, to hang him *after* he had had a chance to recover naturally. "Why was it so essential that he be hung . . . ? "[58] This, from the newspaper that had been clamoring for Gordon's execution since his first trial, and had exulted in it only two days before.

Not surprisingly, the news was avidly read and believed. Even George Templeton Strong, the insightful diarist, was not immune, and wrote in his journal, "Gordon, poor wretch, made a pitiful exit. He went to the gibbet half-dead with a dose of strychnine . . . and more than half-drunk with brandy. The doctors dosed him with stimulants and thus kept life in his body for the law to extinguish in due form." Strong, however, fully supported the execution, adding, "Serves him right. . . . *Vivat lex,* and may it promptly exterminate every man who imports niggers into this continent."[59]

Marshal Murray's account answers the charges that Gordon went to the scaffold drunk and near death:

> No unprejudiced, reasoning spectator of that execution, who heard Gordon's last speech—so cool, deliberate, and emphatic—can, for one moment, have supposed him to have been under the influence of liquor. The slight tremor in his frame, and the weakness in his knees were the effects of strychnine, not of intoxication. Although his arms were bound, he refused support, even to the last moment and seemed quite offended when it was volunteered by one of the marshal's deputies.[60]

A letter to Murray from Abbott Hodgman and John Simmons, two of the physicians who had labored to revive Gordon after his suicide attempt, stated the case clearly and credibly:

> Sir: Reports being in circulation that Nathaniel Gordon was intentionally made drunk previous to his execution[,] we think it is a duty we owe to you and to ourselves to correct such error by stating the facts as they occurred. . . .

The doctors then provided a detailed, hour-by-hour account of their efforts to resuscitate the stricken prisoner until 11 A.M., when further treatment was considered unnecessary.

[Gordon] then conversed freely, and stated that he had taken strychnine at 3 o'clock a.m. with the intention of destroying his own life.
Before coming out of his cell he remarked "As the poison has not
taken effect, and I am now ready to die, the sooner it is over the better.
Let it come as soon as possible." On leaving his cell . . . and in a
firm, clear voice, [he] made the speech reported in the newspapers of the
day. He was not carried to the gallows, as alleged, but walked in the
usual manner . . . and there stood without support until the last
moment.[61]

This was the age of the Victorian morality tale, and what better way
to portray the death of a slaver than cowering before his fate, supported on the gallows by the stalwart officers of the law? It made for a
morally appropriate resolution, and one that satisfied a basic need in
the reader. It was also untrue. His limbs were certainly shaky, and there
must have been some light-headedness. Gordon was a small man,
made considerably smaller by a year and a half in prison and further
weakened by an extraordinarily painful and debilitating poisoning.
He was also preparing to leave his family, as well as his very existence,
in a manner certain to bring shame on his loved ones and infamy to
his name. Considering these circumstances, and despite the fact that
he went to his death an unredeemed and unrepentant felon, it is fair
to say that Nathaniel Gordon bore up rather well during his final
moments.

The Gordon case would be news for one more day. His funeral took
place at the home of Captain Woodside, at 119 South Eighth Street,
Williamsburg, Brooklyn, on February 22, 1862. The press reported that
"an immense crowd of spectators surrounded" Woodside's home. Some
of these were supporters, but almost certainly a larger number were curiosity seekers. Gordon was then brought to Cypress Hills Cemetery in
Brooklyn.[62] He was buried on a hillside in lot 403, section 4, grave #13,
in the plot of a family named Hetfield.[63] No record exists of the connection between Gordon or Woodside and the Hetfields. Today, the lot,
long neglected and overgrown, contains 19 gravesites; Gordon's was
the first. If there was ever a stone, it no longer survives, nor does any
other indication of a grave.

After the execution, Elizabeth Gordon continued to live for a time
with the Woodsides. Marshal Murray honored his promise to Gordon
and did his best for Elizabeth and her five-year-old son. He initiated

a subscription, by which he managed to raise $115 for them. A ben-efit was held in their behalf at the Bowery Theater, which realized them another $300. "Still," as Murray recorded in his account of the case, "it would be a true charity if some beneficent individual would supply her the means to commence a small business and to educate her child, as the poor woman remains in very precarious circum-stances."[64]

Nothing is known of Elizabeth once she left New York. It is unlikely that she returned to Portland as there is no mention of her in any of the Portland—or Maine—directories, nor is she buried in any of Portland's cemeteries. She is not listed in any of the U.S. federal census reports for 1870 through 1910, nor in the Canadian census reports through the 1880s. In fact, no information at all exists on Elizabeth Annie Kenney Gordon before 1855, or after 1862. Even her true birthplace remains a mystery; various census reports, newspaper articles, and government documents list her place of birth alternately as New Brunswick, Nova Scotia, and England.[65]

Interestingly, genealogical research reveals that her son eventually made his way back to Portland, living only a mile from his former fam-ily home. He earned his living as a hard-hat marine diver; an 1890 newspaper article described his business as "lucrative," and he was considered "the city's most noted submarine diver."[66] In his later years, he owned a grocery store. Married twice, he was the father of one child and the grandfather of two. But as with his mother, his vital information is muddled. Although his birth certificate correctly states that he was born in Cape Elizabeth in April 1857, the June 1860 census—taken while his father was sailing the *Erie* on its fateful voyage toward the west coast of Africa—lists his birthplace as Illinois, as does the census of 1900. The Maine census reports of 1880 and 1920 have him born in New York. He died in Portland in 1922, and his death certificate, in all likelihood filled out by his second wife, correctly lists his parents' names, but claims his place of birth as Green Bay, Wisconsin; it has his birth day correct, but the year wrong by one year.[67]

His son—the slaver's grandson—was the sixth and last Gordon to have the name Nathaniel. His friends knew him as Ned. He was reput-edly a highly intelligent and appealing man with a lively sense of humor, and was well liked within the community. Ned Gordon served as managing editor of Maine's three Gannett newspapers from 1927 until 1945, and died in 1948. Both his children are gone as well, but according to Maine genealogist Kenneth Thompson, "there are an unknown number of Captain Gordon's great-great-grandchildren alive . . . in the 50's to late 60's age range, none of whom I suspect know anything of their infamous ancestor." [68]

## CHAPTER XII

## TO HANG A SLAVER

It would be difficult to find a person with worse luck than "Lucky Nat" Gordon. Fortune failed him from the moment he sought clearance from Consul Charles J. Helm, the U.S. consul general in Cuba, until he stood on the gallows a year and a half later. There is simply no logical explanation for why this one man attracted so much negative attention from people who never met him. Three cabinet secretaries, two federal judges, a U.S. attorney, a federal marshal, and finally, the president made Gordon's fate their personal agenda. Even his capture defies logic. The fact that the *Erie* was spotted, stopped, and taken by a ship of the woefully unsuccessful African Squadron speaks to Gordon's bad fortune.

Having been indicted and jailed in New York, the least likely venue to convict a slaver, Nathaniel Gordon—his life and livelihood—should have been safe. As the single largest center in the world for the financing and outfitting of slaving expeditions, New York had little reason to want Gordon executed. Men like him had been part of the city's financial infrastructure for years. However, the election of a Republican administration and the subsequent appointments of E. Delafield Smith to the office of U.S. attorney and Robert Murray to the position of U.S. marshal changed the climate. The timing of the war—coming so near Gordon's indictment—further lessened his chances of survival. With

(left, above) HARPER'S WEEKLY ON-SITE DEPICTION OF THE GORDON EXECUTION, SHOWING HANGMAN BILL ISAACS FIXING THE ROPE AROUND THE SLAVER'S NECK.

(left, below) NEW YORK ILLUSTRATED NEWS ON-SITE ENGRAVING OF THE GORDON EXECUTION, DEPICTING THE BODY OF CAPTAIN GORDON HANGING FROM THE CROSSBEAM OF THE "UPRIGHT JERKER."

Northern warships blockading Southern ports and the issue of slavery establishing itself as a major factor in the conflict, the wartime attitudes of people who once had looked the other way were changing; a more ominous view was taken of the slave trade. Despite the fact that laws forbidding it had been on the books for 68 years, suddenly people were awakened to the horrors of the trade, in large measure due to the publicity given trials such as Gordon's.

Significantly, for the first time, the five links necessary to hang a slaver were solidly in place: he was arrested by American officers; he remained in jail long enough to face trial (although he had many opportunities to escape); despite a hung jury in the first trial, he eventually faced a jury willing to convict; the prosecution's case was sufficiently sound that no technicality could be cited to cancel the verdict; and Gordon was proven to be an American officer serving aboard a laden slaver. The links were strong, and the chain held. With the president's denial of clemency, Gordon's fate was sealed.

But surely other captured slave-ship captains and mates were equally guilty. Why was Gordon the *only* slaver to die on the gallows? The constant failure to actively pursue and end the slave trade by the U.S. government, the navy, and the courts explains why no one was punished in the decades *before* the Gordon case, but why weren't the slavers who were captured *at the same time* as Gordon, and *after* Gordon, and even *along with* Gordon, dealt with as harshly as he? After all, Smith's masterful handling of this case should have paved the way for further capital convictions.

In fact, Smith had no intention of hanging every slaver he brought to trial; he was out to set examples. What he saw as vital in his efforts to break up the slave trade were the successful prosecution and conviction of the three types of men most crucial to the traffic's success: those who owned and outfitted the vessels; those who sailed them; and those who bonded them so that they might sail again. The slave trade in New York was, in the words of one of Smith's predecessors, "carried on with a regular machinery to evade the law," relying on "lies, fraud, and perjury . . . , agents and foreigners . . . having no design but to circumvent justice."[1] Smith's master plan was to unravel this skein of deceit by attacking its main facets.

In a letter to Postmaster General Montgomery Blair in November 1862, he states his intentions clearly:

Three things are required to end the slave trade at this port: First, to stop the fitting out; Secondly, to restrain American officers and seamen from serving on slave ships; and Thirdly, to extirpate "Straw Bail" for vessels seized for the offence and then bonded or bailed and discharged.[2]

Smith carefully chose his three examples: Nathaniel Gordon, Albert Horn, and Rudolph Blumenberg. Gordon had already been hanged. Horn, a New York merchant, owned and had fitted out the *City of Norfolk,* a 572-ton steamer that was taken in October 1860 with 560 slaves aboard.[3] Horn and his captain, Henry C. Crawford, were both arrested. Horn was indicted under the Act of 1818, which prohibited the fitting out of vessels "with intent to employ" them as slavers. The specified penalty was a fine and imprisonment.[4] Crawford, however, was indicted as a pirate, under the same act that would hang Captain Gordon.[5]

Delafield Smith had Crawford dead to rights. But he agreed to drop all charges against him if he would testify against Horn. Naturally, Crawford jumped at the chance; Horn was convicted and sentenced to five years' imprisonment, and Crawford left court a free man. The prosecutor who had sent one slaver to the gallows let another go free, for helping him win a five-year sentence against a ship owner.

Rudolph Blumenberg's story is tied directly to that of the notorious slaver *Orion.* The vessel had been captured, libeled in New York, bonded, equipped for another slaving voyage, and captured once again. The firm of Beebe, Dean, and Donahoe defended the crew, and convinced then–U.S. Attorney Roosevelt that there was insufficient evidence to justify pursuing a trial. The men were all released, but the ship was libeled. However, Congress had passed a law in March 1847, in an effort to "reduce expenses of proceedings in Admiralty," that allowed the owners of libeled vessels to post bond in order to regain custody of their ships. This legislation created a number of loopholes, all of which worked to the benefit of the slavers. It allowed a ship owner to bail out his libeled ship and send it to sea on another slaving voyage while the fate of the vessel was still being decided in court. The only stipulation set by the law was that the vessel not engage in illegal activities. If captured again, the bond would be forfeit.

During this period of frenetic slaving activity, bondsmen did not have to pay before they bailed out a ship; it was common practice for a bondsman to swear an oath promising the sum required to bond a vessel, with virtually nothing to back it up. The laxness of the courts allowed this to continue, while the offending bondsmen went unpunished—until the *Orion* and the bondsman who'd freed her to pursue her final voyage: Rudolph Blumenberg. He swore before Judge Betts's clerk that he had the $17,923 required to back up the vessel's bond; he lied. When the *Orion* was recaptured with a cargo of nearly 1,000 Africans aboard, she was again libeled. This time she was condemned and destroyed. The court demanded that Blumenberg forfeit the bond. When it became evident that he had neither sufficient money nor property, he was charged with perjury and brought to trial in circuit court.[6]

Smith was determined to send Blumenberg to jail, but he had to try the man three times; the first two trials ended in hung juries. The third resulted in Blumenberg's conviction in May 1861. Justice Nelson sentenced him to five years in Ossining, "as a warning to others."[7]

In his letter to Postmaster General Blair, Smith continued:

> The first will be accomplished in the conviction of the merchant, Albert Horn; the second, by the execution of Gordon; and the third, by the punishment of Blumenberg. The exertions now on foot to relieve Horn, will render *his* pardon necessary, if Blumenberg is released. And the discharge of them or either of them would make the execution of Gordon an idle and therefore a cruel ceremony.[8]

Smith was understandably concerned with the necessity of keeping Horn and Blumenberg in prison, to send a clear message to all owners and bondsmen of slave ships. Ironically, Smith's grand design would be foiled by the one man who had ensured his success in the Gordon case. Convicted in October 1862, Horn served less than seven months of his five-year sentence—he received a presidential pardon due to ill health.[9] Rudolph Blumenberg actually served a little over two years of *his* sentence, before Lincoln awarded *him* a pardon in early 1863 for supplying Marshal Robert Murray with information about the slave trade in New York.[10]

Smith's determination to vigorously prosecute only one defendant from each of his three target groups explains his less-than-forceful efforts against other slavers. But there was another reason why they weren't punished with the same vigor as Captain Gordon. Although the links were all in place for Gordon's conviction, and the chain held, such was not the case with most of the other slave traders brought to New York at around the same time, despite the fact that all their vessels were captured laden.

The record is clear: the *Bonita*'s sailors, all foreigners, were quietly released after Smith decided to nol-pros their indictments. The *Cora*'s captain and first mate escaped custody; the remaining two mates were allowed to plead to a lesser charge and were each sentenced to ten months and a $500 fine. William Carter, captain of the schooner *Josephine,* was released on $3,000 bond, then promptly disappeared. Delafield Smith nol-prossed the indictment of the *Wildfire*'s owner, Pierre Pearce, so that he could stand trial in Boston; once there, he posted $10,000 bail and left for parts unknown. The captain and owner of the bark *Kate* each posted bond, and fled. In the case of the *Nightingale,* any chance Smith might have had to convict third mate Minthorne Westervelt was compromised when Justice Nelson took it upon himself to speak to the jury of the defendant's youth and good breeding. The jury was deadlocked, as it was with the ship's other two mates, and the charges against all three men were dropped.[11] Appleton Oaksmith, owner of the *Margaret Scott,* was released in New York, then indicted and convicted in Boston, only to break jail. Oaksmith's captain, Samuel Skinner, was actually convicted of fitting out a slave ship and sentenced to five years. He quickly turned informant and was pardoned by Lincoln.[12]

In nearly all these cases, at least one—and often more—of the five vital links in the chain was missing. When Smith elected to nol-pros a defendant, it was usually because he was aware of the likelihood of either an acquittal or a hung jury due to lack of evidence or proof of citizenship. There were, however, a few instances in which Smith had a clear-cut case, yet refrained from pressing his advantage. The most glaring was the case of Nathaniel Gordon's two mates.

After Gordon was executed, first mate William Warren and second mate David Hall still languished in the Tombs, no doubt anticipating a similar fate. After all, there was nothing to distinguish their cases from that of their late captain. At trial, their lawyer, Gilbert Dean, pointed out to the court that the defendants were penniless, having had their needs paid for by Captain Gordon "as long as the money lasted." Delafield Smith nol-prossed the piracy indictment and allowed each to plead guilty to the lesser charge of violating the Act of 1800. The captain had been hanged, as per Smith's plan; he saw no need to kill the mates as well. The court determined that they had served more than half the two-year sentence for the offense; Judge Shipman sentenced Warren to an additional eight months and Hall to nine months, and gave each man a token fine of one dollar. In sentencing Hall, Shipman said, "You may congratulate yourself upon getting off so easily. The crime you were engaged in was a very heinous one, and if caught engaged in it again, the punishment [will] be severe."[13]

The last slave trade case to be adjudicated in New York City was that of Erastus Booth, captain of the bark *Buckeye.* Indicted under the acts of both 1800 and 1820, Booth was tried in February 1862, the month of Gordon's execution. Surprisingly, he was immediately released on bail and—even more surprisingly in light of recent events—chose to wait around for his trial. After the chief prosecution witness left New York, Delafield Smith sensed that he did not have enough evidence to prove a capital case for piracy and dropped that charge in favor of the lesser count. The case was still so weak, however, that Judge Shipman instructed the jury to bring in a verdict for acquittal. Erastus Booth left circuit court a free man. According to one historian, "This debacle was a fitting end to American prosecutions of slave-trading pirates. . . . Only the disappearance of the slave trade brought an end to the government's inability to enforce its laws."[14]

The war against the slave trade was over. As the *New York Times* had predicted on the day after Gordon's execution, the government had "fired a ball cartridge" at the traffic, and indeed had "followed it up with blanks." The administration needed an example, and through the perfect confluence of timing and circumstances, they found it in Nathaniel Gordon. There would not be another.

But the last question that should be addressed is, to what extent, if any, did the hanging of Captain Gordon actually help to bring about an end to the slave trade? In fact, by late 1862 the African trade was dying anyway. An American naval officer visiting the Congo River in September found the trading centers "in a very depressed condition . . . and slave prices . . . fallen to one-third or one-fourth their 1860 levels." Within a year, the "fifteen slave 'factories' at Punta da Lenha [were] on the verge of collapse" and the slave traders were "at their wits' end" due to the scarcity of vessels looking for product.[15]

This was due to a number of circumstances unrelated to Gordon. For one, the markets were either drying up or inaccessible. Brazil had been closed to slavers since 1852; the one slave ship that tried to unload its cargo thereafter was driven off at every port, until a Brazilian warship finally captured her, released the slaves, and arrested the crew.[16] The British patrols off Havana were gradually eliminating Cuba as a market. Also, the Seward-Lyons treaty finally gave the British the right of search and seizure. And the Union blockades along the southern coast of the United States made it virtually impossible to deliver slaves, even if there were a demand, which at this time there clearly was not.

Further, it was becoming increasingly apparent to the president— and ultimately, to the nation—that the Civil War was as much about slavery as it was about union, and that a Northern victory would have a major impact on the institution. The country was in the process of making a sharp turn into a new era, in which "manstealing"—the horrific trafficking in humans—would no longer find acceptance.

In his account of the Gordon case, U.S. Marshal Robert Murray wrote that "the slave traders recognized in the Execution of Gordon their defeat, and a general exodus to Cuba ensued."[17] While it is tempting to envision the slavers leaving the country en masse, it is likelier that a number of the Lower Manhattan entrepreneurs simply took up residence in other Northern ports, where they could attempt to pursue their trade at less risk. Nearly four months after Gordon's death, Murray wrote to Secretary of the Interior Caleb Smith:

> Since entering upon the duties of this office, I have made an earnest effort, at least, to check the Slave Trade from the Port [of New York]. This City had become the principal depot for vessels in this traffic, and I felt that here the attempt must be made to arrest the Slave Trade. The seizures and arrests thus made have had the effect of stopping, at least temporarily[,] the fitting out of Slavers in this Port. But from reliable information in my possession, I am satisfied that the parties interested have removed their operations from New York to the ports of New London, New Bedford, and Portland. Allow me to draw your attention to this, so that steps may be taken to prevent the clearance of slavers from the New England waters.[18]

Slavers continued to operate, just not out of New York.

Surely the awareness that there was a newfound willingness to hang a man for engaging in slave trading must have given pause to some who might otherwise have considered a voyage to the Congo. But

Gordon's execution, while it sent a shock wave through New York's slaving community, did not have the immediate hoped-for impact. The slave trade was, in fact, dying; but before its demise, it actually took a very brief *upturn* in the spring of 1862, right after Gordon's death. With the price of slaves on the Congo at rock bottom, and the American African Squadron all but defunct, the temptation was too hard for many to resist; despite increased British activity, some American slavers still attempted the run to Cuba. Operating with virtually no American assistance, the British African Squadron captured sixteen American slavers between March and October 1862 as compared to ten in all of 1861.[19] By 1863, however, the flow had become a trickle, and in the following year, the Spanish government reported that not a single slave had been landed in Cuba.[20] The African slave trade under the American flag had ended.

Ultimately, much of the impact of Gordon's execution was perceptual rather than practical. To an administration in the throes of a civil war, a prosecutor facing a heretofore-unvanquished evil, and a city and nation anxious to cleanse their reputations in the world's eyes, the slave trade was very real, and very daunting. Despite the fact that the trade was dying an inevitable death, it was *perceived* at the time that the execution of a slaver was both necessary and long overdue in order to stop the trafficking. The Gordon case provided the first opportunity to claim a decisive victory over this old and insidious foe. When the New York press announced a "death blow to the slave trade," that is exactly how it was seen.

Six years after Gordon's death, the *Atlantic Monthly* retold his story, concluding,

Whatever Gordon's life may have been worth to him or to his friends, I think the country put it to a very good use when she hanged him. . . . All through the little ports and the big ports of the United States it was known that a slave trader had been hanged. And when that was known, the American slave trade ended. All up and down little African rivers that you never heard the names of it was known that an American slave trader had been hanged, and cowardly pirates trembled, and brave seamen cheered when they heard it. Mothers of children thanked such gods as they knew how to thank, and slaves shut up in barracoons, waiting for their voyage, got signal that something had happened which was to give them freedom. That something was that Gordon was hanged. So far that little candle threw its beams.[21]

To the writer at the *Atlantic Monthly,* Gordon's death ended the American slave trade. As time passed this perception grew.

Writing before the turn of the twentieth century, John R. Spears ended his comprehensive history of the slave trade in America with the following comment on Nathaniel Gordon's execution:

For more than three hundred years the oppressed had been crying from the foul hold of the slaver, "How long, O Lord, how long?" But when the axe fell, and the rope creaked to the weight of that dishonored clay, the sweet angel of Mercy was at last able to reply: "Now."[22]

# AFTERWORD

# CAPTAIN GORDON'S LEGACY

On a May morning in southern Sudan, a seven-year-old boy was sent to market by his mother, to sell her peanuts and eggs. The quiet of the day was suddenly shattered as Arab horsemen armed with long knives and rifles descended on the village, killing the men and seizing the women and children. The boy was tied to a donkey for the long trek north, where he was sold into slavery. There, as the property of a wealthy farmer, he suffered beatings, survived on scraps, and lived in constant fear of death. After ten years and two unsuccessful escape attempts, he finally made it to freedom. He did not learn until he was 21 that the same raid that had made him a slave had claimed the lives of his mother, his father, and his two sisters. The young man went on to pursue an education, eventually collaborating on a book that told, in stunning detail, the story of his sufferings—and of his deliverance.

His odyssey is both shocking and inspiring. What makes it all the more remarkable is the fact that his enslavement took place in 1986.

Francis Bok wrote his account, *Escape from Slavery,* in 2003, when he was 24 years old. He is the first escaped slave to testify before the Senate Committee on Foreign Relations, during the course of its research into slavery in Sudan.[1] Before he found his freedom, Bok was one of approximately 27 million human beings throughout the world currently living in slavery—more than twice the number of Africans seized in the three and a half centuries of the transatlantic slave trade. Currently there are approximately 800,000 people trafficked a year, making the modern-day slave trade one of the top three moneymakers for organized crime.[2] *National Geographic,* in a 2003 article on twenty-first-century slavery, listed 116 countries in which people are currently being held in bondage. As one would expect, many are underdeveloped nations; also on the list, however, are Denmark, France, Sweden, Japan, Italy, Greece, Spain, Great Britain, and the United States. It is es-

timated that the slaves of today, through their enforced labor, con-
tribute annual revenues in the neighborhood of $13 billion to the
world's economy.[3]

It is a safe assumption that many if not most Americans believe that
the curse of slavery and the slavers ended with the Civil War and the
laws that presumably banished it forever from our shores. Indeed, the
day is gone when American presidents could look from the windows of
the White House and watch slaves being sold in Washington's infamous "Georgia Pen." The time of the New England slave ships, and the
Charleston auction block, and the lash in the overseer's hand is over;
but slavery still exists, illegally and in vast numbers, in nearly every nation in the world, including our own. Here, slaves are to be found—or,
more accurately, not found—in nearly all 50 states, with the heaviest
concentration of forced labor operations in California, Texas, Florida,
and New York. These victims fill many roles: farmhands, domestics,
sweatshop and factory laborers, restaurant workers, sex slaves and
prostitutes.[4]

These people do not represent a class of poorly paid employees,
working at jobs they might not like. They were bought and sold specifically to work, unable to leave, forced to live under constant threat of
violence. By any definition, they are slaves.

The United States is one of modern slavery's main "countries of destination." People are brought here from Russia and its former states,
from Eastern Europe, from India, from Latin America, from Asia. They
are often kidnapped. Or they are lured by the promise of good-paying
jobs and better lives in America. While many are smuggled illegally
across the Mexican and Canadian borders, others are actually assigned
temporary visas and, with the help of wily traffickers, successfully pass
through the security checks of our major airports on a regular basis.
Some of the visas are legitimate, while others contain fictitious names.
Once the traffickers have introduced their victims into the country, the
promise of betterment vanishes and a life of captivity begins. The Baltimore schooner has effectively been replaced by the 747.

In a 1999 study, State Department analyst Amy O'Neill Richard
wrote, "Trafficking to the U.S. is likely to increase given . . . low risk of
prosecution and enormous profit potential for the traffickers."[5] She
could just as well have been writing about the slave traders of 1850.
Her prediction was accurate. In the words of Kevin Bales, president of
the Washington, D.C.–based nonprofit organization Free the Slaves,

the modern slave trade "does with people what organized crime does with heroin, and often more successfully."[6]

Lately, considerable media attention has been given to the traffic in sex slaves: women forced to work in strip joints and peep shows, and women and children—some little more than toddlers—forced into prostitution. It reflects the abuse of tens of thousands of victims, a growing number of whom run the added risk of exposure to HIV/AIDS and other sexually transmitted and infectious diseases. Not surprisingly, the number of HIV-infected trafficking victims is on the rise.[7]

But sex slavery is only one facet of the slave traffic in America today. There are slaves working in the fruit groves of Florida and California, the farms of Texas and New Mexico, the construction sites of Chicago, and the garment factories and restaurants of New York, as well as in the sex shops, brothels and street corners of Alaska, New Jersey, and Georgia. Slavery and slave trafficking in our country "extend . . . into almost every area of the economy where cheap labor is at a premium."[8] The problem has reached epidemic proportions, and it is growing.

The federal government, in an August 2003 report, estimated that 18,000 to 20,000 people are trafficked annually into the United States, for sexual exploitation or forced labor.[9] John Miller, director of the State Department's Office to Monitor Trafficking in Persons, believes that figure could be low: "What we know is that the number is huge."[10] Kevin Bales estimates that there are, at this moment, between 60,000 and 100,000 people held in slavery in this country.[11] But it is impossible to obtain an accurate figure, he says, because modern-day slavery survives and thrives in the shadows. In the words of Terry Coonan, executive director of the Center for the Advancement of Human Rights at Florida State University, "This is almost an invisible crime because the victims are kept out of the public eye."[12]

Even the government admits, in its 2003 assessment paper, that despite the existence of some studies on trafficking, and the funding for more, "none of these U.S. Government–funded studies will provide a nation-wide estimate of the scope or magnitude of trafficking persons into the United States or comprehensively address trafficking trends to and within the United States." Stressing the obvious, the report concludes that "such analysis would be useful to understanding the scope and magnitude of trafficking in the United States."[13]

Why is slavery on the rise now? According to Free the Slaves, "changes in the world's economy and societies over the past 50 years have enabled a resurgence of slavery." These changes include population growth, urban migration, and the corruption of governments. First, the global population has more than tripled since World War II, with the greatest explosion occurring in the "developing world." This—combined with such natural and man-made disasters as civil war, environmental degradation, ethnic conflict, and the recent tsunami—has resulted in deteriorating living conditions and an increasing number of dispossessed, dispirited, and hungry people. Second, the resultant social and economic changes have driven countless people to urban centers where, unable to find jobs or security of any kind, they become prey to slavers' promises of a better life abroad. And finally, the corruptibility of governments around the world has made it virtually impossible to apprehend or punish the traffickers, despite the fact that there is not a single country in which slavery is legal.[14]

In some countries, the slavers pay off the government. Often, the government itself is an active partner in the enslavement process. The *BBC News UK Edition* of March 7, 2005, headlined an article "Niger Rapped over Slavery Denial." Niger's parliament, under international pressure, had banned slavery in 2003, and made trafficking a crime punishable by up to 30 years in prison. Knowing that virtually nothing had been done to implement the new law, Anti-Slavery International (ASI) scheduled a special event in March 2005 for the liberation of 7,000 of Niger's approximately 43,000 people still living in slavery. To finance the event, ASI sent thousands of dollars to Niger's official human rights committee—which pocketed the money. At the last minute, the Niger government canceled the event, claiming that slavery no longer existed within its borders. They then arrested the country's antislavery activists. Commenting on the government's action, David Ould, deputy director of Anti-Slavery International, observed, "The enactment of legislation that criminalizes and penalizes slavery does not automatically mean it has been eliminated." Again, the same could be said of our own country nearly 200 years ago.[15]

There are clear differences between the slave trade of Nathaniel Gordon's time and the traffic of today. In 1850, the cost of a slave was high; he or she would bring an average price of $1,000, which in today's currency amounts to around $40,000. Nowadays, a slave can be purchased for anywhere from forty to a few thousand dollars, depending in large part upon the intended nature of the work. Because the slaves of the nineteenth century were so expensive, they represented a significant investment, and as such would usually be fed, sheltered, and cared for in such a way as to ensure their continued productivity. Harshly treated though they were, care was taken to prolong the slaves' effectiveness for as many years as possible. Today, slaves are disposable; they are often used to the point of failure—illness, old age, refusal to conform—and then "discarded." Kevin Bales points out that there is "no reason to protect slaves from disease or injury—medicine costs money, and it's cheaper to let them die."[16] Their cost is low, while their capacity to deliver profits is high. At a time when slavery was legal, it was important to be able to establish ownership; today, deniability is the norm. The buyers of slave labor are less slave *owners* than slave *holders*. In our all-things-are-disposable culture, people are just another commodity.[17] The two essential ingredients that link the slave trade of Gordon's day with today's "human trafficking," as it is called, are profitability and violence. And underlying it all is greed.[18]

Who are the modern-day slave traffickers? In the days of the Atlantic trade, the actual institution of slavery in the United States was based on racial and ethnic differences. Whites owned Blacks; that was the social order. An American slaving captain was invariably White—generally a New Englander—with a mostly White crew. There was a strong probability that the captain had acquired his cargo of slaves from an Arab trader. However, it was usually Black Africans themselves who captured, kidnapped, or bought members of their own or neighboring tribes and sold or bartered them into slavery. While some of today's traffickers work within a similar single-ethnicity framework, victimizing their own people, many more prey upon people of other ethnicities. The victims may be of the same country or region as the traffickers, but are of a different "race" or social class.[19]

Although many are freelancers operating alone, traffickers generally operate in organized groups that range in size from small mom-and-pop family enterprises, to large Chinese street gangs, to the Russian and Italian mafias. Generally, the size of the operation helps to dictate the dollar value of the slave: the larger the ring, the higher their expenses; therefore, the greater the selling price.[20] Some of the major slave-trading networks do business on the Internet and maintain their accounts in reputable banks. The computer has modernized the trade to the extent that, according to one expert on sex slavery, "a network . . . has the ability to bargain and complete financial transactions long distance. . . . The parties don't even have to know each other."[21]

It is difficult to draw a portrait of the typical trafficker. As Kevin Bales points out, "The new slavery is a crime with millions of victims but very few identifiable criminals."[22] There is no specific method, no generic technique that applies to all traffickers. Bales tells us that, far from being "clear and distinct," the new slavery is "inconveniently sloppy, dynamic, changeable, and confusing as any other kind of relation between humans."[23] Also, it can be dangerous to inquire too deeply into the workings of trafficking rings. These are people who have killed to protect their businesses.[24] It is safe to assert that the traffickers acquire their victims either through direct violence—kidnapping—or trickery and enticement. When slaves are kidnapped, "they must lack sufficient power to defend themselves against that violent enslavement."[25] For this reason, traffickers pick their victims from among the poor, the dispossessed, the homeless.

When luring people into slavery, the traffickers succeed more through deception than through violence. The State Department's 2003 "Trafficking in Persons Report" states that "they might recruit and find potential victims through advertisements in local newspapers offering good jobs at high pay in exciting cities or use fraudulent travel, modeling and matchmaking agencies to lure unsuspecting young men and women into trafficking schemes."[26] The trafficker is often a prominent member of the community or a "family friend," who offers a vision of the good life in America and convinces credulous parents that their children will have advantages and opportunities beyond the capacity of their home and village to provide. False passports and contracts are proffered, but the victims—jobless, rootless, uneducated, gullible—are often required to pay exorbitant prices for their own travel and accommodations. Very few are able to come up with the money. Most let their "benefactors" pay for them; this becomes a "debt" that they are then obligated to repay when they are settled in the United States.[27] Once here, however, they find that they have been sold to brothels, sweatshops, farms, and factories. They are paid little or nothing, brutalized—the women often raped—and poorly fed and sheltered. Hammered constantly with lies about corruption and cruelty in our government, they are made to fear not only their traffickers and their owners, but any American in a position of authority as well. Brainwashed, debased, and malnourished, they are worked long and hard, deprived of any hope of improvement or escape. Attempts at resistance are met with brutality, sometimes even death. Because the per capita cost of slaves is so low, it is often worth more to the slaveholder or trafficker to make examples of recalcitrant workers.[28] And no one will inquire after them. Whereas the Southern slaveholders of the eighteenth and nineteenth centuries kept detailed and precise records of their property, the people who buy today's slaves do not ask for receipts and do not keep records of their lives or deaths.

Former attorney general John Ashcroft described trafficking as

> a transnational criminal enterprise. It recognizes neither boundaries nor borders. Profits from trafficking feed into the coffers of organized crime. Trafficking is fueled by other criminal activities such as document fraud, money laundering and migrant smuggling. Because trafficking cases are expansive in reach, they are among the most important matters—as well as the most labor- and time-intensive matters—undertaken by the Department of Justice.[29]

What is the government doing to recognize and combat the slave trade in the United States today? The law under which Nathaniel Gordon was hanged is still on the books, but it no longer prescribes death as a punishment. As time passed, and the law came to appear less relevant and more archaic, its provisions became less severe. In 1909, Congress amended the Act of 1820, making the offense punishable by life imprisonment. In 1948, legislation was passed that further reduced the sentence to a maximum of seven years in jail and a $5,000 fine. The law was again amended in 1994, then—as the presence of modern-day slavery was making itself known—completely restructured in 2000 under the Clinton administration. It can now be found under the Victims of Trafficking and Violence Protection Act of 2000; referred to as the 2000 Act, it passed almost unanimously, as had the original Piracy Act of 1820.[30] The law is defined as "an Act to combat trafficking of persons, especially into the sex trade, slavery, and slavery-like conditions, in the United States and countries around the world through prevention, through prosecution and enforcement against traffickers, and through protection and assistance to victims of trafficking."[31]

The 2000 Act is actually the grandchild of both the 1820 act and the Thirteenth Amendment (which abolished slavery), and is the government's first significant response to the growing practice of modern-day slavery in the United States. Although other measures and modifications have been implemented since its passage, the act is, according to a report put out in March 2002 by the Protection Project (a legal human rights institute based at Johns Hopkins University), "the first comprehensive law to address the various aspects of trafficking."[32] It attempts to do so in a number of ways.

First, the 2000 Act acknowledges the seriousness of international as well as domestic slave trading, stating specifically that "trafficking in persons is a transnational crime with national implications." It recognizes that, because the victims often do not speak English, are subject to coercion and intimidation, and fear "forcible removal to countries in which they will face retribution or other hardship," they usually don't report the crimes committed against them. The law amends existing immigration legislation to allow victims of slave traffickers to remain in the United States, to provide social services and legal benefits, and to solicit their help in prosecuting offenders. It also addresses the issue of the victims' countries of origin, setting specific minimum standards for the elimination of trafficking and threatening to withhold assistance from those countries that fail to meet them.[33] In a September 10, 2004, White House press release, President George W. Bush announced financial sanctions against Burma, Cuba, Sudan, North Korea, Venezuela, Bangladesh, Ecuador, and a handful of other countries until their respective governments comply with the 2000 Act's minimum standards.[34] Most recently, the government's 2005 "Trafficking in Persons Report" listed four Arab states—Saudi Arabia, Kuwait, Qatar, and the United Arab Emirates—as potential candidates for sanction.[35]

Second, the law provides a broad definition of trafficking by recognizing that both forced labor and the sex trade fall within its parameters. It is no longer necessary that actual physical violence occur in order to define a slaving situation, either; according to the act, "force, fraud, or coercion" can qualify a case as a "severe form of trafficking." The mere threat of abuse is sufficient. In instances of sex trafficking, if the victim who has been forced to perform a commercial sex act is under 18 years of age, none of these other qualifications is necessary for the case to be considered "severe."[36]

Third, the 2000 Act expands earlier concepts of prevention, protection, and prosecution. It works to protect the victims, stating that they should not be "inappropriately incarcerated, fined, or otherwise penalized" for acts committed as victims of trafficking. This was not always the case. Such previous legislation as the Mann Act brought the weight of the law down upon the prostituted woman herself; the 2000 Act seeks to prosecute the trafficker, not the victim.[37]

The law sponsors programs for job training and counseling, education, microlending (the loaning of money to small businesses that cannot get funds from traditional banks), and public awareness. It also helps establish programs in the victims' countries of origin, "to assist in the safe integration, reintegration, or resettlement . . . of victims of trafficking." This represents a departure from the existing strict conditions governing immigration. Should victims wish to remain in the United States, the 2000 Act provides for "T Visas' that grant temporary resident status to 5,000 victims annually. Additionally, some victims are allowed to remain here permanently, after three years as temporary residents, if they can satisfy the government that they would "suffer extreme hardship involving unusual and severe harm upon removal from the United States."[38] To be considered for a green card, it certainly helps if the victim volunteers to serve as a prosecution witness in a trafficking trial. If a liberated slave is willing to testify in court, he or she can come under the umbrella of the Witness Protection Program and be given a new identity as well as housing, employment, money to live on, and "other services necessary to assist the person in becoming self-sustaining."[39] Since the passage of the 2000 Act, the government hasn't come close to finding 5,000 trafficking victims, let alone any who wish to apply for visas.

These provisions would be meaningless unless the 2000 Act also provided for vigorous prosecution and punishment of the traffickers. In fact, it doubles the punishment—from 10 to 20 years—for those convicted of "peonage, enticement into slavery, and sale into involuntary servitude," and virtually open-ends the sentence all the way to life imprisonment in cases of murder, kidnapping, aggravated sexual abuse, or the attempt to commit them.[40]

In addition, the act provides clear definitions and penalties for peonage, slavery, involuntary servitude, and forced labor; sex trafficking of children; and the unlawful use of documents, such as immigration papers and passports, for trafficking.[41] If convicted of any of these offenses, the trafficker or slaveholder may also be required to forfeit all his or her assets. The Ramoses, a family of traffickers in south Florida, are a case in point.

An ideal location for the smuggling and enslavement of farm workers, south Florida has been described by a Justice Department official as "ground zero for modern slavery."[42] A large number of the victims are brought north across the U.S. border from Mexico by traffickers—"coyotes," as they are called—with promises of regular work and decent pay. The coyotes can be independent slavers, or merely the employees of a trafficking ring. The people they smuggle into the country come with no knowledge of American culture or language, and no concept whatsoever of their rights. Once they arrive in Florida, they find themselves confined in barracks and forced to work long hours under the watchful eyes of armed guards. Men who have attempted to aid in their escape have been badly beaten or killed.

Several hundred of these workers were sold by their coyotes to the Ramos family and held in labor camps. The driving force behind the family was two brothers—Juan and Ramiro, nicknamed "El Diablo" for his temper—and a cousin, José Luis. They ruled the camps with the latest assault weapons and the willingness to use them. Four workers successfully escaped in April 2001 and brought their tale of enslavement to the government. Two days later, they were interviewed by FBI agents, who then arrested the three Ramoses. Their defense was reminiscent of the pleas made by the slavers' attorneys in the days before the Civil War: why prosecute only these men? Why not go after the large corporations and the food companies that commissioned them? Were it not for the government's sudden desire to appear proactive, their lawyer claimed, these men would never have been charged in the first place.

The four liberated pickers testified against the Ramoses. The jury deliberated a day and a half, and returned guilty verdicts on all three men. The two brothers each received a twelve-year sentence, while cousin Jose was given a term of ten years.[43] In addition, the U.S. district court judge ordered the confiscation of the family's earnings from their slaving operation—a total of $3 million—as well as considerable land and property.[44]

Other cases have been brought successfully in other parts of the country, reflecting the diversity of occupations to which the victims are put. Ironically, many have occurred in and around the nation's capital. A Washington, D.C., couple was convicted of enslaving a domestic by hiding her passport and visa. The woman, trafficked illegally from Ghana, was forced to work seven days a week performing all the household chores and watching the couple's child. She was allowed neither compensation nor the freedom to leave. After a year and a half of this abuse, the young woman escaped. The man and woman who had enslaved her were charged with arranging to bring her to America under false pretenses, and with forced labor; each was given a prison term.[45]

In March 2002, a Gaithersburg, Maryland, man was sentenced to six and a half years for keeping a Brazilian woman imprisoned as a domestic slave for 20 years.[46] In Silver Spring, Maryland, a couple received a nine-year prison sentence for enslaving a Cameroonian teenager for three years. The girl was forced to work during the day and perform sexual acts at night. When she first arrived in the United States, she was 14 years old.[47]

In August 2003, two "madams" were brought to trial in Newark, New Jersey, for imprisoning four Mexican girls—from 14 to 18 years of age—in their Plainfield, New Jersey, brothel. The judge gave each of the madams seventeen and a half years in prison.

It should be noted that there is no parole in the federal system; all the convicted felons in these cases can expect to serve the full term of their sentences.[48]

One of the oddest cases involved the enslavement of an African boys' choir. A Texas charity group visiting Zambia heard the choir, and Keith Grimes, a Baptist minister in the organization, brought them back to the United States, ostensibly to raise money to build schools in Zambia. He advertised the group as the Z.A.B.C.—Zambian Acapella Boys Choir. When the concert money started coming in, Grimes and his daughter elected to keep it, and made the boys—the youngest of whom was eleven—perform up to five concerts a day. They were housed in a trailer and denied medicine when they fell ill and food when they complained. And in their off-hours, they were forced to dig a swimming pool for their "sponsor." The boys continued to perform for nearly two years, believing that despite their hardships, the money they earned was being sent home to their families. When they ultimately discovered that only $20 a month was being sent to each family and that nothing was being done to build schools, they resisted, whereupon the pastor's daughter and her husband—Grimes had died of a brain tumor—attempted to deport the four oldest boys. At this point, U.S. immigration officials questioned the boys and uncovered the story. Initially, it was hard to believe that a church choir had been trafficked and exploited by a man of the cloth, but when the facts were borne out, the boys were given care and offered new lives in the United

States. Ten of the thirteen boys elected to stay. According to Given Kachepa, the youngest of the boys, most of the ten who stayed have fallen upon hard times. They drink to excess and maintain no contact with their families in Zambia. The oldest is now twenty-four. Because the liberation of the boys took place in January 2000, and the 2000 Trafficking Act did not pass until the following October, no charges were filed against the daughter or her husband. Concerned members of the community attempted to contact the FBI, Janet Reno, and various state and federal senators and congressmen in an attempt to provide services for the boys and punish the couple; they did not receive a single response. Apparently, the official mind-set a mere six years ago dictated that in order for slavery to occur, there must be signs of physical brutality: whip scars, chain marks, cuts, and bruises.[49]

Given was taken in by a loving Texas family, and recently graduated high school in the Dallas–Fort Worth area. He is applying to college; meanwhile, he works at Target and sends a portion of his salary to his family in Zambia. He talks openly about his experience, believing that public awareness is the only way to keep such things from happening to others. How could such a man as Grimes convince the boys' families and community to trust him with their children? "He was a different man in Zambia—well-dressed, polite, and he made promises. He even signed a contract. When he got here, he became pushy, intolerant. When a boy comes to a new country, he will make little mistakes because he doesn't understand its ways; but Mr. Grimes would get extremely angry over the smallest things."[50] Aside from his position in the church, nothing distinguished Grimes from thousands of other traffickers in humans.

Perhaps the most dramatic trafficking case to appear in the last few years—and the largest ever prosecuted—was resolved in January 2004. Kil Soo Lee, owner of Daewoosa Samoa, Ltd., a Korean-run forced-labor garment factory operating in American Samoa, was tried in Hawaii's U.S. district court for keeping more than 200 Vietnamese and Chinese workers in bondage by threats, beatings, and starvation. These workers had each paid between $5,000 and $8,000—the equivalent of five to ten years' pay in their home countries—to their traffickers, for what they were told was steady work at decent pay and good living conditions. They were smuggled into Hawaii, taken to Kil Soo Lee's factory, and forbidden to leave. They worked in 104-degree heat; lived 36 to a room in a dirty, rat-infested barracks; and were denied food for days if they objected. When one woman complained about the conditions, Lee's overseers put her eye out with a broken pipe. On November 28, 2000, Lee demonstrated his power by ordering a mass beating of the workers; his thugs carried out his orders, using pipes and chairs on the helpless victims, most of whom were young women.

When Lee was finally arrested, he and two of his accomplices faced charges including conspiracy to violate individual civil rights, extortion, money laundering, and 11 counts of involuntary servitude. After a three-month trial, they were convicted on 14 counts.[51] Lee himself received a prison term of 40 years.

The day of Kil Soo Lee's conviction saw the resolution of another trafficking case, this one in Edinburgh, Texas. For several months, three brothers named Soto had been running a prostitution ring exploiting women smuggled into the United States from various Central American countries. After an "indoctrination" period involving repeated rapes and beatings, the ring would send the women north to various locations. The traffickers were arrested while still holding as sex slaves four young women, whom they had brutalized mercilessly. The brothers, along with four of their henchmen, received sentences ranging from four months to fourteen years, and were ordered to pay restitution to their victims.[52]

So exactly how successful has the government been in its war against slave trafficking? In a February 15, 2004, letter to the *New York Times Magazine,* in response to a cover article on sex slavery in America, John Ashcroft enumerated the successes thus far achieved by his department, listing cases against 111 traffickers—"a nearly threefold increase over 1998–2000." (He fails to mention that the 2000 Act had not yet been passed.) Ashcroft then stated that the government had opened, in all, 229 investigations in the previous three years, concluding, "Our work continues."[53]

While the increase in cases and investigations might seem impressive at first glance, the numbers pale when placed in the context of the tens of thousands of slaves in the United States today, and the many thousands more who enter the country every year. In December 2004, Free the Slaves and the Human Rights Center of the University of California, Berkeley, coauthored "Hidden Slaves: Forced Labor in the United States," the most comprehensive study of trafficking to date. It shows that despite significant advancements, the 2000 Act falls short in a number of important areas.

By linking visa status to the victims' willingness to testify against their former traffickers, the government treats them more as prosecution witnesses than "individuals who are . . . deserving of protection and restoration of their human rights."[54] In the words of one official, "[The Department of] Health and Human Services is looking for victims, but the Department of Justice is looking for cases."[55] These victims have been damaged, psychologically and physically, and appearing in court before their abusers is a devastating ordeal. In addition, the accused slavers often threaten these survivors with violence—either against them or their families. Frequently, the threats are made good, and the U.S. government is powerless to stop it.

Furthermore, the 2000 Act's awareness programs fall far short of the mark. In truth, ignorance about the slave trade among prosecutors and police is rampant. Given the daily duties of the average policeman, there is neither time nor inclination to go looking for slave cases. As often as not, a law officer would not recognize such a case if he came across one, having virtually no idea what to look for. A classic case is that of multimillionaire real estate tycoon Lakireddy Bali Reddy. Born in India, Reddy settled in Berkeley, California, and proceeded to make his fortune by importing, enslaving, and prostituting young women from his native country. In a trafficking career that spanned a period of 15 years, he "repeatedly raped and sexually abused his victims and forced them to work in his businesses in Berkeley." During this time, at least one teenage girl died. Reddy's activities were finally uncovered in 2000; he pled guilty to immigration fraud and illegal sexual activity, and paid a total of nearly $11 million in restitution to some survivors and their families.[56] He also received a prison term in excess of eight years. And yet, only three years earlier, the Immigration and Naturalization Service had investigated him for possible immigration fraud and found him to be "a professionally educated gentleman, with widespread corporate interests. . . . There was nothing to indicate any criminal conduct."[57]

Training is essential. Ashcroft asserted that "effective interagency and intergovernment cooperation is . . . a key part of our strategy to combat human trafficking, and we are training federal and local law enforcement."[58] Unfortunately, while the government has made a start, it has a long way to go. As the study "Hidden Slaves" makes clear, there is simply not enough being done to train local law enforcement officers so that they can "identify victims and forced labor operations; improve cooperation and information sharing . . between federal and state agencies; revise procedures for the handling of survivors; and provide [them] with protection, benefits, and compensation."[59]

As vital as is the mandate to educate the public and the government's forces of law is the need to reach the shell-shocked, reluctant, and psychologically crippled victims. The 2005 "Trafficking in Persons Report" states that since 2000, "roughly 700 people have been helped with temporary visas."[60] One trafficking hotline director feels that this number is a gross exaggeration, but if it is accurate, it reflects an average of approximately 127 victims per year at the time of this writing.[61] With the law standing ready to grant temporary resident status to 5,000 victims annually, and considering the countless victims lost within our borders, this is not a figure to brag about.

The problem of how to educate the victims is one of the biggest impediments to an effective response to the slave trade. Most of these people live in terror of the law, and in total ignorance of their rights. Many do not even speak English. Those who trafficked them and those who keep them generally have them convinced that if they were to seek help, they would be met with government disinterest at best, corruption and brutality at worst. They often fear return to their own country, and punishment by ours for being here illegally. Even if they did want to seek help, they have no idea how to go about it. All this is assuming they were allowed access to a car or a telephone. It is a truly daunting problem. What is being done to resolve it?

Once again, Ashcroft: "Finally, the government is devoting substantial effort to a public awareness campaign, launching the Trafficking in Persons and Worker Exploitation Task Force Complaint Line ["Trafficking Help Line"] 888-428-7581."[62] I called this number on Sunday, May 22, 2005, and got a recording asking me to leave a name and number. I did so, but received no response. I called again on Wednesday, May 25, leaving the same message. This time I received a call a few hours later. First I confirmed with the "traffic intake coordinator" that this was indeed the victims' help line. I asked her why no one had returned my first call, and she responded that they receive more than 110 calls a day, which are answered in order of priority. I asked how they could possibly determine priority from a recorded response, and was told that was confidential. When I asked if these callers were all victims, at first she said yes, then changed her mind after I pointed out that the victims helped by the government since 2000 numbered only in the hundreds; with hundreds of calls a *week*, why weren't more victims finding assistance? I was then told that not all the callers were victims, and many who were didn't go further than the first call. I asked her what would be the result if a trafficking victim who somehow managed to find this number, placed the call secretly to avoid detection and punishment, and is met with a recording instructing him or her to leave a number? What number could that victim possibly leave? Her response was, "It doesn't work that way." When I inquired what that meant, she again claimed confidentiality. As it turns out, the Trafficking Help Line is available only Monday through Friday, nine to five, and there is only one intake coordinator. Overall, I got a clear sense that even if a trafficking victim had access to this number at all, he or she would ultimately be halted by the response—or lack thereof.

As I subsequently discovered, there *does* exist a 24/7 Human Trafficking Information and Referral Hotline, funded by Health and Human Services and run by Covenant House of New York City. Created in February 2004, it functions as the HHS's only national hotline. Under the directorship of Gil Ortiz, it operates on an annual budget of approximately $180,000, and employs 17 crisis workers, seven supervisors, and a handful of volunteers. (As of this writing, Mr. Ortiz is concerned that the hotline will lose its government funding, which is up for review.) Ironically, most of the calls the trafficking hotline receives are not trafficking-related; they come from homeless people, potential suicides, victims of domestic violence and child abuse, and individuals with immigration problems. They are all referred by the staff to organizations better suited to address their needs. Mr. Ortiz estimates that his hotline has received, at most, 2,500 trafficking-related calls between January 2004 and June 2005, most of which were passed along to the appropriate nongovernmental agencies for follow-up. The great majority of these calls came from "advocates"—concerned citizens—with "less than one-half of one percent" coming from the victims themselves. When asked for an approximate number of victims who he knows for certain have received assistance through his hotline, Mr. Ortiz responded, "Around ten to fifteen." Asked the biggest factor in locating victims, he answered, "Luck."[63]

On the off chance that a victim *is* found, the government's role ends with the investigation and prosecution of his or her traffickers. The task of providing "basic social and legal services to survivors has fallen squarely on the shoulders of nongovernmental organizations (NGOs) and social services," fewer than half of which are capable of handling the job. Housing is one of the major challenges. It's expensive, and the government simply doesn't allocate enough for it. As a result, many of those who are actually provided with housing are placed in homeless shelters and treated as indigents.[64]

Ultimately, the only way the issue of the burgeoning slave trade in America today will be effectively addressed is through widespread public awareness and active involvement. But public knowledge is sparse, reports random. According to Kevin Bales, it is usually the "good Samaritan"—the suspicious neighbor, the hospital worker who treats an abused victim—who reports a slave case to the authorities. At this rate, trafficking will continue to grow in the shadows.

There are organizations in America today that exist specifically to address the issue of slavery. Free the Slaves, in Washington, D.C., is the sister organization of the London-based Anti-Slavery International, the world's oldest human rights and antislavery group. Since Kevin Bales founded the nonprofit organization in March 2000, it has had a positive effect in curtailing such slave-intensive industries as the cocoa harvest of the Ivory Coast, the rug weaving of India, and the charcoal burning of Brazil. These are all areas that have relied—and continue to rely—on slave labor for the generation of their products. In India alone, it is estimated that there are more than 300,000 children stolen from their homes and forced to work at the rug looms. Free the Slaves has set about providing viable, slave-free alternatives to manufacturers and consumers alike, in an effort to both liberate slaves from their bondage and give them the counseling and material help they need after they are freed. "Liberation is only the first step," says Bales. "It must be followed by rehabilitation."[65]

Break the Chains, formerly known as the Campaign for Migrant Worker Rights, is also located in Washington, D.C., and is a self-described "coalition of legal and social service agencies, ethnically-based organizations, social action groups and individuals devoted to protecting the rights of the migrant domestic working community."[66] Under the leadership of Joy Zarembka, it mainly concentrates on those domestic workers—mostly women—who enter the country under temporary visas. Break the Chains maintains that once the migrants arrive, usually from Africa, Asia, and Latin America, the government ceases to take an active interest in their circumstances; many enter immediately into slavery. As the organization asserts, "The visas are valid for occupations such as housekeepers, nannies, cooks, drivers, gardeners, and other personal servants. Nowhere on the list is 'slave.' "[67] Break the Chains works to help these victims, as well as to effect changes in government policies for the better protection of their rights.

One of the more inspiring antislavery movements in the country today is the Coalition of Immokalee Workers—the CIW. A result of the workers' own determination to break their chains, the CIW was born in the fruit groves and farms of southwest Florida in 1994, and has drawn national attention with its efforts to gain fair pay, better housing, and protection of workers' rights under the law. The CIW spearheaded the discovery, investigation, and prosecution of four of the five slavery rings successfully prosecuted in southwest Florida to date. Three of these cases focused on tomato pickers around Immokalee, the worker town where the movement started. In 2001, the CIW initiated a boycott against Taco Bell. In March 2003, farm laborers from the CIW literally camped outside the doors of Taco Bell's Irvine, California, corporate headquarters, and staged a hunger strike in an effort to force the food chain to take responsibility for the fact that its tomatoes are picked by slave labor. Taco Bell's initial response in a radio interview was, "Slavery was abolished years ago . . . in case you didn't know."[68]

Lucas Benitez of the CIW spoke with workers who had been pistol-whipped, beaten mercilessly, and told that their tongues would be cut out if they dared to report the conditions under which they work. "Taco Bell," said Mr. Benitez, "has a policy that it will not buy food from contractors that mistreat animals. All we are asking is that they have the same policy for humans."[69] The CIW's efforts paid off, although it took more than four years. In May 2005, Taco Bell agreed to pay a penny more per pound for Florida tomatoes, to go directly to the pickers. They also "adopted a code of conduct that would allow it to sever ties to suppliers who commit abuses against farmworkers." The CIW is now turning its attention to the other fast-food giants, asking them to adopt a similar policy.[70] If further progress is made, it will be the farmworkers in the CIW who make it. Reliance on government help will accomplish very little; Immokalee is the nation's largest supplier of tomatoes, yet there is only one government labor inspector in the entire county.

• • •

There is so much to be done, and so few committed to do it. In the slaving days of Nathaniel Gordon, public as much as governmental disinterest allowed a heinous system to exist far too long. The slave trade of the early nineteenth century, though horrific, was small compared to the scope of what we are facing today. The problem exists in every corner of the world, in every part of our country. It is illegal everywhere, and is fought successfully practically nowhere. It is practiced by our businessmen, our farmers, and our neighbors. It thrives in darkness.

Kevin Bales states, "The remarkable thing is that we are standing at a unique moment in human history; for the first time in five thousand years we could actually end slavery. The laws are in place, no economy depends on slavery, and the world is united in its belief that slavery must end. We need only awareness and resources." Through its work with the public and the world's governments, Free the Slaves has set total eradication as its goal. "We just have to ask ourselves," Bales says, "are we willing to live in a world with slavery? If not, now is the time to end it." [71]

The days are gone when it was hoped that the hanging of a single man would cast a pall of terror over the traffickers; they are far too numerous, far too diverse, and far too determined. This time, it will require an effort of monumental proportions on the part of our government, and a firm knowledge and commitment on the part of the public, if we are to have an impact on trafficking. The slave trade in America did not die with Captain Gordon; it merely went dormant for more than a century, and now it is back.

# ACKNOWLEDGMENTS

My gratitude must begin with the man who first planted the seed—Professor Kenneth Bernard. If ever a man epitomized the role of history professor, it was he. In appearance, he was a combination of Abraham Lincoln and Gary Cooper—tall and thin, with a slight stoop and a slow, quiet manner of speaking. And when he referred to the historical figure whom he most admired, it was always as *Mister* Lincoln.

I must thank my agent, Victoria Sanders. She is smart, she is tough, and she is funny. As a first-time author, I had no idea whether the book was viable. There are no words to describe my excitement, and my relief, when Victoria called and simply said, "I'm loving this project!" Thank you for your faith and for your knowledge.

There would have been no book without my editor, Malaika Adero. She saw the importance of the story, and then helped me to tell it, constantly showing me the difference between writing and being a writer. From simple criticisms such as "Don't begin a sentence with a preposition" (Oops, did it again!) to guidance in how to structure and present the work, her assistance was invaluable.

This book took me into areas in which I could not begin to claim expertise; many people have been there to help me along, with advice, information, and support. The late professor Jim Shenton of Columbia gave me all three. Our relationship began with the question "Are you sure there's enough material for a book?" and ended with his request for a copy. I only wish he had lived so I could give him one.

Portland, Maine, Nathaniel Gordon's hometown, has a treasure in Ken Thompson, a most extraordinary genealogist and local historian. Always generous with his research, Ken has provided information on Gordon's family, shown me the homes in which the slaver lived, and toured me around a Portland of the past. Ken can tie Gordon's roots to those of famous statesmen, poets, and several U.S. presidents, living and dead. And he never stops digging.

Ken referred me to Karen Needles, who shared—and shares—my interest in the Gordon affair. We became instant friends. Karen was with the National Archives in Washington at the time, and she invited me down for a whirlwind of research and exchanges. She is a fiend for primary sources, and has given me access to material I would never have seen otherwise. Her Documents on Wheels website (www.docu mentsonwheels.com) features a comprehensive chronology of the Gordon case, and is a treasure trove for the scholar. Whom do we tackle next, Karen?

I owe much to Linda Biagi, friend, mentor, and lifelong bookmeister. Linda saw merit in the story long before it resembled a book, and gave me my introduction to the world of publishing.

No reference book can provide the feeling of immediacy a writer gets from a direct personal link to the past. Here, I was fortunate in becoming acquainted with Barbara Brewer and her daughter, Barbara Ardrey, great-granddaughter-in-law and great-great-granddaughter of U.S. marshal Robert Murray. When I first spoke with Ms. Brewer, she was 89, with a keen grasp of events in the marshal's career. "I may be old," she told me, "but I've still got all my marbles!" It was Ms. Brewer's late husband, Walter, who had transcribed his great-grandfather's meticulously handwritten 77-page account of the Gordon case, which was so vital to this work. Ms. Ardrey, of the York County Culture & Heritage Commission in Rock Hill, South Carolina, was kind enough to send me Murray's photograph, as well as copies of his actual writings.

Inevitably, my study of Gordon called for at least a modicum of familiarity with the legal aspects of the various slaving cases. My good friend Paul Marrow brought his expertise, intelligence, and genuine curiosity to the table, as both knowledgeable attorney and all-around gadfly. Paul was, and is, my constant reminder that there is always another point of view.

It would take a chapter-length dedication to thank all the reference librarians and archivists to whom I owe markers. I will simply express my gratitude to the researchers of the National Archives in Washington, D.C., and New York City, and to the Chappaqua, New York, library staff for their seemingly endless patience as I flooded them with requests for 150-year-old newspapers and out-of-print books, and commandeered the microfilm readers.

Kevin Bales, of Free the Slaves, introduced me to the dark new world of modern-day slavery, and made certain that I presented it accurately. I owe him a double debt—first, for his help in ending this book on a timely note, and second, for an awareness on which I can never go back. He taught me that the United States—and the world at large—is facing a terrible, growing danger; knowledge and resolve are the main weapons against it, and we are the soldiers.

There are two sources without which there would have been no book. Clearly, one is Marshal Robert Murray's personal account of the case. How rare to find a man of insight and integrity, dutifully recording an event in which he was a key player. The second, now sadly out of print, is Warren S. Howard's *American Slavers and the Federal Law 1837–1862*. It has been with me since I first met Captain Gordon, and remains the best source extant on the federal government's shamelessly ineffectual response to the Atlantic slave trade. It cannot—and should not—be read without a keen sense of outrage.

Finally, my boundless love and thanks to my wife, Jane, and my daughters, Jesse and Melora, who have lived with Nathaniel Gordon for as long as they have lived with me. There was never a word of exasperation or frustration, only encouragement and sympathy. Now we can lay the ghost to rest.

# NOTES

# AND SOURCES

## INTRODUCTION: ONE FOOT IN THE WATER

1. James Rawley, *The Transatlantic Slave Trade* (New York: W.W. Norton & Co., 1981), p. 303.
2. Don E. Fehrenbacher, *The Slaveholding Republic: An Account of the United States Government's Relations to Slavery* (New York: Oxford University Press, 2001), p. 200.
3. Rawley, *The Transatlantic Slave Trade,* p. 2.
4. John R. Spears, *The American Slave-Trade* (New York: Charles Scribner's Sons, 1900), p. 30.
5. William C. Davis, *Three Roads to the Alamo* (New York: HarperCollins, 1998), p. 56.
6. Kevin Bales, *Disposable People* (Berkeley and Los Angeles: University of California Press, 1999), p. 10.
7. Fehrenbacher, *The Slaveholding Republic,* p. 135.
8. Warren S. Howard, *American Slavers and the Federal Law 1837–1862* (Berkeley: University of California Press, 1963), p. 25.
9. Fehrenbacher, *The Slaveholding Republic,* p. 140.
10. Tobias Barrington Wolff, "The Thirteenth Amendment and Slavery in the Global Economy," *Columbia Law Review,* May 2003, p. 15.
11. Ibid.
12. Fehrenbacher, *The Slaveholding Republic,* p. 147.
13. Ibid., p. 136.
14. William D. Piersen, *From Africa to America* (New York: Simon & Schuster, 1996), p. 66.
15. Peter Kolchin, *American Slavery, 1619–1877* (New York: Hill & Wang, 1994), p. 22.
16. Wolff, "The Thirteenth Amendment and Slavery in the Global Economy," p. 16.
17. Calvin Lane, "The African Squadron. The U.S. Navy and the Slave Trade 1820–1862," *The Log of Mystic Seaport* 50, no. 4, (Spring 1999), p. 2; Fehrenbacher, *The Slaveholding Republic,* p. 150.
18. Lawrence R. Tenzer, *The Forgotten Cause of the Civil War* (Manahawken, N.J.: Scholars Publishing House, 1997), p. 61.
19. Howard, *American Slavers and the Federal Law 1837–1862,* p. 272.
20. Fehrenbacher, *The Slaveholding Republic,* p. 152.
21. Howard, *American Slavers and the Federal Law 1837–1862,* p. 4.

22. Ibid.

23. Lane, "The African Squadron," pp. 2ff.

24. Ibid., p. 4.

25. Fehrenbacher, *The Slaveholding Republic,* p. 174. There is evidence that the secretary of the navy underestimated the number, which might have been closer to 20—still pitifully small by any reckoning. Howard, *American Slavers and the Federal Law 1837–1862,* pp. 214–16.

26. Howard, *American Slavers and the Federal Law 1837–1862.*

27. Ibid., pp. 224–35.

28. Fehrenbacher, *The Slaveholding Republic,* p. 198.

29. Howard, *American Slavers and the Federal Law 1837–1862,* p. 144.

## CHAPTER I: LUCKY NAT

1. Robert Murray, "The Career of Gordon the Slaver," transcribed by Walter Brewer (1950, unpublished), p. 63; also, "The Execution of Captain Nathaniel Gordon, the Slave Trader," *Portland Advertiser,* Feb. 24, 1862, p. 1. The various newspapers agreed on Gordon's height and general appearance, although they usually got his age wrong, often by several years. Even his death certificate was off by two years.

2. *The New England Historical and Genealogical Register 1935,* vol. 89 (Boston: New England Historic Genealogical Society, 1935), p. 200.

3. Ibid., p. 199.

4. *New York Times,* Feb. 22, 1862, p. 8.

5. *The Colored American* (New York), July 7, 1838, p. 1.

6. James A. Rawley, "Captain Nathaniel Gordon, the Only American Executed for Violating the Slave Trade Laws," *Civil War History,* Sept. 1993, p. 219.

7. William Willis, *The History of Portland from 1632 to 1864* (Portland, Me.: Barley and Noyes, 1865), pp. 769–70.

8. Edward O. Schriver, *Go Free* (Orono: University of Maine Press, 1970), p. iv.

9. Ibid., pp. 50ff.

10. Ibid., p. 110.

11. Ibid., p. 40.

12. Warren S. Howard, *American Slavers and the Federal Law 1837–1862* (Berkeley: University of California Press, 1963), pp. 85–90.

13. FTM Online Genealogical Society, *History of the Treman, Tremain, Truman Family in America,* vol. I, no. 15550, Dr. Levi H. Fenner (unpublished). According to the family history, Fenner soon returned east with a "moderate fortune after his sojourn in California." Settling in Cleveland, he studied medicine and graduated from Cleveland Medical College. He also held a captaincy in the local militia. Fenner died in 1858 of an undisclosed ailment when still a relatively young man. An interesting line in his obituary mentions that he had "taken up his abode at the Cleveland Water-Cure, hoping to be benefited by a Hydropathic treatment." All efforts failed, and he was "cut down in the full vigor of manhood."

14. Howard, *American Slavers and the Federal Law 1837–1862,* pp. 46–47.

15. Murray, "The Career of Gordon the Slaver," p. 25.

16. Rawley, "Captain Nathaniel Gordon," p. 220.

17. Howard, *American Slavers and the Federal Law 1837–1862,* pp. 28–29.

18. Don E. Fehrenbacher, *The Slaveholding Republic* (New York: Oxford University Press, 2001), p. 177.
19. Howard, *American Slavers and the Federal Law 1837–1862*, p. 248.
20. Murray, "The Career of Gordon the Slaver," p. 25.
21. Hugh Thomas, *The Slave Trade* (New York: Simon & Schuster, 1997), p. 291.
22. Howard, *American Slavers and the Federal Law 1837–1862*, p. 1.
23. This was the "stowage" method employed by Gordon.
24. Captain Theodore Canot, *Captain Canot, or Twenty Years of an African Slaver* (New York: D. Appleton and Company, 1854), p. xii. Theodore Canot was arrested in 1847 while in command of the slaving bark *Chancellor*, indicted under the Act of 1818, and prosecuted in New York City. Judge Samuel Betts and Justice Samuel Nelson dismissed the charges, due to a "technical defect in the indictment."
25. Howard, *American Slavers and the Federal Law 1837–1862*, p. 238.
26. William D. Piersen, *From Africa to America* (New York: Simon & Schuster, 1996), p. 30.
27. Howard, *American Slavers and the Federal Law 1837–1862*, p. 104.
28. James A. Rawley, *The Transatlantic Slave Trade* (New York: W.W. Norton & Co., 1981), p. 298.
29. John R. Spears, *The American Slave-Trade* (New York: Charles Scribner's Sons, 1900), pp. 145–46.
30. Calvin Lane, "The African Squadron: The U.S. Navy and the Slave Trade 1820–1862," *The Log of Mystic Seaport* 50, no. 4 (Spring 1999).
31. *New England Historical and Genealogical Register,* p. 199.
32. *New York Times,* Feb. 22, 1862, p. 8.

## CHAPTER II: SLAVERS AND THE LAW

1. Maria Luisa Lobo Montalvo, *Havana: History and Architecture of a Romantic City* (New York: The Monacelli Press, 2000), pp. 16ff.
2. Clifford L. Staten, *The History of Cuba* (Westport, Conn.: Greenwood Press, 2003), p. 24.
3. Don E. Fehrenbacher, *The Slaveholding Republic* (New York: Oxford University Press, 2001), p. 180.
4. Staten, *The History of Cuba,* p. 24.
5. Warren S. Howard, *American Slavers and the Federal Law 1837–1862* (Berkeley: University of California Press, 1963), p. 58.
6. Karen Needles, "United States vs. Nathaniel Gordon." Documents on Wheels. Available online at www.documentsonwheels.com/gordon/index.htm.
7. Robert Murray, "The Career of Gordon the Slaver," transcribed by Walter Brewer (1950, unpublished), p. 2.
8. Howard, *American Slavers and the Federal Law 1837–1862,* pp. 31ff.
9. Murray, "The Career of Gordon the Slaver," p. 7.
10. James A. Rawley, *The Transatlantic Slave Trade* (New York: W. W. Norton & Co., 1981), pp. 291–95.
11. Howard, *American Slavers and the Federal Law 1837–1862,* p. 16.
12. Calvin Lane, "The African Squadron: The U.S. Navy and the Slave Trade 1820–1862," *The Log of Mystic Seaport* 50, no. 4 (Spring 1999), p. 7.
13. E. Delafield Smith, quoted in Tobias Barrington Wolff, "The Thirteenth Amendment and Slavery in the Global Economy," *Columbia Law Review,* May 2002, p. 18.

14. Howard, *American Slavers and the Federal Law 1837–1862,* p. 30.
15. Barry Unsworth, *Sacred Hunger* (New York: W. W., Norton & Co., 1993), p. 300.
16. Howard, *American Slavers and the Federal Law 1837–1862,* pp. 28ff.
17. Fehrenbacher, *The Slaveholding Republic,* p. 164.
18. Howard, *American Slavers and the Federal Law 1837–1862,* pp. 33–35.
19. Daniel Weiser, "The Case of Nathaniel Gordon: Success for the United States, Tragedy for an Individual" (unpublished paper for Columbia University course, May 5, 1986), p. 118; Howard, *American Slavers and the Federal Law 1837–1862,* pp. 111–23.
20. HED #7, Dec. 27, 1858, pp. 292–99, as quoted in Weiser, "The Case of Nathaniel Gordon," p. 118, and Howard, *American Slavers and the Federal Law 1837–1862,* p. 119.
21. Murray, "The Career of Gordon the Slaver," pp. 5, 6.
22. Ibid., p. 3.
23. Ibid., pp. 2, 3.
24. Ibid., pp. 3, 4.
25. Ibid., p. 4.
26. Ibid., p. 6.
27. Fehrenbacher, *The Slaveholding Republic,* pp. 166–67.
28. Howard, *American Slavers and the Federal Law 1837–1862,* pp. 122–23. Within a year, following the outbreak of the Civil War, Helm would leave his post to assume a new position as chief purchasing agent in Cuba for the Confederate States of America.
29. Murray, "The Career of Gordon the Slaver," p. 11.
30. *Jackson Mississippian,* Mar. 31, 1854, p. 2.
31. Murray, "The Career of Gordon the Slaver," p. 17.
32. Ibid., pp. 19, 20.
33. Fehrenbacher, *The Slaveholding Republic,* pp. 165–71.
34. J. Taylor Wood, "The Capture of a Slaver," *Atlantic Monthly* 86 (1900), p. 451.
35. Fehrenbacher, *The Slaveholding Republic,* pp. 165–71.
36. Lane, "The African Squadron," p. 8.
37. Ibid., p. 10.
38. Howard, *American Slavers and the Federal Law 1837–1862,* pp. 41–43.
39. Lane, "The African Squadron," p. 12.
40. Ibid.
41. Fehrenbacher, *The Slaveholding Republic,* p. 174.
42. Howard, *American Slavers and the Federal Law 1837–1862,* pp. 41–43.
43. Lane, "The African Squadron," p. 12.
44. Howard, *American Slavers and the Federal Law 1837–1862,* pp. 131, 132.
45. Fehrenbacher, *The Slaveholding Republic,* p. 9.
46. W. E. F. Ward, *The Royal Navy and the Slaves: The Suppression of the Atlantic Slave Trade* (New York: Pantheon Books, 1969), 46–47.
47. Fehrenbacher, *The Slaveholding Republic,* 176.
48. Ibid.
49. Howard, *American Slavers and the Federal Law 1837–1862,* 132, 133.
50. Ibid., pp. 218, 230.
51. Ibid., p. 134.
52. Ibid., pp. 136–37.

53. "Squadron Letters: African Squadron" 1841–1866. National Archives and Records Administration Micrcfilm File M-89, Roll 111.
54. "Squadron Letters" M-89, Roll 111.
55. Tobias Barrington Wolff, "The Thirteenth Amendment and Slavery in the Global Economy," *Columbia Law Review* (May 2002), p. 16; W. E. B. DuBois, *The Suppression of the African Slave Trade to the United States of America 1636–1870* (New York: The Social Science Press, 1954), p. 169.
56. "Squadron Letters" M-89, Roll 111.
57. Howard, *American Slavers and the Federal Law 1837–1862,* pp. 132–35.
58. Murray, "The Career of Gordon the Slaver," pp. 19–20.
59. "Squadron Letters" M-89, Roll 111.
60. Howard, *American Slavers and the Federal Law 1837–1862,* p. 138.
61. Ibid., p. 111.
62. Lane, "The African Squadron," p. 14.
63. Howard, *American Slavers and the Federal Law 1837–1862,* pp. 170–76.
64. Ibid., p. 232.
65. Lane, "The African Squadron," p. 15.
66. Howard, *American Slavers and the Federal Law 1837–1862,* p. 105.
67. Ibid., p. 108.
68. John P. Spears, *The American Slave-Trade* (New York: Charles Scribner's Sons, 1900), p. 129.
69. Fehrenbacher, *The Slaveholding Republic,* p. 176.
70. Howard, *American Slavers and the Federal Law 1837–1862,* p. 59.
71. Fehrenbacher, *The Slaveholding Republic,* pp. 187–89.
72. Joseph K. Tellewoyan, *The Years the Locusts Have Eaten: Liberia 1816–1996,* pp. 9–10.
73. Allen Huffman, *Mississippi in Africa* (New York: Gotham Books, 2005), pp. 45–46.
74. Ibid., pp. 47–48.
75. Tellewoyan, *The Years the Locusts Have Eaten,* p. 14.
76. Huffman, *Mississippi in Africa,* pp. 45–46.
77. Danna Harman, "Liberia: From Oasis of Freedom to Ongoing Civil War," *Christian Science Monitor,* June 12, 2002, p. 7.
78. Tellewoyan, *The Years the Locusts Have Eaten,* p. 14.
79. Fehrenbacher, *The Slaveholding Republic,* p. 187.
80. Howard, *American Slavers and the Federal Law 1837–1862,* p. 63.

## CHAPTER III: ONE DOLLAR A HEAD

1. Melvin Maddocks, *The Atlantic Crossing* (Alexandria, Va.: Time-Life Books Inc., 1981), pp. 89–93.
2. *New York Times,* Feb. 21, 1862, p. 5.
3. Mel Fisher, "The Last Slave Ships: African Slavery" (Mel Fisher Maritime Heritage Society Inc., 2002), p. 2.
4. *New York Times,* Feb. 21, 1862, p. 5.
5. Warren S. Howard, *American Slavers and the Federal Law 1837–1862* (Berkeley: University of California Press, 1963), p. 7.
6. J. Taylor Wood, "The Capture of a Slaver," *Atlantic Monthly* 86 (1900), p. 455.
7. *New York Times,* Feb. 21, 1862, p. 5.

8. Howard, *American Slavers and the Federal Law 1837–1862*, p. 252.

9. Captain Theodore Canot, *Captain Canot, or Twenty Years of an African Slaver* (New York: D. Appleton and Company, 1854), p. 102.

10. Ibid., p. 94.

11. *New York Times,* Feb. 21, 1862, p. 5.

12. Philip D. Curtin, ed., *Africa Remembered* (Madison: University of Wisconsin Press, 1968), pp. 331–32.

13. Howard, *American Slavers and the Federal Law 1837–1862*, p. 21.

14. Henry Eason, "Journal," U.S. Sloop-of-War "Marion," 1838–1860, Log 902, GW Blunt White Library, Mystic Seaport, Mystic, Connecticut, March 30, 1860.

15. This total is the result of an error in Godon's calculation. The number of slaves landed at Monrovia was recorded as 867. Accounting for the loss of 30 to 37 on the voyage from the Congo, we can assume the correct number to be around 897. This is the number subsequently used by the courts, as well as by the U.S. marshal.

16. Letters from Commanding Officers and Captains of Cruisers to the Secretaries of the Navy, 1841–1866, National Archives and Records Administration Microfilm File M-147, Roll 65.

17. *New York Times,* Feb. 21, 1862, p. 5.

18. Ibid., Nov. 9, 1861, p. 3.

19. Ibid., Feb. 21, 1862, p. 5.

20. *New York Herald,* June 19, 1861, p. 2.

21. Ibid., Nov. 9, 1861, p. 3.

22. J. Taylor Wood, "The Capture of a Slaver," p. 455.

23. *New York Times,* Feb. 21, 1862, p. 5.

24. *New York Herald,* June 19, 1861, p. 2.

25. Howard, *American Slavers and the Federal Law 1837–1862,* p. 238.

26. William Douglass, to former owners, in "Letters from the Former Slaves of Terrell," University of Virginia Electronic Text Center, MS. of February 5, 1857.

27. Ibid., Mar. 8, 1857.

28. John Seys, MSS. to Secretary of State Lewis Cass, 1860, Records of the Department of State, Record Group 59, Microfilm 169, Roll 2 (February 14, 1858–February 22, 1864).

29. Eason, "Journal," Aug. 10, 1860.

30. Ibid.

31. Letters from Commanding Officers and Captains, File M-147, Roll 65.

32. Letters from Commanding Officers and Captains, File M-89, Roll 111.

33. Eason, "Journal," Aug. 27, 1860.

34. Letters from Commanding Officers and Captains, File M-89, Roll 111.

35. Letters from Commanding Officers and Captains, File M-147, Roll 12.

## CHAPTER IV: NEW YORK AND PRISON

1. Harry Johnson and Frederick S. Lightfoot, *Maritime New York in Nineteenth Century Photography* (New York: Dover Books, 1980), pp. ix–29.

2. John G. Bunker, *An Illustrated History of the Port of New York* (Woodland Hills, Calif.: Windsor Publications Inc., 1979), p. 37.

3. Ibid.

4. Eric Homberger, *The Historical Atlas of New York City* (New York: Henry Holt and Co., 1998), p. 44.

5. James A. Rawley, *The Transatlantic Slave Trade* (New York: W. W. Norton & Co., 1981), p. 385.

6. William Armstrong Fairburn, *Merchant Sail*, 6 vols. (Center Lovell, Me.: Fairburn, Marine Education Foundation, Inc., [date]), vol. 2, p. 915.

7. Don E. Fehrenbacher, *The Slaveholding Republic* (New York: Oxford University Press, 2001), p. 202.

8. Tobias Barrington Wolff, "The Thirteenth Amendment and Slavery in the Global Economy," *Columbia Law Review*, May 2002, p. 16.

9. Edward G. Burrows and Mike Wallace, *Gotham* (New York: Oxford University Press, 1999), p. 861.

10. Warren S. Howard, *American Slavers and the Federal Law 1837–1862* (Berkeley: University of California Press, 1963), p. 195.

11. The spelling varies, depending on the source. The Court Minutes Book for the first trial lists him as "Joachimson," District Attorney Smith spells it "Joachinsen," while various newspapers spell it either "Joachimsen," "Joachimmsen," or "Joachimssen." The correct spelling is "Joachimsen," since it is the one used by the attorney himself.

12. *New York Evening Post*, Nov. 24, 1860, p. 4.

13. Ibid, p. 2.

14. Records of Sale for the "Erie," 1860–1861, National Archives and Records Administration, New York.

15. *New York Times*, Feb. 21, 1862, p. 5.

16. Thomas Keneally, *American Scoundrel* (New York: Doubleday, 2002), p. 30.

17. J. G. Randall and David Donald, *The Civil War and Reconstruction* (Boston: D.C. Heath and Company, 1965), pp. 91–92.

18. Ibid., pp. 114–17.

19. *New York Evening Post*, Oct. 31, 1860, p. 3.

20. Ibid.

21. *New York Times*, Feb. 2, 1862, p. 5.

22. *New York Evening Post*, Nov. 2, 1860, p. 3.

23. Robert Murray, "The Career of Gordon the Slaver," transcribed by Walter Brewer, 1950 (unpublished), p. 63.

24. Howard, *American Slavers and the Federal Law 1837–1862*, p. 58.

25. Ibid., pp. 176–77.

26. Ibid., p. 51.

27. Edward Robb Ellis, *The Epic of New York City* (New York: Kodansha America, Inc., 1997), p. 286.

28. Howard, *American Slavers and the Federal Law 1837–1862*, p. 54.

29. Ibid., p. 55.

30. *New York Evening Post*, Nov. 23, 1860, p. 2.

31. Howard, *American Slavers and the Federal Law 1837–1862*, pp. 128–29.

32. Herbert Asbury, *The Gangs of New York* (New York: Thunder's Mouth Press, 1927), pp. 39–40.

33. Luc Sante, *Low Life* (New York: Farrar, Straus & Giroux, 1991), pp. 260–63.

34. Stephen Longstreet, *City on Two Rivers* (New York: Hawthorn Books, Inc., 1975), p. 53.

35. Theodore Roosevelt, *New York* (New York: Longmans, Green, and Co., 1910), p. 238.

36. Ibid., p. 267.

37. Ibid., p. 287.
38. Burrows and Wallace, *Gotham,* p. 862.
39. Alexander B. Callow, Jr., *The Tweed Ring* (New York: Oxford University Press, 1966), pp. 24–25.
40. Ellis, *The Epic of New York City,* p. 285.
41. Burrows and Wallace, *Gotham,* p. 865.
42. Ellis, *The Epic of New York City,* p. 287.
43. Burrows and Wallace, *Gotham,* p. 865.
44. Sante, *Low Life,* p. 263.
45. Burrows and Wallace, *Gotham,* pp. 862–63.
46. Don E. Fehrenbacher, *The Slaveholding Republic* (New York: Oxford University Press, 2001), p. 196.
47. The supercargo represented the owner on board some vessels, and was responsible for the purchase and sale of the cargo.
48. Howard, *American Slavers and the Federal Law 1837–1862,* pp. 155–60.
49. Ibid., pp. 188–89.
50. Ibid.
51. Ibid., p. 163.
52. Ibid., p. 164.
53. The Revenue Cutter Service was the forerunner of today's Coast Guard. It employed fast, armed vessels, one of whose main duties was to apprehend smugglers.
54. Howard, *American Slavers and the Federal Law 1837–1862,* pp. 165–66.
55. Ibid., p. 167.
56. *New York Daily Tribune,* Nov. 4, 1862, p. 4.
57. Ibid. Also Howard, *American Slavers and the Federal Law 1837–1862,* p.168.
58. *The Rail Splitter* (Cincinnati, Ohio) 1, no. 1 (Aug. 1860).
59. Howard, *American Slavers and the Federal Law 1837–1862,* p. 311, n.9.
60. Karen Needles, "United States vs. Nathaniel Gordon," Documents on Wheels, www.documentsonwheels.com.
61. *New York Evening Post,* Nov. 23, 1860, p. 1.
62. "Minutes Book for the Second Circuit," New Hampshire (Waltham, Mass.), pp. 209–26.
63. Townsend, Letter VI, in George Alfred Townsend, *The Life, Crime, and Capture of John Wilkes Booth* (New York: Dick Fitzgerald, 1865).
64. Charles Dickens, *The Works of Charles Dickens* (New York: Books, Inc., 1867), p. 73.
65. Charles Sutton, *The New York Tombs,* ed. by James B. Mix and Samuel A. Mackeever (San Francisco: A. Roman & Co., 1874), p. 47.
66. Ibid., p. 46.
67. Eric Homberger, *The Historical Atlas of New York City* (New York: Henry Holt and Co., 1998), p. 84.
68. Ibid., p. 81.
69. Ibid.
70. Sutton, *The New York Tombs,* p. 295.
71. *New York Times,* Dec. 24, 1860, p. 2.
72. *Springfield Daily Republican,* Feb. 25, 1862.

## CHAPTER V: FIRST TRIAL

1. Louis Auchincloss, ed., *The Hone and Strong Diaries of Old Manhattan* (New York: Abbeville Press, 1989), p. 193.
2. Eric Foner, *Politics and Ideology in the Age of the Civil War* (New York: Oxford University Press, 1980), p. 53.
3. Ibid.
4. J. G. Randall and David Donald, *The Civil War and Reconstruction* (Boston: D.C. Heath and Company, 1965), pp. 143–44.
5. Auchincloss, *The Hone and Strong Diaries of Old Manhattan,* p. 198.
6. Edward G. Burrows and Mike Wallace, *Gotham* (New York: Oxford University Press, 1999), p. 865.
7. Ibid., p. 866.
8. Ibid.
9. Ibid.
10. Theodore Roosevelt, *New York* (New York: Longmans, Green, and Co., 1910), pp. 202–203.
11. Lloyd Morris, *Incredible New York* (New York: Random House, 1951), p. 37.
12. Auchincloss, *The Hone and Strong Diaries of Old Manhattan,* p. 202–203.
13. Ibid.
14. Ibid., pp. 128–29.
15. Burrows and Wallace, *Gotham,* p. 870.
16. Warren S. Howard, *American Slavers and the Federal Law 1837–1862* (Berkeley: University of California Press, 1963). p. 72.
17. *New York Times,* June 23, 1861, p. 3.
18. *New York Herald,* June 18, 1861, p. 5. Devoutly opposed to the slave trade, Murray had been to Washington the week before this article was published, where he met with three cabinet secretaries, including William Seward. "The Marshal was informed that the present government was determined, at all hazard and at any cost, to break up the slave trade."
19. Howard, *American Slavers and the Federal Law 1837–1862,* p. 72.
20. Ibid., p. 222.
21. *New York Herald,* June 17, 1861, p. 2.
22. Ibid., italics added.
23. John T. Morse, Jr., ed., *Diary of Gideon Welles, Secretary of the Navy under Lincoln and Johnson,* vol. 2 (Boston: Houghton Mifflin Co., 1911), p. 83.
24. Howard, *American Slavers and the Federal Law 1837–1862* p. 200.
25. Ibid., p. 258.
26. Ibid., pp. 258–60.
27. *New York Herald,* Nov. 7, 1861, p. 8.
28. Howard, *American Slavers and the Federal Law 1837–1862,* p. 99.
29. Ibid., p. 196–99.
30. *New York Herald,* June 19, 1861, p. 2.
31. Ibid., June 20, 1861, p. 2.
32. Ibid.
33. *New York Daily Tribune,* June 18, 1861, p. 7.
34. Ibid., June 21, 1861. p. 8.
35. *New York Times,* June 18, 1861, p. 7.
36. Ibid.
37. Ibid., June 20, 1861, p. 2.

38. *New York Herald,* June 20, 1861, p. 2.
39. Ibid.
40. Ibid.
41. *New York Times,* June 21, 1861, p. 5.
42. *New York Times,* June 22, 1861, p. 3.
43. *New York Daily Tribune,* June 22, 1861, p. 4.
44. *New York Times,* June 25, 1861, p. 3.
45. *New York Daily Tribune,* June 22, 1861, p. 4.
46. Ibid., p. 3.

**CHAPTER VI: SECOND TRIAL**

 1. *New York Evening Post,* Feb. 21, 1862, p. 3.
 2. *New York Times,* Feb. 27, 1862, p. 3.
 3. *The National Cyclopedia of American Biography,* vol. 5 (New York: James T. White and Co., 1891), p. 515.
 4. *New York Times,* July 3, 1861, p. 3.
 5. Ibid., July 16, 1861, p. 6.
 6. Karen Needles, "United States vs. Nathaniel Gordon." Documents on Wheels, www.documentsonwheels.com/gordon/index.htm.
 7. Ibid.
 8. Margaret E. Wagner et al., *The Library of Congress Civil War Desk Reference* (New York: Simon & Schuster, 2002), pp. 246–47.
 9. J. G. Randall and David Donald, *The Civil War and Reconstruction* (Boston: D.C. Heath and Company, 1965), pp. 371–72.
10. Ibid., p. 872.
11. Louis Auchincloss, ed., *The Hone and Strong Diaries of Old Manhattan* (New York: Abbeville Press, 1989), p. 205.
12. Ibid., p. 208.
13. Edward G. Burrows and Mike Wallace, *Gotham* (New York: Oxford University Press, 1999), p. 871.
14. Ibid.
15. Ibid., pp. 873–76.
16. Ibid., p. 872.
17. Smith, E. D. ms to G. Whiting, Oct. 7, 1861, Record Group 48 Gen'l Records of the Department of the Interior, Records relating to the Suppression of the Slave Trade.
18. *New York Times,* Nov. 23, 1861, p. 3.
19. Karen Needles, "United States vs. Nathaniel Gordon."
20. Ibid.
21. Ibid.
22. *New York Evening Post,* Nov. 7, 1861, p. 4.
23. Ibid., Nov. 8, 1861, p. 4.
24. *New York Herald,* Nov. 7, 1861, p. 8.
25. Karen Needles: "United States vs. Nathaniel Gordon."
26. *New York Evening Post,* Nov. 8, 1861, p. 4.
27. *New York Herald,* Nov. 7, 1861, p. 8.
28. *New York Times,* Nov. 8, 1861, p. 3.
29. Ibid.
30. *New York Evening Post,* Nov. 8, 1861, p. 4.

31. *New York Times,* Nov. 8, 1861, p. 3.
32. *New York Evening Post,* Nov. 8, 1861, p. 4.
33. Ibid.
34. Robert J. Plowman, "The Voyage of the 'Coolie' Ship Kate Hooper October 3, 1857–March 26, 1858," NARA Prologue (Summer 2001), pp. 2–3, at www .archives.gov/publications/prologue_summer_2001_coolie_ship_kate_hooper _1.html
35. *New York Times,* Nov. 9, 1861, p. 3.
36. Ibid.
37. Ibid.
38. Ibid.
39. Ibid.
40. *New York Herald,* Nov. 9, 1861, p. 3.
41. *New York Times,* Nov. 9, 1861, p. 8.
42. *New York Evening Post,* Nov. 9, 1861, p. 3.
43. *New York Herald,* Nov. 9, 1861, p. 3
44. Ibid., Nov. 11, 1861, p. 2.
45. Karen Needles, "United States vs. Nathaniel Gordon."
46. *New York Herald,* Nov. 9, 1861, p. 4.
47. *New York Daily Tribune,* Nov. 9, 1861, p. 8.
48. *New York Times,* Nov. 9, 1861, p. 4.
49. E. D. Smith ms to C. B. Smith, Nov. 22, 1861, Record Group 48; Karen Needles, "United States vs. Nathaniel Gordon."

**CHAPTER VII: SENTENCING**

1. *New York Times,* Nov. 18, 1861, p. 6.
 2. *New York Herald,* Nov. 18, 1861, p. 5.
 3. Warren S. Howard, *American Slavers and the Federal Law 1837–1862* (Berkeley: University of California Press, 1963), p. 203; *New York Evening Post,* Nov. 12, 1861, p. 4.
 4. Howard, *American Slavers and the Federal Law 1837–1862,* p. 203.
 5. George P. Andrews, *Biographical Sketch of Honorable E. Delafield Smith* (New York: Greer & Co., 1871), p. 11.
 6. *New York Evening Post,* Nov. 14, 1861.
 7. Andrews, *Biographical Sketch of Honorable E. Delafield Smith,* pp. 11, 12.
 8. *New York Herald,* Nov. 21, 1861, p. 8.
 9. Ibid.
10. Howard, *American Slavers and the Federal Law 1837–1862,* pp. 203–204.
11. Ibid., p. 202.
12. *New York Evening Post,* Nov. 26, 1861, p. 4.
13. Ibid., Nov. 30, 1861, p. 4.
14. Ibid., Nov. 22, 1861, p. 2.
15. Ibid., Nov. 19, 1861, p. 2.
16. Ibid., Nov. 30, 1861, p. 4; *New York Herald,* Nov. 30, 1861, p. 4.
17. Letters from U.S. Marshals, June 16, 1862, Record Group 48: Records of the Department of the Interior.
18. Howard, *American Slavers and the Federal Law 1837–1862,* pp. 189, 234
19. *New York Evening Post,* Nov. 30, 1861, p. 3.
20. Ibid.

21. *New York Herald,* Dec. 1, 1861, p. 2.
22. Ibid.
23. Robert Murray "The Career of Gordon the Slaver (1866)," transcribed by Walter Brewer, 1950 (unpublished), p. 40.
24. Ibid.

**CHAPTER VIII: REACTIONS**
 1. *New York Times,* Dec. 1, 1861, p. 4.
 2. Ibid.
 3. W. S. Fitzgerald, "Make Him an Example," *American History Illustrated* (1983), p. 7.
 4. *New York Evening Post,* Feb. 2, 1862, p. 2.
 5. Roy P. Basler, ed., *The Collected Works of Abraham Lincoln* vol. v (New Brunswick, N.J.: Rutgers University Press, 1953), p. 47.
 6. *Daily National Intelligencer,* Dec. 5, 1861, p. 2.
 7. *New York Times,* Nov. 11, 1861, p. 4.
 8. *Daily National Intelligencer,* Dec. 5, 1861, p. 2.
 9. *New York Evening Post,* Nov. 30, 1861, p. 2.
10. Edward K. Spann, *Gotham at War* (Wilmington, Dela.: Scholarly Resources Press, 2002), p. 85.
11. Ibid., pp. 86–87.
12. *New York Evening Post,* Dec. 2, 1861, p. 2.
13. Ibid.
14. Ibid.
15. Ibid., Nov. 30, 1861, p. 2.
16. Ibid., Dec. 2, 1861, p. 2.
17. Ibid., Dec. 7, 1861, p. 1.
18. Ibid., Dec. 4, 1861, p. 2.
19. Ibid., Dec. 5, 1861, p. 2.
20. Spann, *Gotham at War,* pp. 86–87.
21. Ibid., p. 49.
22. Ibid., p. 45.
23. Ibid., p. 3.
24. J. G. Randall and David Donald, *The Civil War and Reconstruction* (Boston: D. C. Heath and Company, 1965), pp. 360–62.
25. *New York Evening Post,* Nov. 25, 1861, p. 3.
26. Randall and Donald, *The Civil War and Reconstruction,* p. 360.
27. Ibid., p. 361.
28. *New York Evening Post,* Dec. 21, 1861, p. 2.
29. Randall and Donald, *The Civil War and Reconstruction,* p. 36.
30. *New York Times,* Feb. 21, 1862, p. 3.
31. Ibid.
32. Harriet Sigerman, *An Unfinished Battle* (New York: Oxford University Press, 1994), pp. 115–25.
33. David Brownstone and Irene Franck, *Illustrated History of Women* (Danbury, Conn.: Grolier Educational, 1999), pp. 57–59.
34. Christine Stansell, *City of Women* (New York: Alfred A. Knopf, 1984), p. 105.
35. Robert Murray, "The Career of Gordon the Slaver (1866)," transcribed by Walter Brewer, 1950 (unpublished), p. 41.

## CHAPTER IX: THE AWFUL CHANGE

1. J. T. Dorris, "President Lincoln's Clemency," *Journal of the Illinois State Historical Society* xx (January 1928), p. 551.
2. Ibid., p. 550.
3. William Lee Miller, "Lincoln's Mercy," *Miller Center Report,* Scholar's Corner, University of Virginia (Summer 2001), p. 30.
4. Harold Holzer, comp. and ed., *Dear Mr. Lincoln* (New York: Addison-Wesley Publishing Co., 1993), pp. 71–72.
5. Dorris, "President Lincoln's Clemency," p. 550.
6. Ibid. p. 84.
7. Ibid., p. 548.
8. Ibid., p. 550.
9. Miller, "Lincoln's Mercy," p. 32.
10. Dorris, "President Lincoln's Clemency," p. 551.
11. Miller, "Lincoln's Mercy," p. 10.
12. Dorris, "President Lincoln's Clemency," p. 553.
13. Miller, "Lincoln's Mercy," p. 12.
14. Dorris, "President Lincoln's Clemency," p. 554.
15. J. G. Randall and David Donald, *The Civil War and Reconstruction* (Boston: D. C. Heath and Co., 1965), pp. 302–304.
16. Dorris, "President Lincoln's Clemency," p. 558.
17. Miller, "Lincoln's Mercy," p. 32.
18. William Lee Miller, *Lincoln's Virtues* (New York: Alfred A. Knopf, 2002), p. 16.
19. Miller, "Lincoln's Mercy," p. 30.
20. Dorris, "President Lincoln's Clemency," p. 556.
21. Southern Historical Publication Society, U.S. Biographies Project, Biographies of Jefferson County, W.V., "John Yates Beall" (Richmond, Va.: 1909), vol. XI, pp. 61–62.
22. Don E. Fehrenbacher and Virginia Fehrenbacher, eds., *Recollected Words of Abraham Lincoln* (Stanford, Calif.: Stanford University Press, 1996), pp. 40–41.
23. *New York Times,* Feb. 21, 1862, p. 5.
24. Robert Murray "The Career of Gordon the Slaver (1866)," transcribed by Walter Brewer, 1950 (unpublished), p. 41.
25. Reverend J. W. Chickering ms. to Abraham Lincoln, University of Chicago Library, African American Studies Collection, Lincoln Miscellaneous Mss Coll., Barton Collection of Lincolniana, Box 2, Folder 1.
26. Rev. William Hayesward, ed., *Abraham Lincoln: Tributes from His Associates* (New York: Thomas Y. Crowell & Co., 1895), pp. 167–68.
27. *New York Daily Tribune,* Dec. 2, 1861, p. 7.
28. *New York Evening Post,* Feb. 4, 1862, p. 3.
29. *New York Times,* Feb. 6, 1862, p. 5.
30. Ibid., Feb. 8, 1862, p. 5.
31. As it turned out, Haines was tried twice, each trial ending in a hung jury. Ultimately, he posted bail, and nothing further transpired. Warren S. Howard, *American Slavers and the Federal Law 1837–1862* (Berkeley: University of California Press, 1963), p. 204.
32. Ibid., pp. 192–96.
33. *New York Herald,* Dec. 2, 1861, p. 4.
34. *New York Times,* Jan. 28, 1862, p. 4.

35. *New York Herald,* Feb. 4, 1862, p. 1.
36. U.S. Library of Congress, The Abraham Lincoln Papers at the Library of Congress, Series 1, General Correspondence, 1833–1916.
37. Beverly Wilson Palmer, ed., *The Selected Letters of Charles Sumner* (Boston: Northeastern University Press, 1990), pp. 99–100.
38. Fehrenbacher and Fehrenbacher, *Recollected Words of Abraham Lincoln,* p. 153.
39. Edward Waldo Emerson and Waldo Emerson Forbes, eds., *Journals of Ralph Waldo Emerson, 1856–1863* (Bridgewater, N.J.: 1999), pp. 377–78.
40. Stuart Lutz, "Lincoln Let Him Hang," *Civil War Times,* March 1998, p. 37.
41. *New York Times,* Jan. 28, 1862, p. 4.
42. *Union & Journal* (Biddeford, Me.:), Feb. 21, 1862, p. 1.
43. Fehrenbacher and Fehrenbacher, *Recollected Words of Abraham Lincoln,* p. 41.
44. Lutz, "Lincoln Let Him Hang," p. 37.
45. Roy P. Basler, ed., *The Collected Works of Abraham Lincoln* (New Brunswick, N.J.: Rutgers University Press, 1953), vol. III, p. 39.
46. Eric Foner, *Politics and Ideology in the Age of the Civil War* (New York: Oxford University Press, 1980), p. 50.
47. Basler, *The Collected Works of Abraham Lincoln,* vol. II, p. 268.
48. Ibid., pp. 273–75.
49. Ibid., p. 492.
50. Ibid., p. 421.
51. Ibid., p. 492.
52. Ibid., pp. 492–93.
53. Ibid., vol. III, p. 79.
54. Ibid., vol. II, p. 281.
55. Ibid., p. 266.
56. Ibid., p. 546.
57. Ibid., vol. III, pp. 39–42.
58. Ibid., vol. IV, p. 183.
59. Ibid., vol. III, p. 435.
60. Ibid., vol. II, p. 449.
61. Ibid., vol. III, p. 305.
62. Ibid., p. 451. This was the same Roger Pryor who, as a Confederate general, would one day visit Lincoln on behalf of the ill-fated John Yates Beall.
63. Ibid., p. 265.
64. Ibid., p. 239.
65. Fehrenbacher and Fehrenbacher, *Recollected Words of Abraham Lincoln,* p. 2.
66. Michael Burlingame, *The Inner World of Abraham Lincoln* (Urbana: University of Illinois Press, 1994), p. 23.
67. U.S. Library of Congress, The Abraham Lincoln Papers at the Library of Congress, Edward Bates to Abraham Lincoln, February 4, 1862, Case of Nathaniel Gordon.
68. Howard K. Beale, ed., *The Diary of Edward Bates* (Washington, D.C.: Government Printing Office, 1933), p. 229.
69. U.S. Library of Congress, The Abraham Lincoln Papers at the Library of Congress, "Proclamation Granting Nathaniel Gordon Temporary Stay at Execution," Feb. 4, 1862.
70. Margaret E. Wagner et al., eds. *The Library of Congress Civil War Desk Reference* (New York: Simon & Schuster, 2002), p. 14.

71. Ibid., p. 147.
72. Ibid.
73. *Springfield Daily Republican,* Feb. 21, 1862, p. 4.
74. Basler, *The Collected Works of Abraham Lincoln,* vol. V, p. 186.
75. John G. Nicolay and John Hay, *Abraham Lincoln* (New York: Century, 1890), p. 99.
76. *New York Times,* May 2, 1862, p. 4.
77. Miller, *Lincoln's Virtues,* p. 21.
78. Randall and Donald, *The Civil War and Reconstruction,* pp. 372–73.

## CHAPTER X: LAST ATTEMPTS

1. *New York Times,* Feb. 7, 1862, p. 1.
2. Records of the Department of the Interior, Record Group 48, Letters from U.S. Marshals, Feb. 18, 1862.
3. *New York Times,* Feb. 6, 1862, p. 5.
4. Robert Murray, "The Career of Gordon the Slaver (1866)," transcribed by Walter Brewer, 1950 (unpublished), pp. 64–65.
5. Dr. Levi H. Fenner, "History of the Treman, Tremaine, Truman family in America," FTM Online Geneological Society, vol. 1, no. 15550 (unpublished). Marshal Murray was a dedicated and honorable man, and as different from his predecessor, Isaiah Rynders, as one could possibly be. Murray so hated the slave trade that, in collaboration with Senator Charles Sumner, he authored his own proposed legislation to aid in its demise. It is impossible to determine to what extent the Gordon case provided the motivation, but it is a matter of record that Murray wrote his bill during the last month of Nathaniel Gordon's life. No copy of the actual bill survives, other than this cover letter, sent to Attorney General Bates:

Sir,

I have the honor to enclose herewith copy of a bill for the more effectual suppression of the African Slave trade drawn up by me at the solicitation of the Honorable Charles Sumner of the U.S. Senate.

I shall be happy to receive your opinion of the same, and would feel grateful for any suggestions which you may please to offer that will add to its efficacy.

There is no record of Bates's official response, nor did the attorney general see fit to record the communication in his diary. On the back of the letter, presumably in the hand of Bates's secretary, is a brief explanation of the contents, under the notation "not official."

Throughout Lincoln's presidency, Robert Murray would distinguish himself through various deeds, some more controversial than others, but all marked by strength, conviction, and initiative. During New York City's days-long Draft Riots of 1863, two dozen members of the rampaging mob descended on his home. Murray drew two pistols and handed one to his wife, "instructing her not to fire until he should utter the word." He walked out of the house to confront the mob, which "perhaps, respecting the character of his little army of one, made haste to depart" (*New York Times,* July 17, 1863).

On another occasion, acting on President Lincoln's orders, Murray illegally seized and deported a Spanish slaver, José Arguelles, who had been living in New York. Since no extradition treaty existed with Spain, Murray was indicted for kidnapping by a New York grand jury. He told the court that he had acted on a presidential directive, and the indictment was ultimately quashed ( John G. Nicolay and John Hay, *Abraham Lincoln* [New York: Century, 1890], vol. 9, p. 47).

It is clear that Lincoln valued Murray highly. In order to obtain evidence of slaving activities, the marshal resorted to "bribing captain, masters, sailors, stevedores . . . and deckhands." Because he obviously could not present signed vouchers of his expenses, he stood to lose his investment. Lincoln stepped in and authorized full reimbursement (ibid.).

After Lincoln's assassination, Murray interviewed one of the conspirators, George A. Atzerodt; within five minutes, he elicited a full confession (*New York Herald,* July 8, 1865).

6.  Murray, "The Career of Gordon the Slaver," p. 65.
7.  *New York Evening Post,* Feb. 6, 1862, p. 2.
8.  W. S. Fitzgerald, "Make Him an Example," *American History Illustrated* (1983).
9.  *New York Evening Post,* Feb. 11, 1862, p. 4.
10. National Archives and Records Administration, Record Group 267, Records of the Supreme Court of the United States, Entry 26, Ex Parte Nathaniel Gordon.
11. Michael Burlingame, *The Inner World of Abraham Lincoln* (Urbana: University of Illinois Press, 1994), pp. 65–67.
12. Howard K. Beale, ed., *Diary of Edward Bates* (Washington, D.C.: Government Printing Office, 1933), p. 233.
13. U.S. Library of Congress, The Abraham Lincoln Papers at the Library of Congress, Rhoda White plea for clemency, Feb. 17, 1862.
14. Murray, "The Career of Gordon the Slaver," pp. 44–45.
15. Ibid., p. 46.
16. U.S. Library of Congress, The Abraham Lincoln Papers at the Library of Congress, Edward Bates to Abraham Lincoln, Feb. 18, 1862.
17. Beale, *Diary of Edward Bates,* p. 233.
18. ref. Chapter X *supra.*
19. William Lee Miller, "I Felt it to be My Duty to Refuse," at talk presented to the Lincoln Forum, Gettysburg, Pa., November 17, 2001 (unpublished), p. 35.
20. U.S. Library of Congress, The Abraham Lincoln Papers at the Library of Congress, Gilbert Dean to Abraham Lincoln, Feb. 18, 1862.
21. U.S. Library of Congress, The Abraham Lincoln Papers at the Library of Congress, Edward Bates to Abraham Lincoln, Feb. 18, 1862.
22. *New York Evening Post,* Feb. 20, 1862, p. 3; also, Murray, "The Career of Gordon the Slaver," p. 46.
23. *New York Herald,* Feb. 21, 1862, p. 5.
24. Murray, "The Career of Gordon the Slaver," p. 46.
25. Ibid.
26. Ibid.
27. *New York Times,* Feb. 21, 1862, p. 5.
28. Ibid, Jan. 31, 1862, p. 5.
29. Ibid., Feb. 21, 1862, p. 5.
30. Ibid.
31. Ibid.

32. Ibid., p. 4.
33. Ibid., Feb. 22, 1862, p. 4.
34. Murray, "The Career of Gordon the Slaver," pp. 43–48.
35. *New York Times,* Feb. 20, 1862, p. 4.
36. Jennifer Fleischner, *Mrs. Lincoln and Mrs. Keckley* (New York: Broadway Books, 2003), p. 231; Emanuel Hertz, ed., *Lincoln Talks* (New York: Bramhall House, 1986), pp. 661–62.
37. Thomas Keneally, *Abraham Lincoln* (New York: Lipper/Viking, 2003), pp. 172–75.

## CHAPTER XI: THE GALLOWS

1. Robert Murray, "The Career of Gordon the Slaver (1866)," transcribed by Walter Brewer, 1950 (unpublished), p. 47.
2. Ibid.
3. *New York Herald,* Feb. 22, 1862, p. 1.
4. Murray, "The Career of Gordon the Slaver," p. 49.
5. *New York Times,* Feb. 22, 1862, p. 3
6. Murray, "The Career of Gordon the Slaver," p. 49.
7. Ibid., p. 50; *New York Herald,* Feb. 22, 1862, p. 1.
8. *New York Times,* Feb. 22, 1862, p. 8.
9. Murray, "The Career of Gordon the Slaver," p. 50.
10. Ibid.
11. *New York Times,* Feb. 22, 1862, p. 8.
12. Murray, "The Career of Gordon the Slaver," p. 52.
13. Ibid., p. 54.
14. Ibid., pp. 67–68.
15. Ibid., pp. 73–75.
16. Ibid., p. 68.
17. Ibid., p. 58.
18. Robert L. Mount, "The Hinge of Reform," *Mankind* 1, no. 4 (1967), pp. 46–48.
19. *New York Herald,* Feb. 22, 1862, p. 8.
20. Stuart Banner, *The Death Penalty* (Cambridge: Harvard University Press, 2002), p. 150.
21. Ibid., p. 158.
22. Ibid., p. 157.
23. Meyer Berger, *The Eight Million* (New York: Columbia University Press, 1983).
24. Paul Davenport, *South Riding Tunebook,* vol. I (Maltby, England: SRFN Publications, 1997). Also, June Lazare, "Folk Songs of New York," Folkways FH5276 (1966). Originally printed by H. De Marsan, Publisher of Songs and Ballads, 38 and 60 Chatham St., New York, 1860.
25. *Portland Advertiser,* Feb. 24, 1862, p. 1.
26. Murray, "The Career of Gordon the Slaver," p. 71.
27. Ibid.
28. Geoffrey Abbott, *The Book of Execution* (London: Headline Book Publishing, 1994), p. 240.
29. Banner, *The Death Penalty,* pp. 156–57.
30. Ibid., p. 171.
31. Ibid.
32. Ibid., p. 172.

33. Ibid., p. 173.

34. Ibid.

35. Murray, "The Career of Gordon the Slaver," p. 57.

36. *New York Times,* Feb. 22, 1862, p. 8.

37. *New York Herald,* Feb. 22, 1862, p. 8.

38. Murray, "The Career of Gordon the Slaver," p. 58.

39. *Portland Advertiser,* Feb. 24, 1862, p. 1.

40. Murray, "The Career of Gordon the Slaver," pp. 58–59.

41. *New York Times,* Feb. 22, 1862, p. 8.

42. "Lines" was a word used to refer to one's lot in life; "hard lines" is an archaic expression meaning "difficult conditions," "rough treatment," or "bad luck."

43. Murray, "The Career of Gordon the Slaver," p. 60.

44. *New York Times,* Feb. 22, 1862, p. 8.

45. *New York Herald,* Feb. 22, 1862, p. 8.

46. *New York Times,* Feb. 22, 1862, p. 8.

47. This type of break, frequently seen nowadays as a result of auto accidents, is still referred to as the "hangman's fracture."

48. *New York Evening Post,* Feb. 22, 1862, p. 3.

49. *Richmond Examiner,* Feb. 25, 1862, p. 3.

50. Murray, "The Career of Gordon the Slaver," pp. 74–75.

51. *London Daily News,* Mar. 8, 1862, p. 5; also quoted in Murray, "The Career of Gordon the Slaver," pp. 75–77.

52. *New York Times,* Feb. 22, 1862, p. 4.

53. *New York Evening Post,* Feb. 22, 1862, p. 3.

54. *Springfield Daily Republican,* Feb. 22, 1862, p. 8.

55. *Portland Advertiser,* Feb. 24, 1862, p. 1.

56. *New York Herald,* Feb. 22, 1862, p. 8.

57. *New York Times,* Feb. 22, 1862, p. 8.

58. Ibid., Feb. 24, 1862, p. 4.

59. Allan Nevins and Milton Halsey Thomas, *Diary of George Templeton Strong, The Civil War 1860–1865* (New York: Macmillan, 1952), pp. 208–209.

60. Murray, "The Career of Gordon the Slaver," p. 66.

61. Ibid., p. 67.

62. *New York Daily Tribune,* Feb. 23, 1862.

63. Records and Documents of Cypress Hills Cemetery, Brooklyn, New York, 1862–present.

64. Murray, "The Career of Gordon the Slaver," pp. 68–69.

65. Interview with Kenneth Thompson, Portland, Me., genealogist, author, and historian, Feb. 10, 2004.

66. W. H. Bunting, *A Day's Work* (Gardiner, Me.: Tilbury House Publishing, 2000), pp. 204, 268.

67. Interview with Kenneth Thompson, May 27, 2005.

68. Ibid.

## CHAPTER XII: TO HANG A SLAVER

1. Tobias Barrington Wolff, "The Thirteenth Amendment and Slavery in the Global Economy," *Columbia Law Review* (May 2002), p. 18.

2. U.S. Library of Congress, The Abraham Lincoln Papers at the Library of Congress, E. Delafield Smith to Montgomery Blair, Nov. 19, 1862.

3. Warren S. Howard, *American Slavers and the Federal Law 1837–1862* (Berkeley: University of California Press, 1963), p. 251.
4. Ibid., p. 160.
5. Ibid., pp. 233–34.
6. Ibid., pp. 170–76.
7. Ibid.
8. U.S. Library of Congress, The Abraham Lincoln Papers at the Library of Congress, Smith to Blair.
9. Howard, *American Slavers and the Federal Law 1837–1862*, p. 234.
10. Ibid., p. 176.
11. Ibid., pp. 231–35.
12. Roy P. Basler, ed., *The Collected Works of Abraham Lincoln* (New Brunswick, N.J.: Rutgers University Press, 1953), vol. VI, p. 294.
13. *New York Times,* Feb. 26, 1862, p. 3.
14. Howard, *American Slavers and the Federal Law 1837–1862,* p. 205.
15. Ibid., p. 64.
16. Ibid., pp. 46–47.
17. Robert Murray, "The Career of Gordon the Slaver (1866)," transcribed by Walter Brewer, 1950 (unpublished), p. 65.
18. Records of the Department of the Interior, Record Group 48, Letters from U. S. Marshals, Feb. 18, 1862.
19. Howard, *American Slavers and the Federal Law 1837–1862,* p. 286.
20. Ibid., p. 65.
21. *New York Daily Tribune,* Dec. 17, 1868, p. 3.
22. John R. Spears, *The American Slave Trade: An Account of its Origin, Growth and Suppression* (New York: Charles Scribner's Sons, 1900), p. 223.

## AFTERWORD: CAPTAIN GORDON'S LEGACY

1. Francis Bok, *Escape from Slavery* (New York: St. Martin's Press, 2003), pp. 1–278.
2. Interview with Kevin Bales, Free the Slaves, June 6, 2005. Bales is one of the world's foremost antislavery activists. He began his study of international slavery more than 12 years ago, when its existence was practically unknown. Today, he is a professor of sociology, a trustee of Anti-Slavery International, a consultant to the United Nations Global Program on Trafficking Human Beings, to the Economic Community of West African States, and to the U.S., British, Irish, Norwegian, and Nepali governments. His book *Disposable People* was nominated for the Pulitzer Prize in 2000, and the film which was based upon it, "Slavery: A Global Investigation," won a Peabody Award in 2000. That same year, Bales won the Premio Viareggio for services to humanity. (Bales, "The Social Psychology of Modern Slavery," *Scientific American* [April 2002].)
3. Andrew Cockburn, "21st Century Slaves," *National Geographic* (September 2003), pp. 12–20. Cockburn refers to Kevin Bales's *Disposable People* for all current statistics on modern-day slavery.
4. Free the Slaves and University of California, Berkeley, "Hidden Slaves: Forced Labor in the United States," Human Rights Center, University of California, Berkeley, 2004 www.freetheslaves.net. pp. 1, 10.
5. Amy O'Neill Richard, "International Trafficking in Women to the United States:

A Contemporary Manifestation of Slavery and Organized Crime," Washington, D.C., Center for the Study of Intelligence, 1999, p. iii.

6. Kevin Bales, *Disposable People* (Berkeley and Los Angeles: University of California Press, 1999), p. 250.

7. U.S. Department of Justice, *Trafficking in Persons Report June 2003,* www .state.gov/documents/organization/21555.pdf.

8. Cockburn, "21st Century Slaves," p. 23.

9. U.S. Department of Justice, *Assessment of U.S. Activities to Combat Trafficking in Persons* (Aug. 2003), www.state.gov/g/tip/rls/rpt/23495.htm.

10. Peter Landesman, "Sex Slaves on Main Street," *New York Times Sunday Magazine* (Jan. 25, 2004), p. 32.

11. Interview with Kevin Bales, Feb. 11, 2004.

12. CNN.com Member Services, "Modern-day slavery is alive and well in Florida" (Feb. 25, 2004), p. 2, www.cnn.com/2004/us/south/02/25/human.trafficking.ap/ index.html.

13. U.S. Department of Justice, *Assessment of U.S. Activities to Combat Trafficking in Persons,* p. 4.

14. Bales, *Disposable People,* p. 232.

15. BBC News World Edition, "Niger Rapped over Slavery Denial," Mar. 7, 2005, www.news.bbc.co.uk./2/hi/africa/4327497.stm.

16. Bales, *Disposable People,* p. 15.

17. Ibid., p. 25.

18. Ibid., p. 234.

19. Interview with Kevin Bales, June 6, 2005. Only 1 or 2 percent of the traffickers who bring people into the United States are American by birth, while another handful—mostly Russians—are naturalized.

20. Bales, *Disposable People,* p. 234.

21. Cockburn, "21st Century Slaves," p. 10.

22. Bales, *Disposable People,* p. 237.

23. Ibid., p. 19.

24. Cockburn, "21st Century Slaves," p. 10.

25. Bales, *Disposable People,* p. 32.

26. U.S. Department of Justice, *Trafficking in Persons Report June 2003.*

27. Since 9/11, heightened security at American airports and border checkpoints seems to have reduced the number of slaves smuggled into the country; the bad news is, this has virtually doubled the price charged by traffickers to send or take people into the United States, thereby making the slaves' "debt bondage" all the more impossible to pay off. Cockburn, "21st Century Slaves," pp. 10–18.

28. Bales, *Disposable People,* pp. 19–20.

29. Ibid.

30. Law Cases and Codes: "18 U.S.C. 1593."

31. Victims of Trafficking and Violence Protection Act of 2000, Public Law 106–386, Oct. 28, 2000: Cong. Rec., Vol. 146 (2000).

32. The Protection Project, "A Human Rights Report on Trafficking of Persons, Especially Women and Children." Mar. 2002, Available online at http.//209.190 .246.239/ver2/cr/us_pdf.

33. Ibid., p. 587.

34. Memorandum for the Secretary of State, Sept. 10, 2004.
35. *Trafficking in Persons Report June 2005,* p. 42.
36. The Protection Project. "A Human Rights Report," pp. 588–89.
37. Ibid., p. 590.
38. Ibid., p. 591.
39. Ibid., p. 592.
40. In 2003, President Bush signed the Protect Act into law, further raising the penalty to 30 years for crimes relating to sex tourism involving children (Landesman, "Sex Slaves on Main Street," p. 32). Shortly thereafter, Democratic congressman Rahm Emanuel of Illinois introduced a bill into Congress proposing the death penalty for "kingpins of child sex slave trafficking enterprises" (H.R.3913, 108th Cong., 2d Session). It did not pass.
41. The Protection Project, "A Human Rights Report," p. 593.
42. John Bowe, "Nobodies," *The New Yorker* (Apr. 21, 2003), p. 2
43. Ibid., pp. 6–8.
44. Cockburn, "21st Century Slaves," p. 24.
45. *Washington Post,* June 1, 2003, p. B1.
46. Ibid.
47. Ibid. Also, John Ashcroft, "Pathbreaking Strategies in the Global Fight Against Sex Trafficking." Feb. 25, 2003. Available online at http://www.usdoj.gov/archive/ag/speeches/2003/022503sextraffickingfinal.htm, p. 2.
48. Ashcroft, "Pathbreaking Strategies . . ." pp. 1–5.
49. Interview with Kevin Bales, June 6, 2005; interviews with Given Kachepa, youngest member of the boys choir and a recent high school graduate, and his adoptive mother, Sandy Shepherd, June 8 and 9, 2005.
50. Interview with Given Kachepa, June 9, 2005.
51. John Ashcroft, "Prepared Remarks of General Ashcroft Regarding Human Trafficking," Jan. 29, 2004. Available online at http://www.usdoj.gov/archive/ag/speeches/2004/12904aghumantrafficking.htm, pp.1, 2.
52. Ibid.
53. Ashcroft ms to *New York Times Magazine,* Feb. 15, 2004, p. 6.
54. Free the Slaves, "Hidden Slaves," p. 2
55. Interview with Gil Ortiz, director, Human Trafficking Information and Referral Hotline, June 8, 2005.
56. Free the Slaves, "Hidden Slaves," p. 7.
57. Ibid., p. 25. As Kevin Bales points out, "The 2004 amendment to the TVPA allows victims to bring civil suits against traffickers." In the Reddy case, it netted the victims a significant settlement. However, since traffickers generally "flee or have few seizeable assets," there is little to be gained. Interview with Kevin Bales, June 6, 2005.
58. Ashcroft ms to *New York Times Magazine,* Feb. 15, 2004, p. 6.
59. Free the Slaves, "Hidden Slaves," p. 2
60. Interview with Kevin Bales, June 6, 2005.
61. Interview with Gil Ortiz, June 8, 2005.
62. Ashcroft ms to *New York Times Magazine,* Feb. 15, 2004, p. 6.
63. Interview with Gil Ortiz, June 8, 2005.
64. Free the Slaves, "Hidden Slaves," p. 3.
65. Interview with Kevin Bales, Feb. 11, 2004. Free the Slaves can be contacted via

their website, at www.freetheslaves.net, or by phone, at 866-324-FREE. Their information package should be made mandatory reading in all this country's schools.

66. Institute for Policy Studies, Campaign for Migrant Domestic Worker Rights, "Who We Are" website: www.ips-dc.org./campaign/WhoWeAre.htm.

67. Ibid.

68. Greg Asbed, "For Pickers, Slavery Tastes Like Tomatoes," *Palm Beach Post,* Op/Ed (Mar. 30, 2003), pp. 1–3.

69. Ibid.

70. NBC2 News, "Immokalee Workers Celebrate," May 21, 2005, www.nbc-2 .com/articles.

71. Interview with Kevin Bales, Feb. 11, 2004.

# BIBLIOGRAPHY

## PUBLISHED SOURCES

Abbott, Geoffrey. *The Book of Execution: An Encyclopedia of Methods of Judicial Execution*. London: Headline Book Publishing, 1994.

*American President: The Series, Presidential History Resources, The* [online], 2002. www.americanpresident.org.

Anbinder, Tyler. *Five Points*. New York: Plume Books, 2002.

Andrews, George P. *Biographical Sketch of Honorable E. Delafield Smith*. New York: Greer & Co., 1871.

Asbed, Greg. "For Pickers, Slavery Tastes Like Tomatoes." *Palm Beach Post* Op/Ed (March 30, 2003).

Asbury, Herbert. *The Gangs of New York: An Informal History of the Underworld*. New York: Thunder's Mouth Press, 2001.

Ashcroft, John. Letter. *New York Times Magazine* (February 15, 2004): 6.

Auchincloss, Louis, ed. *The Hone and Strong Diaries of Old Manhattan*. New York: Abbeville Press, 1989.

Bales, Kevin. *Disposable People: New Slavery in the Global Economy*. Berkeley and Los Angeles: University of California Press, 1999.

———. "The Social Psychology of Modern Slavery." *Scientific American* 286, no. 4 (2002): 80–88.

Banner, Stuart. *The Death Penalty: An American History*. Cambridge: Harvard University Press, 2002.

Basler, Roy P., ed. *The Collected Works of Abraham Lincoln*. 9 volumes. New Brunswick, N.J.: Rutgers University Press, 1953.

BBC UK News Edition. "Niger Rapped over Slavery Denial," March 7, 2005, http://news.bbc.co.com.uk/1/hi/africa/4327497.stm.

Beale, Howard K., ed. *The Diary of Edward Bates*. Washington, D.C.: Government Printing Office, 1933.

Berger, Meyer. *The Eight Million*. New York: Columbia University Press, 1983. Also available online at www.nycvisit.com.content/index.cfm? page Pk-669.

*Biographical Directory of the American Congress, 1774–1996*. Washington, D.C.: Government Printing Office, 1997.

Bok, Francis. *Escape from Slavery*. New York: St. Martin's Press, 2003.

Bowe, John. "Nobodies." *The New Yorker*, no. 21, April 2003, 106–133.

Bunker, John G. *Harbor and Haven: An Illustrated History of the Port of New York*. Woodland Hills, Calif.: Windsor Publications Inc., 1979.

Bunting, W. H. *A Day's Work: A Sampler of Historic Maine Photographs 1860–1920, Part II*. Gardiner, Me.: Tilbury House Publishers, 2000.

Burlingame, Michael. *The Inner World of Abraham Lincoln*. Urbana: University of Illinois Press, 1994.

Burrows, Edward G., and Mike Wallace. *Gotham: A History of New York City to 1898*. New York: Oxford University Press, 1999.

Callow, Alexander B., Jr. *The Tweed Ring*. New York: Oxford University Press, 1966.

Canot, Capt. Theodore. *Captain Canot, or Twenty Years of an African Slaver*. New York: D. Appleton and Company, 1854.

Castaneda, Ruben. "Couple Enslaved Woman: Ghanaian Forced to Work for No Pay." *Washington Post* (June 10, 2003): B1.

Chase, Harold, et al., comp. *Biographical Dictionary of the Federal Judiciary*. Detroit: Gale Research Co., 1976.

*Christian Recorder, The*. Philadelphia, Pa.

CNN.com.member services. *U.S. Report: Modern-day slavery is alive and well in Florida*. February 25, 2004, www.cnn.com/2004/US/South/02/25/human.trafficking.ap/index.html.

Cockburn, Andrew, "21st Century Slaves," *National Geographic* (September 2003): 2–29.

*Colored American, The*. New York, N.Y. July 7, 1838, Item 3728.

Curtin, Philip D., ed. *Africa Remembered*. Madison: University of Wisconsin Press, 1968.

*Daily National Intelligence, The*. Washington, D.C.

Davenport, Paul. *South Riding Tunebook*. Vol. I. Maltby, South Yorkshire, England: SRFN Publications, 1997.

Davis, William C. *Three Roads to the Alamo: The Lives and Fortunes of David Crockett, James Bowie, and William Barret Travis*. New York: HarperCollins, 1998.

Dickens, Charles. *The Works of Charles Dickens: American Notes*. New York: Books, Inc., 1867.

Dorris, J. T. "President Lincoln's Clemency," *Journal of the Illinois State Historical Society*, no. 20 (January 1928).

Douglass, William. Mss to former owners, in "Letters from the Former Slaves of Terrell, 1857–1866." Richmond: University of Virginia Electronic Text Center.

Dow, George Francis. *Slave Ships and Slaving*. Salem, Mass.: Marine Research Society, 1927.

DuBois, W.E.B. *The Suppression of the African Slave Trade to the United States of America 1636–1870*. New York: The Social Science Press, 1954.

Eason, Henry, "Journal," in U.S. Sloop-of-War *Marion*, 1858–1860, Log 902. G.W. Blunt White Library, Mystic Seaport, Mystic, Conn.

*Eastern Argus, The*. Portland, Me.

Ellis, Edward Robb. *The Epic of New York City*. New York: Kodansha America, Inc., 1997.

*Elmira Daily Advertiser, The*. Elmira, N.Y. December 3, 1861.

Eltis, David. *Economic Growth and the Ending of the Transatlantic Slave Trade*. New York: Oxford University Press, 1987.

Eltis, David, and Richardson, David, eds. *Routes to Slavery*. Portland, Ore.: London, 1997.

Eltis, David, and James Walvin, eds. *The Abolition of the Atlantic Slave Trade*. Madison: University of Wisconsin Press, 1981.

Elwell, Edward Henry. *The Boys of '35: A Story of a Seaport Town*. Boston: Lee & Shepard, 1884.

Emerson, Edward Waldo, and Waldo Emerson Forbes, eds. *Journal of Ralph Waldo Emerson, 1856–1863*. Bridgewater, N.J.: Replica Books, 1999.

*Evening Press* (Portland, Ore.) (October 8, 1970): 15.

Ewen, Frederic. *The Poetry of Heinrich Heine*. New York: Citadel Press, 1969.

"Execution of Gordon, the Slave Trader, The." *Harper's Weekly* (March 1862): 167.

Fairburn, William Armstrong. *Merchant Sail*. 6 vols. Center Lovell, Me.: Fairburn Marine Educational Foundation, Inc., 1955.

Fehrenbacher, Don E. *The Slaveholding Republic: An Account of the United States Government's Relations to Slavery*. New York: Oxford University Press, 2001.

Fehrenbacher, Don E., and Virginia Fehrenbacher, eds. *Recollected Words of Abraham Lincoln*. Stanford, Calif.: Stanford University Press, 1996.

Fiske, John, and James G. Wilson, eds. *Appleton's Cyclopedia of American Biography*. New York: Appleton's, 1889 (for biographies of Sylvanus W. Godon, Gilbert Dean, and E. Delafield Smith).

Fite, Emerson David. *Social and Industrial Conditions in the North During the Civil War*. New York: Frederick Ungar Publishing Co., 1968.

Fitzgerald, W. S. "Make Him an Example." *American History Illustrated* (1983): 40–45.

Fleischner, Jennifer. *Mrs. Lincoln and Mrs. Keckley*. New York: Broadway Books, 2003.

Foner, Eric. *Free Soil, Free Labor, Free Men*. New York: Oxford University Press, 1970.

———. *Nothing but Freedom: Emancipation and Its Legacy*. Baton Rouge: Louisiana State University Press, 1983.

———. *Politics and Ideology in the Age of the Civil War*. New York: Oxford University Press, 1980.

———. *The Story of American Freedom*. New York: W. W. Norton & Co., 1998.

Foner, Eric, and Olivia Mahoney. *A House Divided: America in the Age of Lincoln*. Chicago: Chicago Historical Society, 1990.

Franck, Irene, and David Brownstone. *Illustrated History of Women: Opening Doors: 1870–1899*. Danbury, Conn.: Grolier Educational, 1999.

Free the Slaves. *27 Million Slaves—How Did We Get Here*. Washington, D.C.: 2003. www.freetheslaves.net/slavery_index.html.

Free the Slaves and the Human Rights Center of the University of California, Berkeley. "Hidden Slaves: Forced Labor in the United States." Human Rights Center, University of California, Berkeley, 2004. www.freetheslaves.net.

Harman, Danna. "Liberia: From Oasis of Freedom to Ongoing Civil War." *Christian Science Monitor* (June 12, 2002).

*Harper's Weekly*. New York.

Hearn, Daniel Allen. *Legal Executions in New York State: a Comprehensive Reference, 1639–1963*. Jefferson, N.C.: McFarland & Co., Inc., 1997.

Hershkowitz, Leo. *Tweed's New York*. New York: Anchor Press/Doubleday, 1991.

Hertz, Emanuel, ed. *Lincoln Talks: An Oral Biography*. New York: Bramhall House, 1986.

Holzer, Harold, comp. and ed. *Dear Mr. Lincoln: Letters to the President*. New York: Addison-Wesley Publishing Co., 1993.

Homberger, Eric. *The Historical Atlas of New York City*. New York: Henry Holt and Co., 1998.

Howard, Warren S. *American Slavers and the Federal Law 1837–1862*. Berkeley: University of California Press, 1963.

Huffman, Alan. *Mississippi in Africa*. New York: Gotham Books, 2005.

Inskeep, Carolee R. *The Graveyard Shift: A Family Historian's Guide to New York Cemeteries*. Orem, Utah: Ancestry Publishing, 2000.

Institute for Policy Studies, Campaign for Migrant Domestic Worker Rights, "Who We Are," 2004. www.ips-dc.org/campaign/index.htm.

*Jackson Mississippian*. 1854.

Jenrich, Charles H. "An Error in Flags." *Naval Institute Proceedings* (January 1968): 138–41.

Jensen, Derrick. "The New Slavery: An Interview with Kevin Bales." *Sun Magazine* (October 2001): 5–12.

Joachimsen, P. J. *An Address Delivered on Request of the Congregation*. New York: Slater & Riley, 1865.

Johnson, Harry, and Frederick S. Lightfoot. *Maritime New York in Nineteenth Century Photographs*. New York: Dover Books, 1980.

Johnson, Rossiter, ed. *The Twentieth Century Biographical Dictionary of Notable Americans*. Boston: The Biographical Society, 1904.

Keneally, Thomas. *American Scoundrel*. New York: Doubleday, 2002.

Keneally, Thomas, and Sandy Shepperd. *Abraham Lincoln*. New York: Lipper/Viking, 2003.

Klein, Herbert S. *The Atlantic Slave Trade*. New York: Cambridge University Press, 1999.

Kolchin, Peter. *American Slavery, 1619–1877*. New York: Hill & Wang, 1994.

Landesman, Peter. "Sex Slaves on Main Street." *New York Times Sunday Magazine,* (January 25, 2004).

Lane, Calvin, "The African Squadron, the U.S. Navy and the Slave Trade 1820–1862," *The Log of Mystic Seaport* no, 4 (Spring 1999).

Lankevich, George J. *American Metropolis: A History of New York City*. New York: New York University Press, 1998.

Lanman, Charles. *Biographical Annals of the Civil Government of the United States During its First Century; from Original and Official Sources*. Washington, D.C.: James Anglim, 1876.

Larson, Thomas. "Reina's Story." *San Diego Reader*, no. 32 (2003): 1, 32–53.

*Lewiston Journal Magazine* (March 28, 1970): 8A.

Lobo Montalvo, Maria Luisa. *Havana: History and Architecture of a Romantic City*. New York: The Monacelli Press, 2000.

*London Daily News*.

Longstreet, Stephen. *City on Two Rivers: Profiles of New York—Yesterday and Today*. New York: Hawthorn Books, Inc., 1975.

Lutz, Stuart. "Lincoln Let Him Hang." *Civil War Times* (March 1998): 34–38.

Maddocks, Melvin. *The Atlantic Crossing*. Alexandria, Va.: Time-Life Books Inc., 1981.

*Maine Sunday Telegram* (February 15, 1987), p. 19A.

Mathieson, William Law. *Great Britain and the Slave Trade 1839–1865*. New York: Octagon Books, Inc., 1967.

McDonald, Forrest, Leslie E. Decker, and Thomas P. Govan. *The Last Best Hope: A History of the United States*. Reading, Mass.: Addison-Wesley Publishing Co., 1973.

Miers, Suzanne. *Slavery in the Twentieth Century: The Evolution of a Global Problem*. Walnut Creek, Calif.: Alta Mira Press 2003.

Miller, William Lee. "Lincoln's Mercy." *Miller Center Report*, "Scholar's Corner," University of Virginia, Summer 2001

————. *Lincoln's Virtues, An Ethical Biography*. New York: Alfred A. Knopf, 2002.

Morris, Lloyd. *Incredible New York: High Life and Low Life of the Last Hundred Years*. New York: Random House, 1951.

Morse, John T., Jr., ed. *Diary of Gideon Welles, Secretary of the Navy Under Lincoln and Johnson*. Boston: Houghton Mifflin Company, 1911.

Mount, Robert L. "The Hinge of Reform." *Mankind*, no. 4 (1967): 46–48.

*National Cyclopedia of American Biography, The, Volume 5*. New York: James T. White and Co., 1891.

*National Police Gazette, The*. New York.

NBC2 News. "Immokalee Workers Celebrate," May 21, 2005: www.nbc-2 .com/articles.

Nevins, Allan, and Milton Halset Thomas, eds. *The Diary of George Templeton Strong: The Civil War 1860–1865*. New York: The Macmillan Company, 1952.

*New England Historical and Genealogical Register 1935, The*. Vol. 89. Boston: New England Historic Genealogical Society, 1935.

*New York Daily Tribune*. New York.

*New York Evening Post*. New York.

*New York Herald*. New York.

*New York Times*. New York.

Nicolay, John G., and John Hay. *Abraham Lincoln, a History*. New York: Century, 1890.

Palmer, Beverly Wilson, ed. *The Selected Letters of Charles Sumner*. Boston: Northeastern University Press, 1990.

Piersen, William D. *From Africa to America: African American History from the Colonial Era to the Early Republic, 1526–1790*. New York: Simon & Schuster, 1996.

Plowman, Robert J. "The Voyage of the 'Coolie' Ship Kate Hooper October 3, 1857–March 26, 1858." *Prologue*, National Archives and Records Administration, 33, no. 2 (Summer 2001). Available online at www.archives.gov/publications/prologue-summer-2001-coolie-ship-kate-hooper-1.html.

*Portland Advertiser, The*. Portland, Me.

Protection Project, The. "A Human Rights Report on Trafficking of Persons, Especially Women and Children." March 2002. Available online at http://sos.vrm.It:81//files//Hungary.pdf.

Quarles, Benjamin. *Lincoln and the Negro*. New York: Oxford University Press, 1962.

*Rail Splitter, The*. Cincinnati, Ohio.

Randall, J. G., and David Donald. *The Civil War and Reconstruction*. Boston: D. C. Heath and Company, 1965.

Rawley, James A. "Captain Nathaniel Gordon, the Only American Executed for Violating the Slave Trade Laws." *Civil War History* (September 1993): 216–24.

————. *The Transatlantic Slave Trade: A History*. New York: W. W. Norton & Co., 1981.

Richard, Amy O'Neill. "International Trafficking in Women to the United States: A Contemporary Manifestation of Slavery and Organized Crime." Washington, D.C. Center for the Study of Intelligence, 1999.

*Richmond Examiner, The*. Richmond, Va.

Roosevelt, Theodore. *New York*. New York: Longmans, Green, and Co., 1910.

Rowe, William Hutchinson. *Shipbuilding Days*. Portland, Me.: Marks Printing House, 1924.

Sandburg, Carl. *Abraham Lincoln: The War Years*. New York: Harcourt, Brace & Company, 1939.

Sante, Luc. *Low Life: Lures and Snares of Old New York*. New York: Farrar, Straus and Giroux, 1991.

Schriver, Edward O. *Go Free: The Anti-Slavery Impulse in Maine, 1833–1855*. Orono: University of Maine Press, 1970.

Sigerman, Harriet. *An Unfinished Battle: American Women 1848–1865*. New York: Oxford University Press, 1994.

Smith, Linda, and Mohamad Mattar. "Creating International Consensus on Combating Trafficking in Persons: U.S. Policy, the Role of the U.N. and Global Challenges." *The Fletcher Forum of World Affairs* (Winter 2004).

Southern Historical Publication Society. U.S. Biographies Project, Biographies of Jefferson County, W.V., vol. XI, "John Yates Beall." Richmond, Va., 1909.

Spann, Edward K. *Gotham at War*. Wilmington, Del.: Scholarly Resources Press, 2002.

Spears, John R. *The American Slave-Trade: An Account of its Origin, Growth and Suppression*. New York: Charles Scribner's Sons, 1900.

Speer, Lonnie R. *Portals to Hell: The Military Prisons of the Civil War*. Mechanicsburg, Pa.: Stackpole Books, 1997.

*Springfield Daily Republican, The*. Springfield, Mass.

Stansell, Christine. *City of Women: Sex and Class in New York 1789–1860*. New York: Alfred A. Knopf, 1984.

Staten, Clifford L. *The History of Cuba*. Westport, Conn.: Greenwood Press, 2003.

Sutton, Charles. *The New York Tombs; Its Secrets and Mysteries, Being a History of Noted Criminals, with Narrative*. Edited by James B. Mix and Samuel A. MacKeever. San Francisco: A. Roman & Co., 1874.

Tellewoyan, Joseph K. *The Years the Locusts Have Eaten: Liberia 1816–1996*. Available on CD-ROM, Library of Congress Registration #TX 5-550-052, 2000.

Tenzer, Lawrence R. *The Forgotten Cause of the Civil War: A New Look at the Slavery Issue*. Manahawken, N.J.: Scholars' Publishing House, 1997.

Thomas, Hugh. *The Slave Trade*. New York: Simon & Schuster, 1997.

Townsend, George Alfred. *The Life, Crime, and Capture of John Wilkes Booth* (a collection of letters by the author). New York: Dick and Fitzgerald, 1865.

*Union & Journal, The*. Biddeford, Me. (collections of the Maine Historical Society).

*United States Democratic Review* 42, Issue 12. New York: J. & H.G. Langley, 1859.

Unser, Barry, *Sacred Hunger*. New York: N.W. Norton & Company, 1993.

Wagner, Margaret E., et al., eds. *The Library of Congress Civil War Desk Reference*. New York: Simon & Schuster, 2002.

Ward, W. E. F. *The Royal Navy and the Slavers: The Suppression of the Atlantic Slave Trade*. New York: Pantheon Books, 1969.

Ward, Rev. William Hayes, ed. *Abraham Lincoln: Tributes from his Associates: Reminiscences of Soldiers, Statesmen and Citizens*. New York: Thomas Y. Crowell & Company, 1895.

*Washington Post, The*. Washington, D.C.

*Washington Star*. Washington, D.C.

Wiley, Bell I. *Slaves No More: Letters from Liberia 1833–1869*. Lexington: University Press of Kentucky, 1980.

Willey, Rev. Austin. *The History of the Antislavery Cause in State and Nation*. Portland, Me.: Brown Thurston Hoyt Fogg & Donham, 1886.

Williams, Eric Eustace. *Capitalism and Slavery*. Chapel Hill: University of North Carolina Press, 1944.

Williams, Glenn. "The Crowning Crime: The International Slave Trade," Small Museums Association, April 30, 2002. Available online at www.smallmuseum.org/articlecrime.htm.

Willis, William. *The History of Portland from 1632 to 1864*. Portland, Me.: Bailey and Noyes, 1865.

Wilson, Douglas L. *Honor's Voice: The Transformation of Abraham Lincoln*. New York: Alfred A. Knopf, 1998.

Wolff, Tobias Barrington. "The Thirteenth Amendment and Slavery in the Global Economy." *Columbia Law Review* (May 2002): 973.

Wood, J. Taylor. "The Capture of a Slaver." *Atlantic Monthly* 86 (1900): 451–63.

## UNPUBLISHED SOURCES

Bales, Kevin. President, Free the Slaves. Telephone interviews by author, February 9 and 11, 2004; May 28, 2005; June 3 and 6, 2005.

Catlin, Kristen. "The Slave Trade, and Captain Nathaniel Gordon." Senior thesis written for University of Massachusetts course given by Professor William Strickland, May 20, 1991.

Chickering, Reverend J. W. Ms. to Abraham Lincoln. University of Chicago Library, Special Collections Research Center, Lincoln Manuscripts Collection, Box 2, Folder 11.

Fenner, Dr. Levi H. "History of the Treman, Tremaine, Truman Family in America," FTM Online Genealogical Society, vol. 1, no. 15550.

Fisher, Mel. "The Last Slave Ships: African Slavery." Mel Fisher Maritime Heritage Society, Inc., 2. Available online at www.melfisher.org/lastslaveships/africa.htm.

Flaherty, Paul Arthur. "Effect of the Civil War upon Portland, Maine." M.A. thesis, University of Maine at Orono, 1996.

Kachepa, Given. Telephone Interview by author, June 8 and 9, 2005.

Lize, Steven. Primary researcher, Free the Slaves. Telephone interview by author, February 9, 2004.

Miller, William Lee. "I felt it to be my Duty to Refuse," a talk presented to the Lincoln Forum, Gettysburg, Pa., November 17, 2001.

Murray, Robert. "The Career of Gordon the Slaver." With copies of the original manuscripts from Murray's great-granddaughter, Barbara Ardrey, to the author: 1866. Transcribed by Murray's grandson, Walter Brewer, 1950.

Needles, Karen. "United States vs. Nathaniel Gordon." Documents on Wheels. Available online at www.documentsonwheels.com/gordon/index.htm.

Ortiz, Gil, director. Human Trafficking Information and Referral Hotline. Telephone interview, June 8, 2005.

"Petition to the President of the United States, from the Citizens of New York City." New York Public Library.

"Petitions to the President of the United States, from the Citizens of Portland, Me.," December 1861. National Archives, Washington, D.C.

Records and Documents of Cypress Hills Cemetery. 1862–present, Brooklyn, N.Y.

Thompson, Kenneth. Portland, Maine, historian, genealogist, and author. Telephone and personal interviews. February 28, 2002; August 9 and 19, 2002; October 10, 2002; January 20, 2004; February 10, 2004; May 3, 2004; May 18, 19, and 27, 2005.

Weiser, Daniel. "The Case of Nathaniel Gordon: Success for the United States, Tragedy for an Individual." Paper written for Columbia University (N.Y.) course, "Ethnicity in America," with Professor James Shenton, May 5, 1986.

## GOVERNMENT DOCUMENTS

The Abraham Lincoln Papers at the Library of Congress, Series 1. General Correspondence, 1833–1916. Available online at http://memory.loc.gov/ammem/alhtml/malhome.html.

   *United States v. Nathaniel Gordon* (Extract of Minutes), November 30, 1861, Case of Nathaniel Gordon.

   William Seward to Abraham Lincoln, February 3, 1862, Case of Nathaniel Gordon.

   Edward Bates to Abraham Lincoln, February 4, 1862, Case of Nathaniel Gordon.

   Abraham Lincoln, February 4, 1862, "Proclamation Granting Nathaniel Gordon Temporary Stay of Execution."

   William B. Lawrence to John McKeon, February 15, 1862, legal opinion re Nathaniel Gordon.

   Rhoda White to Abraham Lincoln, February 17, 1862, plea for clemency re Nathaniel Gordon.

   Gilbert Dean to Abraham Lincoln, February 18, 1862, Appeal re Nathaniel Gordon.

   Edward Bates to Abraham Lincoln, February 18, 1862, Case of Nathaniel Gordon.

   Edward Bates to Abraham Lincoln, February 19, 1862, Case of Nathaniel Gordon.

   William H. Seward to Abraham Lincoln, February 21, 1862, Case of Nathaniel Gordon.

   E. Delafield Smith to Montgomery Blair, November 19, 1862, re slave trade.

Appeal to Circuit Court, Southern District, NY, in case #15,231: *U.S. v. Gordon,* 25 Fed. Cas., November 1861.

Appeal to Supreme Court of the United States, National Archives and Records Administration, Record Group 267, Records of the Supreme Court of the United

States, Entry 26, Original Jurisdiction Opinions, 1835–1909, #6 Original, Ex Parte Nathaniel Gordon.

*Federal Cases.* Case No. 15,231 *United States v. Gordon,* Circuit Court S.D. New York. Nov. 8, 1861; Nov. 30, 1861, pp. 1364–68.

Joint Explanatory Statement of the Committee of Conference, House Conference Report 106–939. Reprinted in 2000 U.S.C.C.A.N. 1380 & Admin. New 1380 (2000).

Law Cases and Codes: "18 U.S.C. 1593"

"Letters from Commanding Officers of Squadrons and Captains of Cruisers to the Secretaries of the Navy, 1841–1866." National Archives and Records Administration, Microfilm File M-147, Roll 65.

"Minutes Book for the Second Circuit, New Hampshire." Waltham, Mass.

Pardon Case Files, 1853–1946, National Archives and Records Administration, Microfilm File A-391 for Nathaniel Gordon.

Record Group 48: Records of the Department of the Interior:
  Records relating to the Suppression of the African Slave Trade
  Letters Received and Other Records 1854–72
  Letters from U.S. Marshals
Record Group 59: Records of the Department of State Dispatches from U.S. Consuls in Monrovia, Liberia 1852–1906
  M-169, Roll 2
  February 14, 1858–February 22, 1864
Record Group 267, National Archives and Records Administration, Washington, DC. "Records of the Supreme Court of the United States," Entry 26, Original Jurisdiction Opinions, 1835–1909, #6 Original, Ex Parte Nathaniel Gordon.

"Records of Indictment and Minute Books for the Circuit Court of the Southern District of New York," 1860–1862. National Archives and Records Administration, New York.

Records of Sale for the "Erie," 1860–1861 (includes misc. lists of expenses, contents of ship, etc.), National Archives and Records Administration, New York.

Seys, John. Mss to Secretary of State Lewis Cass, 1860, Washington D.C.: Records of the Department of State. Microfilm 169, Roll 2, February 14, 1858–February 22, 1864.

"Squadron Letters: African Squadron," 1841–1866. National Archives and Records Administration, Microfilm File M-89, Roll 111.

United States Department of Justice. *Accomplishments in the Fight to Prevent Trafficking in Persons,* February 25, 2003. Available online at www.usdoj.gov/opa/pr/2003/February/03_crt_110.htm.

United States Department of Justice. Attorney General News Conference, "Worker Exploitation," March 27, 2001. Available online at www.usdoj.gov/archives//ag/speeches/2001/032701/workerexploitation.htm.

United States Department of Justice. Prepared remarks of Attorney General John Ashcroft, National Conference on Human Trafficking, July 16, 2004. Available online at www.usdoj.gov/ag/archive/speeches/2004.

United States Department of Justice. Remarks of Attorney General John Ashcroft, "Path-breaking Strategies in the Global Fight Against Sex Trafficking," February 25, 2003. Available online at www.usdoj.gov/ag/archive/speeches/2003.

United States Department of Justice. *Trafficking in Persons Report June 2003.* Available online at www.state.gov/documents/organization/21555.pdf.

United States Department of Justice. *Trafficking in Persons Information.* February 2004. Available online at www.usdoj.gov/trafficking.htm.

United States Department of Justice et al. *Assessment of U.S. Activities to Combat Trafficking in Persons.* August 2003. Available online at www.state.gov/g/tip/rls/rpt/23495.htm.

United States Department of Justice, Civil Rights Division. *New Legislation.* 2000. Available online at www.usdoj.gov/crt/crim/traffickingsummary.html.

United States Department of Justice, Civil Rights Division. *Trafficking in Persons and Worker Exploitation Task Force* 2002. Available online at www.usdoj.gov/crt/crim/tpwetf.htm.

United States Departments of Justice and State. *Departments of Justice and State Issue Human Trafficking Regulation and Guidelines for Prosecutors and Investigators.* July 18, 2001. Available online at www.usdoj.gov/opa/pr/2001/July/331ag.htm.

United States Department of the Navy. "Report of the Secretary of the Navy," 1860. Washington, D.C.: Government Printing Office, 1860.

United States Navy Department Library, ZB Files.

United States House of Representatives, Committee on International Relations. Testimony of Ralph F. Boyd, Jr., Assistant Attorney General for Civil Rights. *Implementation of the Trafficking Victims Protection Act.* November 29, 2001. Available online at www.usdoj.gov/crt/speeches/1129testimony.htm.

# ILLUSTRATION

# CREDITS

# INDEX